D1034594

NO MEN ARE STRANGERS

BY THE SAME AUTHOR

Robert Minor: Artist and Crusader

No Men are Strangers

By JOSEPH NORTH

INTERNATIONAL PUBLISHERS, NEW YORK

To Beila, who is All Mothers

Library of Congress Catalog Card Number: 58-11504

PRINTED IN THE UNITED STATES OF AMERICA

Contents

1	THE MAKING OF AN AMERICAN	7
2	A SHIPYARD—AND A UNIVERSITY	22
3	A GENTLEMAN OF THE PRESS	34
4	THE ROAD TURNS LEFT	48
5	HUNGRY AMERICA	56
6	SOME TATTERED SCHOLARS	71
7	MY MARCH THROUGH GEORGIA	76
8	I HELP FOUND A MAGAZINE	90
9	NO STRIKE IS EVER LOST	104
10	NEWSMEN AND A NEWSPAPER	116
11	CENTER OF THE WORLD	124
12	GATHERING OF HEROES	137
13	TO THE BRINK AND OVER	148
14	IMPERIALISMO YANQUI	157
15	GONE FOR A SOLDIER	170
16	MARCHING THROUGH DIXIE	189
17	TO A BELOVED RAGAMUFFIN	205
18	IT HAPPENED IN LONDON	218
19	RED ROSES FOR PARIS	236
20	RESURRECTION IN DACHAU	247

1

The Making of an American

WHAT GOLDEN LAND, my father asked. He settled in a shipyard town on the Delaware River, that broad, silvery stream that flowed majestically to the ocean, so like the rivers of his childhood in ancient Ukraine, that too, tumbled through lovely lands to his native Nikolaiev, that sun-lit naval base near the Black Sea where ships came and went—and were built. Strange, I remember him saying, that a man should travel across continents and oceans to live in a town that was as twin brother to the one he had fled. Here he was rearing a family in a small Pennsylvania city, swinging his blacksmith's hammer as he had in the land of the Tsars. "It is certainly a world that is round," he laughed.

He did not know that the blond Swedes had arrived first in the seventeenth century and felled the forests of maple and oak on the sullen heights they named Ooplandt, a mile from our home. I knew, but he never did, that William Penn, the Quaker nobleman, came some decades later, a somber, dignified believer, in a marcelled wig and lace sleeves, to oversee his empire that rolled west from the river to the wild Monongahela and the Allegheny, virtually at world's end. The trunk of the big oak to which Penn fastened his stout frigate still stands, a few feet from the tracks of the Reading Railroad that skirts the waterfront, and my father passed it many a time on his way to work, walking the ties. A rusty, iron fence around the site bears a bronze plaque and the inscribed legend. But my father never could read the inscription. When I was seven, I read it to him when he walked with me, one Sunday, my hand in his, and he murmured, "William Penn? A strange name."

Like his predecessors here, my father was a simple man. In the Old Country they called this the Golden Land, but during his first ten years here he felt the bite of hunger often enough.

Long months had passed before he entered the lofty gateway of the Baldwin Locomotive Works to hammer iron. No worldling passed through the Pearly Gates to his reward more happily. For bread was as rare here in the Panic of 1907, as it had been during the famines of his youth when the chanting priests swung censers over the dust of the Ukrainian fields after the deadly droughts.

Soon he found that the boss spoke a different tongue from the bosses of his youth under the Tsar but the meaning was unmistakably the same. And this riled him: as a skilled mechanic in the Frenchman's shipyard along the Bug he had finally earned enough, working from dawn to dark, to bring his apple-checked bride, my mother, to a neat, two-roomed apartment above a cobbler's shop near the riverside. This he remembered as his bright and happiest time. He had traveled across half the world to find work in a mythical land of gold, and once again he lived —in a slum—along a waterfront, and the rewards were less than they were under the Tsar. This, I remember, perplexed him as we sauntered along the river banks on Sundays listening to the lonely clang of the bellbuoy in midstream. He shrugged his wide shoulders. Well, a man does what he must; he was here, and here he would stay. Why complain? After all, it could not be worse in the long run, than it had been under Nikolai Romanoff. He had no illusions about Holy Mother Russia who was truly a harsh stepmother to her children. Certainly to him. Often he spoke long into the night with his good friend, the gay and chattering Fedyos, over countless glasses of tea and lemon. "No pogroms," my father said. "Besides, it is said a workingman here can even become the President." And both men laughed as they scanned the calendar that hung on the kitchen wall, and saw a vast, triple-chinned president they called Weelyom Toft. The Tsar's governors too had their share of chins and bellies.

But this was a new land, my father murmured. You could move about without the rigamarole of passports and police inspections, papers and wax seals; no abracadabra of kowtowings, "your Excellencies," "your humble servant," and all the rest—save, perhaps, an inevitable bit of that in the shop. Otherwise, it was very possible that a man could be a man. He was ready to gamble. No, he had no illusion: this earth was no poor man's paradise. But he told Fedyos that here no Jew had a need to crouch behind the cellar walls when the Black Hundreds ran through the streets brandishing axes. He had enough of that.

He was a Jew, but he did not deal in commerce, as his neighbors expected of those who worshipped the Jehovah of Moses. He was master of a trade, as his father and brothers had been: one cobbled shoes, another cut saddles, a third tailored clothes. His was the blacksmith's trade and he was well satisfied with it. He loved the glow of the red-hot iron, the shower of sparks, the smell of burning metal and the give of the iron to the blows of his mighty hammer. These blows brought him bread, and he felt confident that he and his hammer could bludgeon a living out of any hard time.

He stood about five eleven, thick and broad at the shoulder and hip, barrelly of chest, heavy of thigh. His rosy face, quick to smile, radiantly, rarely lost the philosophic cheer so characteristically his. "A man carries his heart under his shirt," he said. He bore his hardships stoically, as a man must, wearing the face of one whose world was good, good enough. A thick, drooping, black mustache fell almost to the chin, giving him the stern, wild look of a dark Viking. Yet a pair of merry jet-black eyes shone wide-set in his broad face. His cheeks had a fresh bloom which he never lost until the day he bled to death at the age of thirty-eight, and then it was ashen, for I looked into it his last moment, when he took my hand in his before his eyes closed. He left me a legacy: a thick, silver watch with Roman numerals, his citizenship papers in a heavy mahogany frame, and a bicycle that he had bought—second-hand—which he expected to present to me on my thirteenth birthday.

So his Jehovah endowed him with a span of fifteen sweated years in the Golden Land, during which he built locomotives, mostly. When one of the big layoffs came he found work in the Viscose mill near our town, where he sloshed around in the great fuming vats, wading through the acid in high rubber boots, and heaved the huge barrels which the foremen insisted only Negroes and Slavs could handle, and few survived that job. The acid burned the lungs and the heavy barrels strained the guts. Big men wilted after a few years, each in his turn confident that it couldn't happen to him, and it happened. We buried him in the cemetery on high ground overlooking the river and the railroad tracks.

I remembered a profound pride of craft he had. We would walk along the railroad and watch the trains roar by. When he saw a locomotive of the make he worked on his eyes brightened. "Your father made that," he said, pointing. Early in my life I sensed in him a dignity that rejected the code which held the worker inferior. He knew no trains would run without the skill of men like him, and he expected his due.

"The worst job," he would say, "is asking for one." When men got the sack and the faces of mothers grew haggard, the fathers' sullen, his was the most forbidding face of all on our street. His bold eyes flashed, his mustache seemed fiercer, and we kept out of his way. He sat in the house, brooding, at the kitchen table, cursing the Company, the super, the foreman. When my mother suggested finally that he go and see about work he replied: "They know where I live." My mother would put on her shawl and go sternly across the street where the foreman lived and pleaded, in her pidgeon-English, for her husband's job. My father, I believe, pretended ignorance of her intervention. She would return and say quietly, looking away, "He says they need you there." My father never replied, but the next morning he was up before dawn to catch the yellow No. 37 trolley that ran to the plant.

Like most workingmen I knew, he asked for little. A tender, sunny-tempered giant of a man, generally, he would carry us upstairs on his back to the unheated rooms, in the winter, and he would crawl into the ice-cold sheets to warm them for us. I regarded that as a parental rite and I was surprised to discover that other fathers did not always do the same for their young.

My father never had a day's schooling, but, like all immigrants, he yearned to spread the newspaper before him and read. Everything in this world conspired against that. Work began at dark and he came home at dark, with no margin of energy or time for study. He spoke a strange farrago of Ukrainian and Yiddish, peppered by a rare English word, pronouncing it in a slightly nasal tone which he considered the essential quality of the American speech. Most of the men in the foundry were foreigners, Slavs mainly, and he had few opportunities to learn. For a long time he could not write his name.

One day he furtively took me aside, in the kitchen, and handed me a sheet of paper and a pencil. "Write my name," he said, "write it big." I wrote. He wet the pencil on his tongue and painfully traced the script I had written. Again and again, he went over the letters of his name, the stub lost in his big paw. And one night he confided in me. "A workingman in America can vote if he can write." He would become a citizen and he would vote: that was his right, and it was a great discovery. A neighbor helped him get the "papers" that would certify that he was now an American. When the certificate of citizenship arrived we had a holiday, wine flowed, Fedyos came, and my father hung it, in the heavy frame he had gotten for it, on the parlor wall. He stood off a few feet, his big hands on his hips and he surveyed his triumph.

The election campaign of 1912 came and I heard a new name spoken in the house, spoken respectfully: Eugene Debs, the name was, the name of a great man, my father said, "who stands with the poor against the rich." That seemed to be all my father knew about the man, for I do not recall any talk of political philosophy, of socialism, (though that year Debs received nearly a million votes, and in a time before women gained the right to the ballot). A companion, "a Yankee," at the foundry had told my father, "Debs is a leader of workingmen," and that was enough. The Yankee may well have been an adherent of socialism but evidently could not get the idea across to the foreigner.

Ours was a solid Republican town where the ward-heelers always displayed an enthusiastic devotion to the people on our street a few days before elections. Then came the torchlight parades, the drinking, and I recall my father's aggrieved tone when he said "they" were handing out five-dollar bills for a vote. Election day came and he slicked his shiny black hair, combed his imposing mustache, dressed in his good black serge suit and marched to the polls with the air of a crusader. And he went prepared for his initiation into the rites of America's political life. He knew by now that the letters D-E-B-S did not spell T-A-F-T, the fat one with the chins, and he knew that the third candidate had a strange, outlandish name of nine letters R-O-O-S-E-V-E-L-T. Mrs. Watkins, the undertaker's wife down the street who occasionally visited our home, taught him that. He worried for several weeks before election day that he might confuse the four letters of Debs' name with the four of his detested opponent, "the banker" Taft. Mrs. Watkins wrote Debs' name, in large block letters, on a slip of paper which he opened, with some apprehension, in the privacy of the voting booth.

He came home, shoulders square, scarcely concealing his

jubilation, and he awaited the election returns. Mrs. Watkins came to inform him of the results in our ward. He listened intently, his head cocked to a side, "And how many for Debs?" he asked. "There was none," she replied. He sat silent, perplexed. "But I voted for him!" Our neighbor regarded the foreigner carefully and said, finally, a cynical edge to her words, that the Republicans might have thrown his ballot in the waste basket. "They do that, you know," she laughed, ironically. He rose from the table, left the room to change into a clean white shirt, donned his good black suit, and trudged heavily to the ward heeler who lived in the big, three-story brick house on the corner. "Where is my vote," my father demanded. The ward heeler looked him up and down, and began to shut the door. "How do I know," he replied warily. "My vote," my father clamored, "I voted for Debs. Where is it?"

The ward heeler, pushing the door hard, shouted, "How the hell do I know where your damned socialist vote is." And he slammed the door shut. My father pounded on it, repeating his demand for his lost vote. "Get away from here," the ward heeler yelled from the other side of the door, "Or I'll get the cops after you."

After a while my father came home. He sat by the kitchen window staring out, at the blank walls of the factory down the street.

Our town proudly called itself The Gateway to the South. It was indeed the first big factory city across the state boundary from Delaware. In those years of the first World War many migrated from the southern states and with them came new and strange customs to those of us who were the immigrants and their children. One day, on the main square, I worked my way through a hushed crowd on the curbstone. A masked man in a long white robe, riding a tall white horse, turned the corner. The emblem of a skull and bones was on his robe and he rode with his arms folded across his chest. Hooded figures followed on foot, five abreast, marching in silence, the shuffle of their feet rustling like a chill wind. Their eyes gleamed through the slits in their hoods. The police shooed the crowd back, and the spectators, foreigners mainly, continued to stare wonderingly at the marchers. "God have mercy on us," a little woman in a shawl whispered, "Who are these?" Another at her side replied in Ukrainian, "I heard someone call them Ku Klux something." "What is it, a masquerade, a lodge, what?" The other woman shrugged her shoulders nervously. "Where do they come from?" the first asked. The other gazed at her, frightened. "How do I know? But I don't like it, that skeleton and all." And they hurried away.

I followed the Klansmen on their silent march through the streets to Bethel Court where the Negroes lived. There the doors were closed, the windows shuttered, and the streets deserted. We talked about the march in our schoolyard the next day and somebody said, "nigger, that's who the Klan hates." It was all very mysterious and scary, but the weeks passed and the memory of the hooded march faded, and we forgot about it.

A shipyard sprang up where the reed birds once wheeled, and now we heard the hammer of rivet-guns night and day. Tankers to carry oil to Europe for the war slid down the ways. The town's skyline became jagged with derricks and cranes and the narrow streets built before the Civil War grew narrower, it seemed, crowded with workmen from all nations: now Mexicans appeared, many Italians, to add their numbers to the Slavs, the Irishmen who had come earlier, to the Negroes who had come long ago, for ours had been a way-station of the Underground Railroad. The shipyard brought prosperity to the town, the local newspaper exulted, and it also brought a big influx of Negroes up from the cottonfields of Alabama and Georgia to work in the yards and in the munitions works on the city's outskirts. And many more white Southerners, "crackers," the Yankee neighbors called them.

One day in 1919, a small Negro boy of eight ran breathlessly into the home of our next-door neighbor, Mrs. Sarah Trippet, crying, "Grandma, Klux shooting at us on Market Street." Mrs. Trippet, a Negro woman of 65, earned her living washing other people's clothes and her home was sanctuary for all children of our polyglot gang. There was always a corn muffin or a larded piece of bread, a smile and a laughing word for the children of the poor, be they white or black. Her grandson, Tom, and I, were playmates since we moved into the neighborhood. Wiry, tall, deft, he stood a head taller than most of us and we had remained close friends at high school. I had seen him rise quickly in the classroom to defend a thin, shy, wide-eyed Negro girl who came recently from the South and whose name was Missouri Roberts. The teacher, a Georgian, had ridiculed her because she signed her name "missouri roberts," omitting the capital letters. She had, Tom told me, three seasons of school in the cotton fields. One day, rendered desperate by the teacher's jibes, she threw her inkwell at him. He ran toward her in screaming rage and would have struck her had Tom not struck first. And for that he was expelled.

Now, Mrs. Trippet flew to my mother, for both were widow-women and their friendship had grown through the years. I remember the two well: the round brown face with the carefully combed gray hair near the broad white face with the carefully combed black hair. I can see them standing by the wooden fence between our yards, hanging the clothes on the line, laughing, and passing the time of day in the spare moments. Though the immigrant woman's English scarcely passed beyond a few hundred words, they made themselves understood in the universal language of the poor.

Now Mrs. Trippet stood there, talking in her low, melodious voice: "It's a lynch mob!" she said, brushing her trembling hand against her brow. "Lynch?" my mother asked. Mrs. Trippet explained. "Oh," my mother cried, clapping her hand to her breast, "a pogrom!"

Mrs. Trippet stared at her: "Tom isn't home; he's on Market Street."

"And Ichiel isn't home," my mother started; he was her youngest and favorite brother whom she had brought from the old country two years before. The two woman stood silent an instant: my mother read the old woman's resolve in her eyes. "No," my mother said, "I will go for them. I am younger." Mrs. Trippet shook her head, "But he is my kin."

My mother, pushing the older woman gently into our house, said, fiercely, "No, me. I walk, I run, I hide. I come back soon." As my mother wrapped her scarf about her head, Mrs. Trippet looked searchingly into her face and said, "Oh, child, do be careful."

The immigrant woman went into the street on her search. Ichiel, a handsome youth of twenty with a fiery temper and a tough pride, had quickly learned to drive a car and now earned his pay ferrying passengers on the jitneys, the poor man's taxi-service. The jitneys parked in the city's center some five minutes away, in the heart of the Negro slums where, doubtless, the Kluxers would focus their fire. Mrs. Trippet said Tom had gone to buy her some groceries on Market Street near the jitney stand. When my mother left, Mrs. Trippet moved quickly from window to window closing the shutters as I watched. She brought her young grandson into the house and we went into the darkened kitchen. She locked the back door, kept a crack open in the curtain through which she could scan the deserted streets. "Everything will be all right," she consoled us, and then, under her breath I heard her say, "God, make it all turn out all right."

I peered through the curtain and saw the small figure of my mother go up the silent street and turn the corner onto the main thoroughfare where they were shooting. It too was deserted and she hurried on, past the big stone bank, past the City Hall with its spire and bronze plaque marking the occasion George Washington stopped here to meet with his officers enroute to the Battle of Brandywine. Farther on she met a policeman on the run, his face sweating, a revolver in his hand. "Go home, lady," he shouted. "Quick, there's trouble on those streets." She shook her head, "No." He shrugged, and ran on saying, "Lady, it's *your* life." She met a neighbor who worked in the shipyard and he was hurrying home, lunch-kit under arm. "Missus," he said, "if I was you I'd get off the street right now." "No," she said. He hesitated a moment, then ran on. Another burst of shots sounded, and as she reached Fourth Street, a score of men, half a block away, ran chasing a slim, tall dark youngster and she knew it was Tom. He raced desperately up the street toward her as the mob's leader halted, got on one knee to take three careful shots at the fleeing figure. The bullets caromed off the curbstone.

Tom stumbled toward my mother, his hands outstretched, and she broke his fall, helped him regain his balance and when the gang leader, who had come up, panting, reached for the Negro boy she stepped between them. Tom sped off, darted up a nearby alley and disappeared. The mob leader, a lanky man of thirty, with a head of sandy hair and a long, red neck, turned on her. "If you warn't a woman," he said, "I'd a blown your brains clean out." She stood her ground, eyeing him. "You brave man," she said, and he raised his hand to slap her, but dropped it under her gaze. He turned and barked a few words to the gang and they scattered up the street. Ten minutes later she returned, dragging her brother by the arm.

When she got into the house, Tom was sitting on the kitchen floor, his shirt a ragged strip about his spare, dark chest, his eyes feverish as he stared at her and at us. My mother took off her shawl, put on her apron. "You Ichiel," she said, a captain taking command of an outpost under fire, "You watch by the door. You," she said, turning to me, "get the iodine and bandage from the closet upstairs." She helped Mrs. Trippet with Tom who lay on the ancient sofa we had in our kitchen by the coal stove. They unlaced his shoes, got his rag of a shirt off, and bathed his head. After dark we heard the klaxons of many cars speeding through the neighborhood firing into the shuttered windows of Negro homes. And the occasional dry bark of an answering shot. We sat silent, the lights out, a small candle flickering behind the drawn curtains. I sat beside Tom, my heart beating hard. Later, after midnight, three men crept through the dark, into our yard. Ichiel, stationed by the window, beckoned to us as he peered through the crack. The two women crowded forward to look and I rose to peek, too, through the pane. The men crouched behind our big wooden fence and I saw what they held in their hands. "It's all right," Mrs. Trippet whispered. "My people have come." The three remained there, in the shadows, throughout the night, and we found them there at dawn, when, as the light grew we saw National Guardsmen in khaki, toting rifles, patroling the streets in squads of three: martial law had been declared. Daylight found the children asleep on the floor, Tom, motionless on the kitchen couch. I was by the door with Ichiel and I fell asleep near dawn, waking to find the three Negro men at the kitchen table, drinking coffee, eating sandwiches the women had made for them. The men chewed silently, their eyes to the crack between the curtains. "Don't you worry now, Missus," a dark, stocky man of thirty said. "Nothing's gonna happen now." About noon, everything had quieted down, and they stole through the backyard and disappeared.

Our grocer, Mr. Wallach, who lived a block away, entered the house. An immigrant, the father of three sons, my playmates too, he said, stuttering to my mother, "How could you? You are a widow with f-f-our orphans. You risked your life, your children's lives, f-f-or a stranger?" My mother stared at him: "When I saw him running in the street, I saw my own children running in the street," she said. "No children are strangers."

And yet, not long after the war ended, and the dancing in the streets, we were staunchly American. In those evenings under the flaring gas lamp in the whitewashed kitchen I roused the New England countryside with Paul Revere, had fired my musket by the embattled bridge, had fought down the gray tide at Gettysburg, and had heard the pistol crack in Ford's theater. I saw Old Abe fall.

I regarded myself as native as any who were born in the red-brick homes of Boston's Beacon Street. The Founding Fathers were mine, too, drew their swords for me. I counted myself as native as Daniel Boone. True, I could not ignore our poverty or that we were Jews and that my parents spoke with the accent of the newcomers. There were those who saw that I should not forget that. I fought them, those who called me "sheeny" on my way to school every morning and on my way home every afternoon, a daily routine of my life and I kept a careful record of my wars, in a lined notebook, graded my battles "won," "draw," or "lost."

The bruises of the street did not, however, erase the words of the books, or the affectionate ministrations of the teachers whom I revered. At sixteen I believed the U.S.A. was indisputably the world's greatest and freest land. Oh, there were Kluxers, and those who despised Jews, there were race riots, and there was poverty, but all that would pass away. I could recite the words from the sacred parchment the forefathers had signed and nobody need persuade me that all men are created free and equal. Not far away was Valley Forge which our class visited; and I sat, bareheaded, and very quiet, in Constitution Hall, an hour by trolley-car from our home. Our country's traditions inspired me and streaked bright colors into the gray of our poverty. We were on the move forward. "Excelsior," all my classmates and my cronies believed that, my gang, the sons of immigrants and of Negroes—tow-headed Ukrainians, blue-eyed Irishmen, jet-eyed Italians, curly-headed Jews, laughers, players, brawlers, philosophers, and historians who feared no future. Before we were twelve we re-lived the Revolutionary War every February around the time of Washington's Birthday, in bright pageants at our grade school, strutted in three-cornered hats, wigs, carrying wooden swords and broomsticks for muskets. And one day the teacher said to me, "And you are Thomas Jefferson."

"Mom," I burst into the kitchen that afternoon, "I'm Thomas Jefferson."

She looked away from the big pot in which soup bubbled, and stared questioningly at me. "You know, Mom, the man who wrote the Declaration of Independence. He said all men are free and equal."

"M-m-m," she said, continuing to stir the soup. "But Mom, he wrote the Declaration of Independence. I'm going to wear a hat like he wore, like George Washington on the calendar. You got to make a coat for me like our forefathers wore." I brought her my history book, thumbed through the pages excitedly and thrust at her the great men who assembled that memorable day at Independence Hall. That evening she sat sewing under the gas-lamp, while I watched intently, and when she finished, I strutted proudly before her in Colonial garb. "It is very becoming," she laughed after scrutinizing the child of the Ukraine who was, now, so passionately an American.

School I revered, as though it were a temple, and nobody studied more ardently. I took to learning with zeal and read everything that came my way. I floated down the Mississippi with Jim and Huckleberry, and stalked deer with Cooper's feathered Algonquins: as familiar to me as the Delaware were the shores of Gitchee Gumee. I read at dusk and sneaked a few pages at dawn, like a young monk at Scriptures. The tall, kindly spinster at the Public Library put books aside for me which she felt were to my taste, or that I should read: Poe, Longfellow, Twain, Hawthorne, Melville, Stevenson. My mother, fearful for my eyesight, forbade reading after dark, and once, bursting into my room on suspicion I had disobeyed her stern injunction, she tossed Hiawatha out the window and was horrified when I bolted out the window after him. Fortunately my room opened on a shed half a dozen feet beneath.

I set my sights, under my folk's prodding, on the university—the dream of the immigrant. Despite my mother's fear of overdoing it, she encouraged me to study, for learning was the key to a richer future than hers. If the New World fell short in some ways, it had one virtue they trusted. It gave their sons the opportunity to unlock the wonder of books. None reverence learning so much as the illiterate.

The high school stood on a hillside, a graystone, turreted building from which you saw the river and the passing ships.

I loved every stone of the building, a castle whose rooms held all mysteries for me to master. I studied the declensions of Latin and followed Caesar through Gaul; set up my retorts in the chemistry laboratory and reveled in the literature classes. I have never encountered a fiercer adherent of Shakespeare's than the little, withered, strawberry-blonde teacher whose eyes shone as she read aloud from Macbeth, Hamlet, Julius Caesar. She entranced us as she enacted witch, Highland lord, Roman tribune. A classroom full of immigrant children whose parents could scarcely talk the King's English strutted through the corridors declaiming that they had come not to praise Caesar but to bury him, or, hissing, asked when we three witches shall meet again.

Naturally, not all our teachers were paragons of virtue: there was the principal, who tiptoed through the halls, peering into the faces of the passers-by, who had a patently artificial smile he turned on and off like a faucet. He beamed on the scions of the town's upper crust, and managed a feeble smile for the poor. If a teacher fell ill, he mounted the little platform and taught, and if a Montgomery stumbled over Euclid's triangles he smiled benevolently as he corrected the child: not so with the son of a Jones or a Rosenberg. Then, often as not, his words were acid and the perceptive young understood him very well, and despised him.

But his malevolence was the exception, for in the main, the teachers were truly dedicated to knowledge which they handed on, like torches, to the young whom they respected and who, in turn, regarded them affectionately.

The four years passed like an afternoon and the solemn day of graduation approached. I was given an invitation to take the examination for a four-year scholarship to the University of Pennsylvania, the plum of our school awards. The town's Rotary Club had announced its generous offer for which it received generous commendation on the front pages of our daily newspaper. I took the test, and in due time—great day!—the immigrant's son won the honor, became a neighborhood celebrity, his name and picture appeared on the front page. The neighbors came into our house to congratulate my mother whose eyes sparkled with delight and she embraced me repeatedly. "We will have a party," she said happily. Mrs. Trippet came from next door, Fedyos, my father's old crony, who tweaked my cheek in the Old Country fashion, came from the other end of the city. "I saw your picture in the papers," he said, and drew a bottle of whiskey from his coat. The grocer and his wife came, the undertaker's wife from down the street, my friend Tom and many others. The phonograph played its two worn records and even Mrs. Trippet took a turn around the parlor with Fedyos. The immigrants, the Negroes rejoiced; for one of their own had won the great prize.

The next day I received a note, in class, to appear in the principal's office after school. He rose from his desk, flashed his most effulgent smile, shook hands in congratulations, and then closed the door carefully. He sat down, smoothed the half dozen gray hairs of his pink, shiny head and cleared his throat. I sat, awaiting words of tribute.

"That scholarship," he said, staring at the desk, "that scholarship, as you know, was given by the Rotary Club. The merchants are proud of you, as I am, for your fine record, which is what we expect of our students. Ours is the land of opportunity, where all come from the ends of the earth, to share the bounty of our great and beautiful land. We teach and we mold character. Character," he said, "is more important than success. America needs men of spine, son, and you have it, you have it. Backbone: you can take the outrageous slings and arrows of fortune, as Shakespeare said, along with your triumphs."

I shifted in my chair, uneasily, and glanced out the window, catching a glimpse of a big black freighter heading downstream to the Atlantic. He rose from his chair, walked to the window, fumbled with his spectacles, wiped them, and then turning again toward me, said, "What I must tell you isn't pleasant but it is my duty." I stared hard at him, apprehensive now.

"What I have to say is this. You know the Rotary Club consists of merchants of a certain faith in this town which happens not to be yours. They met last evening and they came to a decision. They admire your fine record, mind you, a grade of 92 for the examinations is exemplary, but they regret they had to come to a decision."

I sat on the edge of the chair, my heart beginning to pound. "I may as well come to the point," he said, as though to himself. "They feel there are enough merchants in this town, of your own honorable faith, of your own kind, to tender you a scholarship. Your co-religionists are justly famed for their generosity to their own. So Rotary regrets it is obliged to withdraw the scholarship in your case, confident in the knowledge that your faith will practice its traditional altruism toward you."

I was cold, by now, turned hollow inside, and I asked slowly, "You mean, sir, I don't have a scholarship?" He averted his eyes. "Well, I would not say that exactly. I mean that the Rotary Club has come to a decision, you understand, that your faith should provide for its own. I am certain you need merely suggest it," he said, rising and beaming upon me, "and I am certain, we are certain, that you will have your scholarship, which, of course, you richly and rightly merit."

I sat silent, staring at him a long moment. "I see," I replied and rose. I left the school, walking slowly, bewildered. I feared to return home, felt, somehow, a sudden panic of exile. I passed the City Hall with its fine bronze plaque commemorating the visit of the Father of His Country, passed Welsh Street with its ancient, square, red-bricked building on the corner, with its plaque that said it had been a way-station for runaway slaves, passed the high picket fence of the shipyard, and heard the hoarse blast of the tugboats and the nervous hammer of the riveting guns. Yet the familiar had suddenly become strange, for I walked as an outcast, and my bewilderment passed into stinging anger. I had won fairly, hadn't I? Nobody said the exam was for Christians only, had they? Everybody in the upper quarter of the class had been asked to take the exam, hadn't they? What Jewish merchants? I knew none of them and my pride forbade me to even consider approaching them as the principal had suggested. That was panhandling, and I had won fairly.

I came home, flung my cap on the floor and sat down in the kitchen. When I told my mother, she sat down before me, her eyes narrowing to gleaming slits. "You'll go to college," she said finally. "And you will not beg anybody. You won and they cheated you. They can burn in the hot fires of hell which awaits them. I've sewed, I've scrubbed, I can do it again. You will go to college." She rose convulsively and went to the stove, fumbled around with the pots and pans. "Don't think about it," she said, her back toward me. Then she turned abruptly, her eyes dim and wet. "What do you want for supper?" She named my favorite dishes. "Tonight we'll feast, we'll have a banquet."

"A banquet," she repeated, her voice rising. "May their souls burn in hell." I went outside and sat on the steps.

2

A Shipyard—and a University

FOR A LONG time afterward, I trusted no man, blundered through the days and in the nights I walked alone on the waterfront, listening to the lonesome clang of the bellbuoy rocked by the waves of the passing ships, dark masses on a dark stream, heading out to a dark sea.

I was a Jew, I reflected bitterly. Is that a curse? And nobody had a sure answer. But, in truth, I was not even part of Jewry. We had never set foot in a synagogue after my father's death. When he lay on his bier, a pale, handsome figure in his black serge suit, my mother said, dry-eyed, to the grocer, "Let those who want to believe, believe. I am finished with believing." She would not worship a God who could take a father of four children, a beautiful man, a man in the prime of his life. "When it came time to live, he died. Call that a God?" The grocer, taking a step back from this blasphemy, replied that God's ways are inscrutable and she said quietly, "One thing I know. My children had a father and now they have none. If God can explain that to me I will listen to Him." And I agreed with her. So I would have no part of a God who had repudiated me. But what about Man? We had fallen away from the Jews and now the Christians dealt perfidiously with us. I was engulfed in a self-pity that had no bounds. I dreamed of taking one of those dark ships out to sea to far-off lands: dreamed of lying deep beneath the river.

My mother's anger changed to anxiety; she wheedled and cajoled in her effort to restore my spirit; she jested and tempted me with an astonishing variety of dishes. I ate them dutifully, even appreciatively, for my excess of woe did not, somehow, diminish my appetite, but I shuffled, nonetheless, through the day, morose, unsmiling, in a state of shock and melancholia. The sorrow of adolescence when the boy is changing into a man has its own agony, but mine seemed beyond the power to endure. Overnight my trust in men withered. Yes, name me one man, one woman (aside from my mother) who might not turn out to be a cloaked enemy about to ambush you. I suppose the betrayal of my confidence, my trustfulness, hurt even more than the loss of the scholarship.

My mother, noting well that the succulence of her dishes and her forced heartiness had little success, decided to shame me. What sort of man, she asked suddenly, one night, did I expect to be if this first setback could destroy me? What made me believe that life would be all honey and almonds? And beneath the gas-light, the shadows flickering across the room, she recalled her father, and mine, the trials they had endured: the Black Hundreds, the pogroms at Easter, the round of famines in the old country, the hardships of the new homeland —unceasing and back-breaking toil, the uncertainty of the job, the poverty—and yet they had endured.

She spoke of her father, whom I knew she revered: "a cobbler who worked hard every day of his life for his brood, and yet a wise and learned man, a saint." Even the peasants came to him for counsel which he gave over his awl, stroking his long forked beard. They trusted him. She told again a story I had heard many times in my childhood. "When my father was a young man in the time before Tsar Nikolai, he lost his way one winter night in a blizzard and he wandered in circles like a blind man." The old man knew that unless he found his way home soon he would be a corpse by dawn. Nothing in the howling dark gave him a hint; he was alone in a wide white world, and he heard, above the wail of the wind, the soft voice of the Angel of Death. Finally, his strength failing, he slipped to his knees, flung out his hands for something to stay his fall. And his finger-tips felt a wooden post. He grasped it, held fast and rose slowly to his knees, recognizing, as he struggled upward that he had stumbled onto an ikon of Christ on the cross which the peasants had built a mile outside the village, at the crossroads. He had his bearings now, and the knowledge poured strength into his veins. He plunged on through the drifts and soon he saw the faint ray of light from the lamp in his window and he was safe. He told his daughter, my mother, afterward, "I, a Jew, was granted life by the Gentile God. It is an omen that requires deep consideration."

"Now," my mother smiled reflectively, for I knew, by her many tellings of this tale her love for it, "now you know well that I am no believer in these things, but your grandfather had a deep wisdom." She said his piety was renowned throughout the countryside, yet even his fellow-Jews understood that he trusted the Gentile God too, and he trusted the Gentiles. "Now this I saw," she added, accenting each word, "saw with my own eyes. Gentiles took us in and hid us in their cellars when the hooligans ran through the streets with axes to chop down Jews. Gentiles risked their lives for us. No, son," she concluded, "not every Gentile is an enemy. And what good is life if you believe all men are evil?" After a long silence, she began again, a fierceness coming into her words, "now is the time to strike back, to show your mettle." She was no fool, she said, no babe in the woods to trust all men, for there are more than enough who are bad, and the world has perhaps more in it of thorns than flowers, but we are here, why, she for one did not know, but this she did know: the good of the world made life worth-while. Life, with all its woes, is well worth the try, as I would come to see. "Your father enjoyed life, this blacksmith who was no Rothschild, a poor man working all his years. Alone he made his way to a new world across the ocean. How did he feel, when he left me, his bride, and an unborn baby, while he traveled to the other side of the world to make a new life for us, trusting his own strong right arm. He asked for no favors and he got none, he worked for all that he got. And that man did not want to die. The doctor said his heart went on pumping even after the rest of him was dead: they said in the hospital they had never seen so strong a heart. Yes, he made a fight of it to his dying day. He was a man and a good man. And he loved you with all his mighty heart."

Her words had their gradual effect, and, of course, I had the natural resilience of youth. Tom, next door, said, "Buck up man, you only lost a scholarship: I got expelled. You can go on to school: me, they stole that school right out from under my feet." And Mrs. Trippet, one day, glancing sharply at me and away, said, "Son, that was a mighty mean trick they played; but you'll trick them when you go on to school in spite of them." I suspected that my mother had a hand in their ministrations and when Fedyos came and laughed at those fools who think they can keep you out of college, I was certain of her hand. Fedyos took me aside and said he had some savings which were mine anytime I decided to go on to college. "I'm a bachelor-boy," he grinned, "and I will only spend it on whiskey." Their words moved me out of the worst of my sorrow, and my mother, noting well that she had gained a point, pushed on with maternal implacability. "We decided, did we not, that you will go to the University?" She gently insisted that I write away for the pertinent information to enter.

And so I did. The college prospectuses came, and she sat down, in her rocking chair under the lamp, sewing, while I studied them. I plowed through the rhetoric in the preface that paid homage to the muses, extolling Aristotle, Plato, Goethe, Shakespeare, the whole pantheon. And then I came to the gist, added up the dollars per point. "It will take a lot of money," I said to my mother. "We'll get it," she snapped, laying down her sewing. "How much?" she asked. When I told her, she mused over the sum and then mapped her plans. She would keep boarders again, as she had before. I would work and we would save.

Well, all right. I had nothing to lose going: nothing to lose not going. Somewhere along the line there would probably be an ambush, for the world was not peopled by men and women like her, like Tom and Mrs. Trippet, like Fedyos. The great god Rotary ruled supreme, and held our likes in contemptuous bondage. But I hankered for the books: they at least could not betray. Or could they? The books quoted Jefferson—all men are created free and equal. Well, still I had nothing to lose. It's six of one and half a dozen of the other, I decided. What the hell. . . .

Okay, I said, I would get up tomorrow and hunt work in the shipyard down the street, and my mother started. All the women of the street dreaded the shipyard for too often the clang of the ambulance woke them in the night. Two neighbors were left widows this past year, their husbands died in "Mr. Pew's slaughterhouse." My mother suggested quickly that I might better try the textile mill nearby where I had worked three summers and where, she felt, the dangers were less. Many of our friends worked in the mills and nobody had brought them home in a sheet. "But it doesn't pay enough," I argued, we would need much more than I could earn in the textile mill, twice as much probably. Two of my cronies worked in the yard as passer-boys tossing rivets and I had wanted to try the work. I had no fear of work: I was strong, lithe, and remembering my father, respected the work of hands. The Jewish tradition, I was told, respects only the work of the head. I sensed that, in the regard my family held for the scholar's pursuit. But we never revealed a bias against labor of any sort. All labor, like bread, was honorable.

The job was simple enough: my tongs grasped the glowing red-hot rivets which I tossed to another boy who caught them in a bucket. The rivet was jabbed into a round hole drilled through the steel plate by the reamer whose machine screamed like a mad animal. The riveter spread his legs, leaned hard against the gun, pulled the trigger and pounded the piece of hot steel into place. Iron and steel weighed down from all points over you, yet in a few days I grew accustomed to the din and the steel. To watch the hull of a ship take shape, to help it take shape, was bright adventure. I got on familiar terms with the great oblongs of steel that swung about our heads from the cranes which we cozened and jimmied into place. Soon I too passed nimbly in and out among them, shouldering an overhanging plate of steel as though it were a bedsheet that hung from my mother's clothesline. Working on the open deck, under the sky, the sparkling river below exhilarated me.

But one noontime as we sat eating our sandwiches beneath the great cranes in that strange silence that comes after the din of the machines, my riveter stared at me curiously. He came from North Carolina, a "down-homer," had a lean, long bluish jaw and when he worked nothing existed but the rivet against which he pitted his hundred and ninety pounds of muscle and bone. Man and riveting gun became one piece. This lunchtime he wolfed his sandwiches, washed them down with a thermos of coffee, wiped his mouth with the back of his hand, and then rattled off a few monosyllabic words, a strange smile on his thin lips.

"You-all Italian?" he asked. I shook my head, glancing at him warily. "Greek?" "No." "Then what in tarnation are you?" I hesitated a moment then replied, "Jewish." He stared at me, his blue eyes widening and his mouth took on an ironic grin. He turned to his holder-on. "Looka what we got here," he exclaimed. "A Jewish Hebrew passing rivets." The holder-on regarded me as something fished up from the deep. And the riveter said, "I thought Jews buy and sell, make money, make money," he rubbed his thumb against his forefinger in a hateful gesture I had seen before. I rose, hot and angry. "If I'm a Jew, it is my own affair, not yours nor anybody else's and you can shut your mouth about it." The two men laughed. "Well, Ikey," the riveter said, "Now don't you-all be getting on your high horse, or we-all might have to get you down off it. Jes don't forgit that."

Several days afterward I heard him say to his partner, "Ikey brung us luck. Never made so much money since he been on the gang. Jew's like a humpback: rub him and you get good luck." The blood came to my face but I pretended not to hear. All summer long his jibes maddened me, yet I had no recourse but to clench my fists and feign indifference, or deafness. I bridled many a blind rage to rush at him, for I knew that he could knock me sprawling with one swipe of his arm. So I learned much of patience, that hairshirt weak and suffering Man has worn through the ages until in desperation, he tears it from his back and lashes out at his tormenter. Sometimes I thought, after the long workday as I lay in my bed, perhaps if I reasoned with him, explained. . . . Explained what? And how? I could hear my own stammering words fall on his heedless ears, and see the contemptuous stare of misunderstanding should I try to talk of justice, righteousness. Suppose I tried to say, look here, you worship God for I know you are a Baptist, and is it not true that Jesus Christ was a Jew? I had said that once to a boy my own age when he had called me "kike," but it did no good; on the contrary. We had to fight it out with our fists, for he became all the more enraged, shouting to his cronies that this kike just called Jesus Christ a kike.

So I swallowed the insult, for my primary purpose was to work on through the summer, put my savings aside for the university fees, thinking all the while, yes, it is six of one and half dozen of the other.

The summer concluded in one realization: it mattered little that I did not regard myself as a Jew; others did, and acted accordingly. And, meeting an ardent leader of the Young Men's Hebrew Association one evening, I filled out a membership card, and attended his meetings. I was surprised that they knew of me, of the business about the scholarship, and one young, curly-headed lady whose soulful eyes attracted me, said, as I walked her home after a social, that she had wondered why I hadn't gone to the Jewish merchants to plead my case: they would have helped.

"The trouble is you're too proud," she said, fixing me with her wide and innocent eyes, "you got to be more practical. You have to play the game." Idealism, she went on, philosophically, has a place, of course, "in the synagogue," but you can't live by it. She had no doubt that her father, who owned a sizeable furniture store in town, would have taken me in hand, had I come to him, and given me good advice--and more. And others of his clique would have reacted similarly. In fact, she had heard them refer to the incident with some indignation, but they heard too that we belonged to no synagogue, were, in fact, atheists, and that had deterred them from action. "Are you really an atheist?" the lovely and practical young lady asked. I replied that I had no reason to believe a God existed, and she shook her head in exasperation. "That isn't practical," she said, stamping her foot. I had no proof that He existed, neither could I prove that He didn't. And since I couldn't prove that, why did I not behave like all others. "Nobody likes an atheist," she said, and if she were one, she would merely keep her mouth shut about it, and go to synagogue, at least for the high holidays, where the townfolk could see her, and realize she belonged with them. That was "playing the game," it was "practical," and had I done so, I would doubtless have that scholarship and would have no need to work in the shipyard like the *goyim*.

I listened to her gravely, to the end (she did have beautiful eyes), and I marveled that so much worldliness could be stored behind their innocence. I went off on a tangent, according to her, when I replied I saw nothing demeaning in physical labor, it was as honorable a way of earning a living as selling furniture, perhaps more so. She had her share of patience too, I realized, when she controlled her anger at a remark that could be considered a slur on papa. "But where does it get you?" she asked. No workingman she ever heard of got rich; and didn't I care how my family would live after I got married and had children. Could I give them all the "advantages" they were entitled to, as a laborer in a shipyard?

Though I walked her home a number of times afterward, I

fear that I fell short of her mundane standards; I refused, gently enough, to talk to her father or any of his cronies, and to attend synagogue services, even for appearances' sake, on Passover and Yom Kippur. She met a law student not long afterward and began walking home with him. She said to me the day after the engagement was announced, a shade of impatience and, I fancied, sorrow in her voice, that he had "ideals" too, but he was a practical man. He had it all mapped out: he would go into politics after his graduation, aim for the District Attorneyship of our country, because the Jews were becoming a power in the community. He could practice his idealism after he became a success, she said, a trifle acidly, and he would provide for his family which, after all, is a man's first responsibility. I wished her all the luck in the world with her lawyer, and assured her that the chap would doubtless be a good provider. "And he'll have his ideals, too," she interjected. For my own good, she concluded, it would be well if I learned to play the game. I was a nice fellow, she said, her lovely hand on my shoulder, but I had to learn that you have to play the game, "or pretend to, it adds up to the same thing. That is, if you want to be a success."

Somehow, though I reflected on her advice, I had no ambitions to become a success. For what? To become a member in good standing of the Ohev Sholom Synagogue Association? And move into that social whirl of the elders who patronized the Y.M.H.A.—portly men of snobbish traits, I felt, who displayed a scorn toward folk like mine who dealt in no commerce, and who labored with their hands for their bread. I had an acute sense of class, instinctively. Not only did I reject any imputation that workingmen were inferior, but early my observations convinced me that their intelligence equalled that of the wealthy, and their ethics certainly were superior. But for what? It seemed to me that the supreme injustice of creation lay in the hopeless plight of the poor, of folk like my father and mother, Mrs. Trippet, Fedyos, and all the others I knew. Thus it had been since the days when the Carpenter drove the money-lenders out of the temple, who got their revenge when He ended up nailed to a cross. That was the fate of the poor, yesterday and today, and so it would be tomorrow. The confidence men had the run of this poor globe from way back, I reflected; the first sharpies, the Pharaohs, persuaded them, by whiplash and whatever other ways I did not know, to haul the greatest load of stone in all the world's history, to build the majestic Pyraminds to house the dry bones of royalty. No, the poor were eternal suckers for the fast-talker, the double-crosser.

No God lived on high to help mortal men through Pearly Gates; neither certainty nor right prevailed anywhere on the continents and the oceans. Blind chance ruled like a despot, and if, by accident, great and good men came along, like Washington and Jefferson and Franklin, and great events transpired, like the American Revolution, the wily and the crooked reaped the fortune in due time. So I saw matters on my seventeenth birthday, which I can scarcely describe as a gala occasion.

My university education which lasted three years scarcely changed or improved my view of life. If anything, it confirmed the merited, if mawkish skepticism of my earlier adolescence. True, I was regarded as a good student, good enough to acquire my Bachelor of Arts degree in three-fourths time. I read enormously with voluptuous pleasure (mostly on my own) of classic Greece and Rome; what I read fascinated me, but left me, on graduation day, with a guiding maxim I had learned from my favorite professor, a sad-eyed Frenchman, who said one day, *"Plus ca change, plus c'est le meme."* That seemed to sum it up. It stuck in my mind like Mark Twain's jingle about the trolley-car tickets, nor did I feel compelled, unlike the eminent sage of Hannibal, Missouri, to palm it off on a captive audience and run. That required a greater wisdom than mine.

This is not to say I had no rewarding moments or satisfying experiences. Five or six gifted professors made the years worthwhile; no waste of time; and half a dozen friends I acquired enriched me, lads of similar, and somewhat desolate, outlook. One particularly, a mathematics major who went on to become a world figure in his realm of learning, became my closest friend. But most of the faculty, it seemed to me, could not, for a moment, forget that their bread and butter came from Drexel and Company, the Main Line bluebloods who dominated the school, and whose intellectual and moral loyalties belonged to John Pierpont Morgan and Co., whose Pennsylvania satraps they were. The Wharton School of Finance was their chief pride; and they cared little, if at all, for their stepchild, the College, which a wonderful, tumbledown old scholar by the name of Dean Josiah Penniman headed in my time. He taught the Bible as literature, and I could never forget how his fading eyes caught fire when he read The Song of Songs or Ecclesiastes.

There was another literature professor who taught Chaucer passionately, the early literature of the English, a worldly, well-dressed, dandy of a man, who brought the Nun into contemporary recognition: he transmitted his passion to his students, even to those budding financiers of the Wharton School. And one day, digressing from his topic to speak, for some reason I cannot recall, of Flaubert and de Maupassant, Balzac and Anatole France, he said, astounding most of us, that a woman who goes without benefit of clergy to bed with a man she loves—and even if she does not love him, is not necessarily a fallen woman. The thought was, possibly, not so novel for many of us postwar young, but its expression at Penn certainly was, for a thick overlay of hypocrisy cloaked the university and many of its fledglings.

Strange it was, though, that no glimmer of concern for the public's welfare, for humanity, shone through the swift semesters of my undergraduate days. Not for years did I learn that Dr. Scott Nearing of its faculty had been expelled for opposing World War I, and that others similarly had suffered harsh penalties because they refused to conform to the stock-exchange ethics of J. Drexel and Co. In all my time I never once heard the name of Dr. Karl Marx, or Frederick Engels, spoken or even whispered in a classroom. It was a distinct marvel of concealment, possibly tacit, possibly not.

But, as many know, the faculty is not a university; no few students, certain friends I acquired, taught me more than my professors. There was this young man, about five feet three, beneath whose close-cropped head of hair shone as bright a pair of eyes as I can remember. In all my classes he was indisputably first. The son of a Jewish journalist, his mother a nurse, he came up in an environment where the value of learning surpassed, unlike the code of my town, the value of bread. Eager for knowledge, inquisitive as the proverbial macaw, this math shark came often with me to my home, to my town which entranced him and we knocked around in the waterfront bars, a pair of delighted virgins. He, in turn, introduced me to the wonders of the Philadelphia Orchestra, where I first heard Beethoven, Brahms, Tchaikovsky; to literature: under his prompting, I read Strindberg, Turgeniev, Ibsen, Shaw.

From him I first learned the name of Karl Marx whom,

he said, his father revered. But he, with all his passion for mathematics, could never get past the hypothetical tailor and his garments Marx used to develop the famous theory of labor value. He argued Marxism with a curiously dispassionate air: it sought to save mankind, which was laudable, he said, but to achieve socialism, Marxists cared little whether the lives of the present generation were destroyed in the effort. "I am the present generation," he said, "and I do not intend to be sacrificed to future generations. Of all generations, mine has my loyalty, for it is alive today, and who knows what monsters tomorrow might bring." I brooded over these sentiments, wondering.

I was respectful of his erudition, his culture. He, in turn, insisted he saw the stuff of a poet in me, and inquired almost daily when I would starting writing verse. Goaded by his insistence, I wrote a poem—about the chandelier in the Academy of Music, which he praised, extravagantly, I suspected. He encouraged me to write more poetry, insisting that I had more than promise, it was my forte, and he rejoiced, as I did, when a professor scrawled across a paper I had submitted, "You Can Write!"

Maybe I can, I reflected, and if that were so, matters could be worse. The young, I suppose, find magic in the writer's craft which has for them, a curious aura of romance. To set down on paper the stories of men, of combat and of love, to get human beings into pages so that they became as real—often more real—than the human beings you knew in life, had wonder in it. Building ships and watching little men fit huge steel plates together into the lovely shape of the hull was good too. But writing was best. No boss but yourself; a transaction between you and a clean sheet of white paper, what could be better?

You never make a living at it, my friend said cheerfully, citing his father who had been called the Yiddish O. Henry, but whose earnings rarely enabled him to pay the rent. But we did not worry much about the practical, like my lady friend of the curls and innocent eyes; we knew that Heinrich Heine lived with poverty in garrets all his life, but the glory of his poetry more than compensated for his life-long indigence. Just write the truth and that is satisfaction enough, we agreed. Truth was sad, of course, and life a dubious boon, a prison house, but you are here, trapped, between a cradle and a bier, and why weep tears few see and less care about?

Perhaps it is best, though, my friend said one day, suddenly displaying a surprising degree of canniness, to have some profession to enable you to eat, so that you can write. His father had said that mankind should feed its writers—like the church cared for its priests—so that they need waste no time scrounging for odd and wasteful jobs to earn the leisure to write. Teaching, my sagacious companion advised, had its compensations—long summer vacations, the few hours in class, the sufficient, if meager, pay, the daily association with people, yes, it had its merits. And we decided to set our sights on a target: we would become college teachers.

We sought out our favorite teacher, the afore-mentioned professor of French literature and he listened, gravely, a tall, shambly, bald figure in his carved armchair, one long bony leg crossed over the other. He stroked his long, angular chin contemplatively, glancing at us once or twice as we spoke. His bleak silence, punctuated by a long sigh, was curiously disconcerting. Finally he asked, regretfully, whether we were Jews, and when we nodded, his silence fell again, like a heavy curtain between us. Then, rising abruptly to stare out the window on the green campus below, he said, "You should know that the university is regarded as the last stronghold of the Anglo-Saxon. You will find all too many scholars who fear the Jew, and scarcely conceal their hatred for him. It is a curse that will plague you all your campus years. Passions and prejudices are delicately misted in the halls of learning, but they exist nonetheless." He said our enemy in cap and gown will smile in our face as he holds the stiletto behind him. It is a cruel fact, and we should examine it carefully before decision.

He chilled me, and once again I felt that old hollowness, the sense of ambush, yet it was not wholly unexpected. My friend regained his surprising composure quickly enough, as we walked slowly through the solitude of the pines and elms of the campus.

"Well," he said, "Shma Yisroel. Plain talk even when it is expressed in poetry, never hurt anybody. The old fellow left us no room for misunderstanding. Straight from the shoulder, bang." I found no jest in it, and surveying my glum face, the young mathematician clapped me on the shoulder saying, "they won't make it easy for us Israelites but who expected to discover the Garden of Eden?" We found a crowded, noisy bar where we had more glasses of beer than we ever drank before and got tipsy over our troubles.

3

A Gentleman of the Press

THE BACHELOR OF ARTS, respected graduate of the Universitatis Pennsylvaniansis—the last stronghold of the Anglo-Saxons—finally decided to become a writer; and he turned up as a cub reporter on the busy and flourishing daily newspaper in his home town. The editor, Frank Hickey, was a tall, gruff man with a monk's fringe of rusty hair on a long, lemon-pale face which was also distinguished by a pair of extraordinary sharp eyes whose glance speared you from behind the silver-rimmed spectacles. "So you went to college?" Yes, I said, surprised that his voice had a blunt, accusatory tone, and he replied, "M-m-m," his lower lip jutting out. "Did they teach you something sensible like writing on a typewriter?" Well, no, they had not. He thought not, he snapped, and said that ordinarily he would be found dead in the doorway before he hired a college man, still, he needed a man quickly, and well, he could chance it. I might prove the exception he never found.

He bade me write simply, "like a man talks," and none of this university stuff. He taught me, as best he could, to write a simple English sentence "so any fool can understand." Out went the Latin polysyllables and Addison's stately complex, balanced sentences I loved so well; brief, direct Anglo-Saxon words jumped up to take their place in short, declarative sentences. "And for the love of Jesus, learn to get a man's name right!" He had never seen a university man who could. Names make news, he said curtly, and he advised me to remember that this is a newspaper, not a literary society. If I had a damned impulse to write novels nobody could stop me, but he could see to it that the Great American Novel would not be written on company time. He extended his hand suddenly and smiled brilliantly, "No hard feelings," he said. "It's only that you have to unlearn so much you learn in college." He had come up the hard way and maybe, he laughed, he had a grudge against anybody who "made" college.

He sat me down before a typewriter, and bade me to re-write and condense a long story that had come over the wire. The next day he escorted me into the alley where the news-paper's Ford was parked: Could I drive? No. He shook his head, smiling dourly, and taught me how to start and stop the car, bade me to take off, on my beat, which consisted of a dozen towns on the pike to Philadelphia. I set off, in jerks and starts, fearful for pedestrians, but arrived at my destination, and by the end of the day, felt fairly certain at the wheel. Curiously, I relished the editor's brusqueness; it had a crisp challenge no man could ignore, and I was eager to pick up the gauntlet of battle.

The newspaper was a power in the county as well as the state; I knew it could make or break a politician in this pros-perous region of half a million souls. The Governor of the State owned it (his personal organ) as he owned ten blocks of the city slums, many coal mines, a considerable share of the ship-yard, and the town's oldest bank. Canny politicians nationally realized that the editorials in his paper reflected his views, and since he was a kingmaker in the Republican councils, many met-ropolitan editors commented on his comment.

The paper had been founded a century before; its reporters in beaver hats and gaiters had recorded the battles of Antietam, Bull's Run, Gettysburg, and, I discovered one day looking back into the musty and crumbling files, it had defended John Brown. Today it had achieved the lofty moral eminence of Warren Gamaliel Harding, and grateful merchants placed many more columns of advertising in its pages than news.

Within a year I was something of a provincial celebrity, man with a by-line, which for some reason, many regarded as an honor akin to a ribbon of the Croix de Guerre. The town's elite handed me cigars, greeted me heartily on the streets, and bought me drinks. The poor, however, knew that a few scribbles on my pad could cause sufficient trouble. The gentle-men of the press were not precisely welcome despite their eminence.

Soon I knew everybody, the mayor, the chief of police, the chief bootlegger, the gamblers and bookies, the ministers, the rabbis, the movers and the shakers.

And soon I discovered that misery was my assignment, for I was in and out of the homes of the poor in search of the hot story. Oh, we knew whom to smear and whom to shield, learned that with the first pay envelope, learned the names of the sacred cows, about whom, if they broke into newsworthy focus, you had a whispered word or two with the city editor. But the poor had no protectors in the king's court.

One day, a year or so after I had learned my trade, the editor looked up at me from under his green eye-shade, saying he had a story he would like me to cover. Two highwaymen had waylaid a respectable citizen of our town on a dark street some months before. Their victim had disobeyed their command to keep his hands high and he struck at one of the thugs who pulled the trigger. The culprits were sentenced to die on the electric chair. The killer, a lad of nineteen, lanky and hollow-eyed, the son of a weaver in the textile mill said on the witness-stand, "I didn't want to shoot, but it went off because the man scared me when he jumped at me." His accomplice was a thirty-year-old veteran who had been shell-shocked and could find no work on his return from war. The execution would be consummated in the penitentiary, democratically situated in the center of the state so that all men were equidistant. "You go along and do a last-mile story," Hickey said.

This was one story I had not anticipated. I had no wish to see a man die or to see him killed by mandate of law. Hickey's sharp-eyed scrutiny discomfited me, as though he were testing my mettle. I knew, as soon as the words were out of his mouth, that I was bound to go. A newspaperman gets his assignment and carries on come hell or high-water. There was a curious elan in the trade: you got your story like the Northwestern Mounties got their man. There were no two ways about it. I conformed to this tradition, for my pride was that I was a good newspaperman. I accepted every assignment uncomplainingly and came back with the bacon; I had gone down into the river in a diver's suit and waded about in the gloom and mud, it was a good story. I had climbed a high church steeple that was cracked by the vibration of the big bronze bells. "Music is stronger than stone," I wrote. It was a good story. I pestered a stunt flier, a local man, to take me up when he had flown home one day to visit his sweetheart. He had scarce patience for my request, he had flown through the clouds to see his girl, not to get publicity, but I badgered him and he consented reluctantly. He made me pay for my temerity: he barrel-rolled, swooped down and curved up, fell to one side and another, looped-the-loop until I scarcely knew if I was upside down or right-side up. Finally, back to terra firma. I staggered out of the plane, dizzy, disheveled, and elated. I had a good story. I went into the ring with George Godfrey, the towering Negro prizefighter many thought merited the world championship: he trained at Leiperville, a nearby suburb. The gladiator toyed with me and then clipped me on the ear explosively. As I went down I rejoiced: I had a good story. All was grist to my mill, the inane, the grand, if it made a story I got it. Well, you had to cover it, even if it was the killing of a man.

A few days before Christmas it was and the snow fell silently. The Yule trees sparkled on the suburban lawns as the sheriff's procession began its journey to the death house. I sat in the car with the younger of the two men who was handcuffed to two husky deputies reeking of whiskey. When we came into the car the condemned youngster asked for a Bible which they brought him dutifully, a great heavy volume which the youth held on his lap the whole way. But he did not talk of Scriptures, not of Job nor Jesus, Heaven or Hell.

The penitentiary gates, high and heavy, as though they were built to accommodate and retain multitudes, swung wide and the cars passed slowly into the prison yard, inched toward the cell block for the condemned. They led the two men away and I stared after the youngster, narrow of shoulder and hunched, hugging his Bible like a shipwrecked man hugs a raft.

I checked in for a room at a nearby inn, an old, gabled Dutch tavern. Filled with local residents merrily singing Christmas carols, it was warm and cozy, but I was cold for reasons other than the icy mountain temperatures. I asked for a rye, and a man beside me said, "Jesus, there's Ellis the executioner." I saw a tall, spare man wearing a gray hat and a long overcoat walk to a table, his eyes lowered. He had an aged and brooding face though he walked straight and stiff like a military man. He hung his hat carefully on the rack and I saw his neat, iron-gray hair, which surprised me. I had perhaps expected the face of Satan, fangs and all, and here this man might have been a clergyman down at the First Methodist Church, or a staid citizen who ran the haberdashery on Market Street. A man's occupation is in his face, I had fancied. I always attempted to guess a man's trade before he declared it, and I had fair success.

Lawyers have a look of circumspect confidence; doctors of a harried control; clergymen wore benignity in their demeanor like priests their collars. But, I thought, the face of this executioner was any man's face.

Lord knows, I had no desire to talk to him, but I knew, as a newspaperman, a good story was in it, in fact, demanded it, and I walked across the room quickly and introduced myself. "Glad to meet you," he said extending his hand. "I like to talk to the newspaper fellows, like to be of help." He lifted his drink with a steady hand. He had just come from Massachusetts. "I had a case there," he said, and it took a moment for me to realize that he was referring to his executions as "cases," like a doctor or a lawyer, a man with a respected profession. After a few moments he excused himself, saying he needed a bit of rest, for he had to be up early so he could leave early to get home in time for Christmas. He had promised his family. . . .

As I lay in bed at midnight, with my somber reflections, I heard a faint knock, and with a sense of growing horror watched the door open inch by inch and the face of the executioner peered in at me. Was this a dream, had I fallen asleep? And then I heard him ask if I would come to his room for a drink, "for Christmas, you know," and he crooked his finger, beckoning me. I rose, and followed him. He tip-toed to his room at the far end of the thick, red-carpeted hallway as dimly lit as the corridors of Purgatory. I was startled by the burst of light and gaiety when we entered his big room where two men and two women sat on the bed drinking whiskey from big tumblers. The executioner introduced me to them as a friend of his, a newspaperman, and we shook hands all around. The younger of the two women who could have been little more than seventeen, giggled, "Oh, Lord, a newspaperman. Can we get our pitchers in the paper?" One man, burly and pink of face, who had the stolid, official look of the courtroom hanger-on was the state witness at executions. The other, a portly, jovial chap of fifty-odd, with a big toothy smile, introduced himself as the undertaker who would return the corpses to the city. The two ladies were prostitutes they had picked up in Altoona to trifle the hours away before they proceeded to their work.

The executioner drank tumbler after tumbler of whiskey but stayed as sober as if that were tap-water that went down his long throat. I made no try to keep pace with him; I was still a novice at the stuff, and beside, I did not overly care for its taste. But I had enough to feel reckless and at about one A.M. I asked him why he followed this . . . this . . . (stumbling for the right word) . . . this profession. His old, weary eyes stared unwinking into mine, and he replied thoughtfully that I was the first one who had ever asked him that.

Slowly, in a kind of stately and deliberate ceremony he pulled the cork from a fresh bottle of Scotch, and poured himself another tumbler-full and then he began his story, readily enough, as though he had been waiting a long time for this opportunity. "I was a poor man's son," he began. His folk migrated from Scotland to settle in the Bronx and he learned the electrician's trade. One winter day, jobless, he answered an ad in the paper for work down at the Tombs, in Manhattan, as an electrician's helper. He grabbed the first subway down, running hard, and he got the job. It wasn't bad at all, he tended the lighting and heating system, but the pay was nothing to write home about. After a couple of years the warden came to ask him if he cared to earn $250 in one evening. "When he said that I knew what he meant. You could only get that much money for doing a certain thing. I knew the official electrocutioner was ailing and old, and I needed money bad, what with the wife sick, another baby on the way and we neck-deep in debt." He figured this way, if it wasn't him it would be somebody else.

After his first case, he substituted for the executioner whenever he was asked, and so he inherited the job. The missus sort of took it hard, at first, but she got used to it, as he had. And that was all there was to his story, he said. "Not much to tell, was it." We sat silently drinking, and I looked away, thinking, and how does he feel when he pulls that switch, and before I knew it, the words were out of my mouth.

His face came alarmingly close and I edged back a bit. Nobody had ever asked him that either, he said, but he would tell me, if I promised him I wouldn't write it up. Of course I wouldn't, I murmured, thinking, simultaneously, that I was promising away perhaps the best part of the story. "I am telling you this because you asked it, son, and I told you I like newspapermen. They understand; they've played square with me, and I got nothing to be ashamed of. Understand?" he repeated,

"Nothing to be ashamed of. I figure this way: I am the law's right hand, I am the thirteenth man on the jury." His words came faster now, as though he had rehearsed them many times before. "The judge pronounces the sentence and the sentence must be carried out. Or else, where would Society be? It's Society's decision. I'm only Society's hand, in a way of speaking. I'm the hand of Society, that's all."

The hand of Society was steady as it tilted the bottle once again. "I am the right hand of the judge, the thirteenth man on the jury," he repeated, and then he asked me if I understood clearly what he was saying. Yes, I said, I understood clearly.

Outside the mountain brook murmured and a night bird cried. The executioner turned his long lean head to listen. "Owls," he said, "there's owls in the mountains."

His voice droned on in the same monotone he had begun, passionless, as though this were a long rehearsed tale, told without contention or certainty. People shunned him doing the job that had to be done, he said, the job somebody had to do. There should be gratitude; his, maybe, was about as hard a job as there is, because he did it knowing there would be no gratitude, and he would never again have a friend. Once he had had friends, and it is a nice thing to have friends, but now he had no friends. Well, a fellow can live without them. But even his children shied from telling anybody what their father did for a living. His only satisfaction was his car, a juiced-up Ford that could go eighty miles an hour.

At three in the morning he mentioned his hardest case. Two men they were, up in Massachusetts, killed a paymaster. It was in the town of Braintree. They were a couple of Eyetalians by name of Vanzetti and Sacco. This fellow Vanzetti had a big mustache and there was a lot about him in the papers a long time. Said they wanted to overthrow the government, anarchists, you must have read about them. "Well, this fellow with the mustache was kind of loco, off his rocker. Wants to make a speech when he gets to the chair. Now I know most times a man says something like God have mercy on my soul. Something from the Bible, which is fitting. But this fellow makes a speech, like a politician. Now how can you do your duty, do it on time, when a fellow's making a speech? You got to stand and wait till he's through talking. And that's bad, the waiting. Usually it's all ship-shape, 1-2-3, you go ahead, do what's got to be done, and it's done. But this Eyetalian!"

He poured another drink and for the first time I noticed Society's right hand was not steady and I sobered up instantly as though somebody had thrown an icy pitcher of water into my face. I had read enough about the anarchists to know the furore that had risen over them and I had read the many statements which questioned their guilt. "And what did this fellow Vanzetti say?" I asked. The executioner shrugged the question off, wearily. "I didn't listen."

I felt exhausted and told him I was dog-tired and had to go. He lay his hand on my elbow and I brushed it off as I headed for the door. "It's just that I need company," he called after me, pleadingly, in the hall, his voice suddenly altered. "Just wait, can't you, till one of the other fellows comes back?" I went on without answering, tip-toed back to my room, a mite unsteadily, and flung myself on the top of my bed, my head rumbling with his words, the thirteenth man on the jury, the Eyetalian making a speech, the juiced-up car.

The executioner was downstairs at dawn, sipping a cup of coffee, and he glanced up at me, nodding politely, inquiring how I slept. He was very official now, sitting at the breakfast table, and what transpired last night had no relation to the right hand of the judge. "We got to be there by 6:30," he said, glancing at me quickly and looking away. "Get some coffee and I'll take you over."

At exactly seven, two sober-faced guards in blue, their eyes bleary as though they too had caroused all night led the younger highwayman into the death chamber which was a great gray cell of a room without windows. I stood huddled with half a dozen newspapermen, pad in one hand and a shaking pencil in the other. The condemned youngster looked about the room; he still hung on to his Bible. The executioner moved soundlessly, a hypnotic intentness blacking his face. He slipped the leather mask over the youngster's face, glanced again at the electrode fastened to the condemned man's calf, and glided toward the open door behind which the switch hung. The condemned man's voice came up from Hell, "May God the Lord have mercy upon my soul."

At that moment I heard the cry of a cock, from afar, penetrating the walls, cock-a-doodle-do, cock-a-doodle-do, and the image of a barnyard, a shingle house and whitewashed fence, a cow, a horse, flashed across my mind, a moment before I heard the fatal whirr. The body leaped against the leather thongs, straining the thongs as though the young vital force of his life would burst them. The whirr filled the room until I felt it would tear through my brain. And then there was silence.

The young body fell back against the uprights of the chair, slack now, empty as a paper bag, and a faint bluish curl of smoke rose to the ceiling. The two guards loosened the thongs, lifted the corpse briskly, its legs and hands flopping like the sleeves of a scarecrow. A few moments afterward they led the older man in. His face had a mysterious smile, the upper lip lifted suddenly in a snarl and seeing us at the far end of the chamber he said in a resounding voice, "Gentlemen of the press. Put this down. You are killing an innocent man. I never had a gun and I never meant to kill. Give me a job and it'd a never happened. Put this in too, and don't forget: you'll be going where I'm going and I'll be there ahead, with a pitch-fork for you, you sonsofbitches." He sat back, stretched his arms on the armrests, tilting his head forward, almost eagerly, to receive the leather mask. The last I saw of his face was the sneer.

On the train home I sat in the smoker, lighting cigarette after cigarette, staring out at the mountains and the tall white firs that stood like rows of shrouded men, and I looked up to see the executioner enter the car, smoking a long thin cigar. He hesitated as he saw me but came to my seat, and stood. Just stood. I could scarcely turn my eyes to look at him and he knew it for he did not sit down. He leaned toward me, a grave look of dignity on his wrinkled face, his gray felt hat careful on his head, his white collar clean and starched and he said in almost a whisper, "I want to ask you a favor, son. Leave my name out when you write up this case, will you? It does me no good to have my name in the papers. It doesn't do my kids good." He stood a moment longer, searching my face and as I remained silent he passed on, smoking his long black cigar.

The execution ticked away in me, like a time-bomb. I tried to ignore it in the routine of my job and I worked harder thereafter with a deliberate and almost passionate vim.

So long as I stayed within certain journalistic precincts I could write as I please, but I steered clear of politics. I supplied, oddly enough, a cultural note to the arid provincial newspaper, writing a daily column now. And one day a letter came from the Baltimore *Sun,* H. L. Mencken's paper, which invited me to come down and talk about a job. I was enormously pleased and I talked to Hickey about it.

I had come to admire him and he adopted me as a sort of junior protege. He told me he had worked on a Pulitzer paper under Claude Bowers, the historian, and I saw that he, too, was an avid reader of history. That we had in common. The editor delved into the riches of our local history, was really an authority on the Underground Railway which flourished here in the 1840's and he spoke of that time when we were alone with a crisp enthusiasm that surprised me. For ordinarily he seemed cold, dry, certainly abrupt and commanding, his red head absorbed solely in headlines that would bring circulation. But in the evenings when he invited me to his home, sat in the living room among tall bird cages full of canaries and yellow warblers, he lifted the veil from his erudition, and spoke of Bancroft, Gibbon, Mommsen and Thucydides as the birds chirped and sang, leaping from perch to perch. He had always kept birds, he said, but he hated keeping them in cages.

I saw, after I came to know him well, that he was a man in a cage. He had strange quirks, long stretches of silence and hostile brooding which seemed, I thought, to come from the boredom bred of the town, the job, I couldn't tell which, and once a month he'd be absent from his desk for two or three days. He was dead drunk, the city editor whispered to me. The gossip in the newsroom had it that he locked himself in his bedroom, away from his wife, and he would regularly down two or three quarts of Bourbon, drinking himself into a solitary stupor. But he never showed up drunk in public, retained his official dignity, his public authority and face. That he kept sacrosanct. When he gave his word, he kept it meticulously, a quality respected by the town's gangsters whom he cultivated on the assumption that they knew everything of politics. "A straight shooter" the mob called him.

Like the others on the staff he was a man without illusion or ideal, an observer, rather than a participant in life. His ambition, he said to me, was modest: to be a big frog in a small puddle. I showed him the letter from Baltimore which he read carefully and then looked at me evenly, the sharp glance going out of his eyes. I had a good choice, he said, but he would refrain from giving advice. All he could say was that if I stayed I could become a big frog in this little puddle too, for the city editor's job would be mine soon. And he would hate to see me go personally, because I was doing a good job. "Maybe you ought to wait a while," he concluded, "you haven't learned everything this newspaper can teach, have you? You've been here, what, three years? You're having fun, aren't you. The first years are always fun in this game. And if you need more money," he said glancing sharply at me, and I suddenly suspected he believed that I showed him the letter for that purpose, "I can arrange that too. But the money isn't bad, is it?"

As a matter of fact it wasn't bad. I got good pay for the trade in those times. I was twenty-four and single and I wasn't worried about the pay. I was flattered that he wanted me to stay and I considered his words. The big city would merely be more of the same, and I could bide my time until I felt a stronger urge to move on. I had no compelling ambition to be a big frog anywhere. I had a variety of excitement, a degree of adventure, the job still had its challenge and my star was in the ascendant even if it was a small heaven. No, I was in no hurry.

I wrote a letter to the Baltimore paper, stalling for time and I continued to roam the county on my own, a provincial troubador who wrote about everything and anything that suited my whim, in my daily column called "Talk It Over." The county was a world and I knew its trade winds, its roadways and bypaths, its green hills and clustered towns with their daily mysteries into which I could delve. Each character on my beat stood out sharp, distinct, a man standing against the sky. I came to love the county and its history which was a trove of riches. I chose the hallowed spots of the locality for my topics and wrote of what I read in the official records at the county courthouse, of its past since the Swedes and Quakers came.

The more I read and reflected upon my readings, the more I discovered a strange division in my estimate of Man's prospects. How diligently my predecessors here had toiled, what unfathomed love of life these Colonials had, and those generations who came after them in the Nineteenth Century. The old deeds in the county courthouse often as not, measured boundaries by tracing a line from "the gnarled apple trees at the foote of the hill where the hemlocks grow to the small running spring of the four weeping willows"; the references to the things of nature had, in these legal documents, a reverence for the soil upon which they came as babes and walked as men and women, and upon which they gazed as death called. But even beyond this I discovered far more evidence of a plain, yet inspiring humanity than I had thought, heretofore, existed.

History, I believe, is best reconstructed from the journals local inhabitants keep, often in intimate diaries, and in the Historical Society you read how this father, or that mother, or grandmother, sent their sons off to the wars, the advice they gave, the words of parting and of home-coming; and how often, far more often than not, they took their stand on the side of the angels. Though Philadelphia itself has been described as a Tory center in the Revolutionary War, certainly the yeomen and artisans of the surrounding territories were, at least from what I read, partisans of Washington's cause.

Not far from my home stood the dwelling of "Mad Anthony" Wayne among great dark oaks which seemed so aged that he may have put them into the earth himself. And in a tumble-down cemetery in the midst of the town's slums stood a simple white shaft over the remains of John Morton, inscribed solely with the dates of his birth and his death, and the single pertinent comment on his life: "He Signed the Declaration of Independence, July 4, 1776." You got the shape of the lives and the quality of their minds from the local records, and how often it was that I encountered a sturdy belief in that which made life worth the living—freedom from tyrants, the equality of men, the search for a happiness that did not base itself upon the enslavement of other men.

A widespread identity of view shaped the community, or almost all of it, into a whole. Yes, these were good people, who wanted good for all men. Then where, I asked myself, did their dream and their labor go astray? Certainly the world I saw about me scarcely reflected their image; the Negroes, I saw, were in a kind of new enslavement; as a Jew I certainly knew that many, maybe most, suffered the sickness of prejudice —against race, against religions, against the money-less folk. The pursuit of happiness? Jefferson's dream of a nation felicitously peopled by independent and thinking farmers, contented with their flocks and acres had shrunk to a rat-race for the job, and *I* knew that the laborer, worthy of his hire, got a pittance.

Reason began to suspect what once my childish faith explicitly believed—that men, Man, was good, and that the evil they did, and the greater evil crushing them, came from some source eluding me.

This began to show itself in my columns that won some considerable local popularity. I told of "Mad Anthony" Wayne's ghost wandering among the elms, and of Penn before him; wrote of the rolling seamen off the low-lying black freighters that bobbed in mysteriously from all the world's ports, comparing them to Ulysses' crew, the shadowy figures of Homer. My columns contrasted oddly with the boiler-plate editorials of our Republican newspaper and I uncovered a considerable public interest in the classics. Even my associates on the paper, generally articulate in their disdain for the long-hair stuff, asked questions. "This fellow Homer," the parchment-dry copyreader asked one night, "what was he all about?" They listened as I told tales from mythology, of Ulysses, Paris, Helen, Ajax, Agamemnon, these sons of John Barleycorn. The sports writer whose red-thatched head had lain in more gutters than I could count, who had no formal education beyond seven grades of elementary school, asked if it was true that the Olympics began in Greece. When I finished my Homeric lecture the police reporter rose, glancing at the clock as though the hour-hand registered the centuries. "It ain't changed in five thousand years," he commented, as he rushed off to the police blotter where he believed all history could be found.

One evening Hickey asked me to wait, and we would go down to Joe's Bar that we frequented. The mob would be on hand, as well as a new floor show. I was to pick him up at six in McBride's office. McBride, the county political boss, was a tall, dour fellow who wore a long dark overcoat that reached to his ankles. He wore it throughout all seasons of the year save midsummer. The townsfolk said no wonder, the man's got ice-water in his heart. Nobody ever saw a smile on his cadaverous face. His office, across the street, occupied the top floor of the town's biggest building, eight stories high-fronted with marble.

I arrived about six and knocked on the heavy, mahogany door, built obviously to lock the whispered consultations in. A rotund police sergeant I often met on my travels through town opened it and greeted me jovially. "Your boss said to hang around, he'll be out soon." I heard the murmur of voices from an inner room as I sank into the big leather chair by the window. A picture of Warren Gamaliel Harding hung on one wall, Penrose on another, the jowled, handsome and controlled faces of the Republican saints.

Somebody walked out and left the door to the sanctum ajar and I caught a glimpse of the men inside. Standing by the long, glass-topped table that stretched halfway across the room was the GOP boss, a police captain, the publisher and the editor. All puffed on heavy cigars, the room was bluish with the reek, but I could see their faces, staring, transfixed, at the table. Dollar bills lay in heaps across its surface, like piles of green leaves. The tall boss sorted them into neat heaps as he counted, licking his thumb frequently. Save for his hands, he was imperturbable, his eyes never wavered from the greenbacks. Another cop entered, drew a wad of bills fram an inside pocket and lay them on the table with ritualistic reverence. The police captain shoved it toward McBride with a mechanical gesture. The boss did not look up, but continued sorting the bills, pushing a rising pile before each man. I had heard of the Saturday-night payoff, the greenbacks that funnelled in from the speakeasies, the whorehouses, the gambling dens, the little browbeaten shopkeepers.

The door closed with a bang and I turned my face. After fifteen minutes or so the editor came out, poker-faced, striding in his slow dignity. "Let's go," he said in a strange voice, glancing at me quickly. We went down, silent, and got into his car. He suggested we take a little spin before going to the Bar, he needed a breath of air. He whizzed through the streets, his face dead-pan. "The big frog in a small puddle," I thought. Was that me, a decade hence?

4

The Road Turns Left

A MAN'S DESTINY awaits no formal introduction: it comes unannounced, in life, as it does in death. One day in early spring, a tall, sandy-haired man of thirty, wearing a red-checkered mackinaw and a cloth cap stopped at my desk to say he represented an organization called the International Labor Defense.

Since, he said, I may never have heard of it, too many people didn't, it defends workingmen and takes its stand for Labor's rights. He had read my columns, he said, and it struck him that I would be interested in what he had to say. When I nodded, he continued on to tell me that the City Council of Bethlehem had just passed an ordinance forbidding free speech. And that was a challenge to his members who had announced that they would read the Constitution before the gates of Bethlehem Steel which was notorious for its treatment of workingmen. He would like some newspaperman who believes in the Constitution to be there when they read it.

He surveyed me in a curious scrutiny. I looked up and his eyes were very blue and very innocent. There was caution in my voice when I replied that Bethlehem was up in Northampton County, which, unfortunately, lay outside my concern. He replied that he thought I was interested in free speech everywhere, and besides, some local folk would be there.

I sat quiet a moment, disturbed. True, my column gave me a latitude beyond the province of straight news, but I knew this topic was forbidden terrain. Like all newspapermen I knew my paper's policy but somehow the blue innocent eyes challenged me. The more I thought, the more I wanted to go.

I consulted with the editor and he replied, abruptly, "Reds," as though that closed the matter, but a moment afterward, he looked up again. "If he said some local people are going up there, maybe you ought to look into it."

The ILD man told me when his people would show up and asked me to keep the hour confidential. I arrived in Bethlehem, a town much like my own, several main streets of jumbled store-fronts, and crowds moving in a nervous bustle, obviously the families of workingmen. Darkened rows of wooden, two-story frame houses spread across the hills, the green of the maples tarred by the smoke of the great funnels that marched for a mile behind the barbed-wire fence of Bethlehem Steel. I noticed too that wherever a smokestack stabs the sky you will find a church steeple near at hand. Bethlehem was a city of churches, the bulbous towers of the Greek Orthodox, the granite of the Roman Catholic, the Gothic spires of the Protestant vied with the smokestacks.

On a vacant lot across the street from the main gate, a guard sat eating an apple which he cut carefully in quarters with a gleaming penknife. I glanced at my wrist watch and exactly at two, three small, canvas-topped trucks rounded the corner, and a score of young folk poured onto the lot, some wearing leather jackets. They set up, in a trice, a small platform, draped an American flag over the rail, and a slim, blonde young woman, eighteen perhaps, ran up the steps.

"Fellow-Americans," she cried in a high-pitched, girlish voice, "We of the International Labor Defense of this county are here to defend the Constitution. The authorities deny workingmen the right to meet and organize. Here is what the Bill of Rights says." She pulled a sheet of paper from her handbag and began reading.

The guard, apple in hand, jumped from his stool, fumbled for his whistle and blew a piercing blast. The crowd of youngsters closed around the stand as a troop of mounted policemen in chin-strapped helmets clattered from nowhere into the street. Two horsemen dismounted and seized the speaker, dragged her across the lot as she shouted, "Congress shall make no law abridging. . . ." A hand came down across her mouth, the slap exploded like a shot and the neat blue ribbon binding her hair came undone.

I suddenly discovered myself tearing at the cop's hand and, at the same moment, I was knocked off my feet by two other policemen, propelled in mid-air across the lot and dragged into a nearby building where I was flung into a cell. I slid across the stone floor and slammed into the opposite wall. The younger of the two cops, ruddy-faced with a small snub nose, stalked toward me. He said he would take care of this Red sonofabitch and he raised his fist. I shouted that I was a newspaperman which halted him a moment as he looked questioningly toward the other, who laughed, saying, "Good, give him something to write up." They pinned my hands behind my back and the younger man beat me carefully, like a blacksmith hammering at an anvil. I twisted and wriggled to free myself but after a few moments the room grew dark and I slumped to the stone floor.

When I came to, the cell, which had an arched ceiling like some ancient dungeon, was in shadows, the setting sun throwing a pale single shaft of light through a small barred window high up. I staggered to a bench and sat there, half stunned. My eyes becoming accustomed to the dark, I saw a man's body in the corner. It stirred and I recognized the checkered mackinaw of the young man who invited me here. He sat up slowly, shook his head as he regained consciousness. I tried to help him rise, but the effort was beyond me and I was suddenly sitting on the floor beside him, staring at a streak of blood coursing down his cheek. His eyes slowly focussed on me, blinked and then he said, his forehead wrinkling. "By God, it's the newspaperman."

We lay propped up on our elbows surveying each other and then he laughed ruefully, saying he had sure got me into a jam. I felt a sudden hot and blind fury as the faces of the two cops, their methodical brutality, returned to memory. They had beaten me without rancor, without anger or any special bitterness which made the matter all the more degrading, for it seemed to deny me any iota of human dignity. I had, for them, the sensibility and the quality of a leather punching-bag and for the first time in my life I sensed a strange and icy hatred.

A voice I could not recognize as mine said: "When I get out I will shoot those two bastards dead." My cellmate rose to his feet at that and helped me up. He fished a handkerchief from his pocket and wiped my face. "There," he said, surveying me unsteadily, "You look a lot better." And a moment afterward, "Now what was that you were saying?" I repeated it and he whistled in astonishment.

Then, in the heavy silence and gloom of the cell he carefully delivered a strange lecture which, as I remembered it through my rage, my frustration and my aching head, was to the effect that my impulse for revenge, natural and comprehensible as he could understand it to be, was sheer and crazy romanticism. You don't shoot cops who beat you up; they were merely instruments, like wooden clubs, in the hands of those who gave them their orders. Nor were these, as individuals, totally responsible: these, in turn, reflected a system, a class, the capitalist class. It was capitalism that was responsible, a way of life that was based upon the exploitation of one man by another, the working class by its employers. I remember him saying this was something that had to do with a struggle between classes; and Marx and Engels said way back in something called the Communist Manifesto that all history was the record of class struggles.

He spoke slowly though evenly, with a ready command of words, almost didactically, like some professors I had had. I remembered wondering what strange manner of creature was this who seemed to have no anger, no bitterness, for he had been beaten as I had been, and yet he spoke with a clinical objectivity as though all this might have happened to two other fellows, and after a while I strained my eyes through the dark to catch a glimpse of him. The flash of my physical pain and my sense of mortification, of shame, in fact, seemed to melt under the slow, steady cascade of his words which I tried hard to comprehend. I sat there, a morose young man, increasingly astonished at the tone of sober paternal authority this young man had, for he was not more than two or three years my senior.

"When we get out," he concluded, "I would like to talk to you. Think it over, and maybe you will want to talk to me." I am not certain which set of emotions dominated me at that moment: my pain and anger, or my wonder over this peculiar young man speaking with such curious detachment. After a while a policeman came and peered through the bars, unlocked the heavy wooden door with a great key. Flashing his searchlight on us, he pointed at me. "You," he said, "come with me." My cellmate pushed me forward, gripping my hand briefly in his. "Scram," he said, suddenly in the vernacular which sounded strange, coming after his discourse.

So they thought you were a Red, Hickey laughed when I returned to the office. He lay a friendly hand on my shoulder as he looked up from his pile of copy. "Heard they worked you over," he said, his bright eyes peering at me through the rimless spectacles. "Any damage?" He caught the expression on my face and his laughter trailed off.

I described my experience in great detail, telling him of this weird young man who seemed to transcend the clobbering he too had gotten, and Hickey replied, pursing his lips, that I should not be surprised for it was the way of the radical to seek martyrdom, that they contrived to get themselves into such plight in order to be crucified. They were unlike ordinary human beings, a streak of insanity ran through them all. "Like Jesus Christ?" I asked. Hickey slipped his glasses from his nose and wiped them. "Listen," he said finally, "take a day or two off. Go out to the ball game, get drunk. Get this stuff out of your mind. Maybe you need a doctor?"

"I don't want to get it out of my mind," I replied. "I want to keep my mind on it."

"Say," he said, "you are in a bad way."

It could well be that the editor was right, for the beating, and the strange performance of my cell-mate seemed to act as a catalytic agent in an unstable solution. All my disordered, nebulous dissents seemed to take form. I hunted up the ILD offices in Philadelphia to talk again with the young man in the mackinaw who invited me to spend an evening at his home. Home was a single, narrow room, with a single rickety chair, a small table on which lay a notebook and pencil and a heap of books and pamphlets. As he hustled about to fix some coffee on the gas burner, I thumbed through the names of the authors of the books—Jack London, Shakespeare, Lenin, Gorky, the Bible. I picked up the Scriptures and glanced at him quizzically. He caught the glance and smiled, saying that his father was a hard-shell Baptist who beat the Good Book into him with a switch. His angular face had a glow through which freckles showed and his smile was boyishly simple, the shy smile of an honest man. I recalled that when I first saw him, that day in the newsroom, I thought of his clear, frank eyes in a face that might possibly belong to a fanatic, but this smile changed it: he seemed a sort of grown-up Huckleberry Finn, cow-lick and all. After we talked a while he reached for a small slim book, the *Communist Manifesto,* and he read the lines which said that all history is a record of class struggles. I must have read it, he said, I had gone to college. When I replied that I had not, had not even heard it mentioned at the University, he said crisply, "Odd kind of education people get." I told him that in all my years at college no professor had ever mentioned the name of Karl Marx. "Well," he smiled that oddly luminous smile again, "your political education begins now."

And so my political education began. I met his friends as well as his books. Some I liked immediately, others seemed possessed by a sort of intellectual arrogance as though their allegiance to the ideas of Karl Marx gave them a kind of Brahminhood. Yet I was rather awed by their awareness and insatiable curiosity about matters political. All of them belonged to an International Labor Defense club of South Philadelphia, and most were the sons and daughters of working class families, an eager, zestful lot, having in common, I felt, a loyalty to matters beyond their immediate experience and association. They talked a great deal, and knowledgeably, about trade unions, standards of living, wage scales, labor leaders, labor fakers, Congress, Washington, London, Moscow. They impressed me with their sense of kinship to the world at large; and though they danced and sang, courted and made love, these essentials of their age, they were in their early twenties, seemed secondary to their involvement with mankind.

I found myself seeking their company more and more, drawn by that quality I rarely encountered elsewhere, of living not primarily for themselves but for a promising future about which they were boisterously, yet serenely, confident. I began to read the illustrated periodical of their organization, the *Labor Defender,* and now and then, saw a copy of the *Daily Worker* which was bizarre to my eye: it was written in a language that was, at once, colloquial and yet strangely intellectual, referring often to economics, philosophy and history which was beyond my ken. I would have taken them somehow as neophytes of some strange and worldly religion, a sort of latter-day following of Epicurus, had I not seen them in all their youthful and ordinary ebulliences—for music, for the movies, for the dance, for ordinary romance. That the girls, often as not, wore leather jackets and seemed somewhat disdainful of fashion, and the boys certainly disregarded the customary sartorial canons, did not escape me. Yet, in a way, I found that attractive, for it seemed a badge of their superiority over the garb and appearance of the Philistine. Tom Paine, too, I had read, cared mighty little about his appearance, lived primarily by his ethic, his principle, and, at the moment, it did not occur to me that others—unlike myself—might be repelled by their buoyant indifference.

One day I learned, accidentally, that my cellmate of Bethlehem had left town in the course of his duties and several weeks later I picked up a newspaper to discover that he was among some twenty-three union leaders and textile strikers arrested in Gastonia, North Carolina. The charge was murder. A chief of police had been shot as he led a gang of armed deputies in a raid on a tent colony of the strikers.

I hastened to the ILD offices to ask if I could somehow be of help to my friend. It did not once occur to me to question his guilt or his innocence. I assumed instantly that he was culpable of no wrong; I had been to Bethlehem. The ILD folk asked if I would help in the publicity department and, agreeing, I spent my evenings writing news releases, drafts of leaflets and statements explaining the issues of the case. Work on my newspaper had now become virtually meaningless and I could scarcely await the end of the day so that I could get to the main job, my volunteer post, the Gastonia case. And one night, several months later, a national leader of the ILD came to my typewriter to tell me that they needed a publicity man in the New York office, the national headquarters. Was I interested?

As a matter of fact I was enormously interested, but I wanted time to consider. This was a crossroad of my life, though I did not regard it as a fateful personal matter then. It came as naturally as the sun rose. Yet the road to New York would lead me to an unknown destination. I suspected I would forego the chance to rise in the world of commercial journalism, but no mundane ambition of that sort burned in me. Dominantly I was occupied with the matter of the men and women of Gastonia, my friend among them, who might die a felon's death. That they had gone to a distant community to help in others' affairs seemed right and just to me even though the Southern authorities and some of the northern newspapers assailed them as interlopers, carpet-baggers, trouble-seekers and trouble-makers. Why should they not pursue the course their consciences dictated? My natural sympathies were drawn as to a magnet by the plight of the southern textile worker which I could easily envisage, for my own experiences among the looms when I ran bobbins for the weavers gave me more than a clue. I remembered the generous, kindly women who mothered me when I was a kid of twelve wheeling my handtruck filled with spindles; and I read that the speedup, the stretchout, as they called it down South, required each weaver to work twice or three times the number of looms he tended before. I knew of the flux, the bleeding of the bowels, caused by a deficient diet. The ILD published photographs of the shacks that housed them, of the company towns that straggled up the Appalachian ranges, the obscure but palpable terrors which beset them. And they needed help from the North and they got it. If the man in the mackinaw could go South to aid his fellows in America, I could go to New York to offer my services for the social good. I decided to leave my job and go, and made the decision with no profound soul searching or inner upheaval. It just seemed time for me to go and that was all.

I explained to my mother that I was offered work in New York and that it attracted me. I did not, not yet, explain the nature of that work, fearing that it might disturb her. She replied, in effect, that I was a man, now, and if I wanted to go, I should go.

I had known that that would be her response. And yet I grieved to leave her. Mother she had been, abundantly, and yet she was more than that. We could talk as friends, man to man, so to speak. Her unfailing good cheer, her courage, her fierce honesty and luminous intelligence had been—and to this day —is, infectious. Her large, black, deep-sunk eyes so quick with understanding surveyed me, looked me up and down. "Yes, it is time for you to go," she said thoughtfully. "It is not good for a son to linger too long in his mother's house. You have wings now, my son, strong ones I believe. Use them. Fly high." I felt a pang of remorse, shame even, that I had not taken her into my confidence but I feared that my unorthodox course might worry her needlessly, and I sought somehow to spare her that. I resolved then to send her literature (she had learned to read in the past few years) and I would return to explain my course to her. But later—when I saw the direction of it more clearly myself. "Write often," she said, in parting, "and come when you can."

5

Hungry America

THE OFFICES OF the International Labor Defense had a quality of most working class headquarters in that time: a shabbiness of furniture, a disarray in cramped and narrow space that belied the fire and zeal of the occupants. The brightness of man's spirit shed a glow that transformed the drab quarters into temples of translucent light. The windows looked out upon the spires of Grace Church on Broadway, across the street, and from another view the spears of Wall Street pierced the skies.

Inside, the place hummed and buzzed and crackled, with militance and tragedy and hope. Through its doors came the disinherited, the injured, the defamed. Aunt Molly Jackson came from the coalfields of Kentucky, a gaunt and singing grandmother, the bard of the mountains through which the fabulous veins of coal ran amid the green pine. After telling of the lot of her folk, she sang the wonderful Coal Miners' Wife Blues and that anthem of the strikers, "Which Side Are You On?" which said, with a poignancy I found almost unbearable:

Come all of you good workers, good news to you I'll tell,
Of how the good old union has come in here to dwell.

Don't scab for the bosses, don't listen to their lies.
Us poor folks haven't got a chance, unless we organize. . . .

They say in Harlan County, there are no neutrals there.
You'll either be a union man, or a thug for J. H. Blair. . . .

Oh, workers, can you stand it? Oh, tell me how you can,
Will you be a lousy scab, or will you be a man? . . .

My daddy was a miner, and I'm a miner's son
And I'll stick with the union, till every battle's won.

And the refrain merely asked four times: *"Which side are you on?"*

Set to an old hymn tune it was composed by the wife of a coal miner during the bitter Harlan strike. Leaders of the striking miners came; tall, almost invariably, kin of Daniel Boone, the sons of coal-miners, descendants of the settlers out of Scotland, England, Wales, Ireland, tough, proud and uncrushed though a muted light of sadness lay in their eyes when they were silent. And when they broke their long silences, for they were taciturn men, they told me chilling stories, in their curious, undramatic manner which allowed the unadorned fact to convey the horror, telling of Buicks toting Chicago gangsters, "thugs," they said, "gun-thugs" who wore armor that clanked beneath their white broadcloth shirts and fine blue serge suits and who fired fusillades at them with machine-guns, insolent and murderous in their knowledge that the law was in collusion with them.

Broadchested Slavs came, in cheap, store-bought suits and broad-brimmed hats from Pensylvania to tell how federal agents battered in their doors with axes, hustled them into cars and held them in remote jails for weeks, incommunicado, until the compliant courts handed down writs to deport them from their homes. Negroes came, and in curiously soft yet brilliantly vivid words, told of the horrors they confronted daily: the constant and unspoken calumny that declared them inferior to neighbors of paler cast, the floggings that loosed the blood to run down their backs, the ritualistic lynch orgy whenever their determination to move forward an inch from the new-fangled slavery ran afoul of their employers' animal fear of them.

I received, as my pay, the very first week I came to work here, some $4.50—a sum which they arrived at by dividing the total in the till by the number of those working in the office. This did not deter me. I *was* taken aback, true, for I had accepted the proposed wage of $35 a week, which was fifty dollars less than I had been earning at the newspaper. But that sum was not available at the moment; bail had to be raised for a striking coal miner in the anthracite that week, the father of seven children, and who, in conscience, knowing that, could reject the only recourse the ILD organizers had? I couldn't, certainly, nor could anyone else in the office. Cheerfully, if disconcerted, they accepted what there was for wages, and tried one way or another to meet the urgent bills for rent and food and raiment.

I found a room in Lower Manhattan in that maze of tenements that were so enormously alive, in these days of hunger (it was shortly after the Stock Market had crashed).

I had just begun to read Marxist periodicals, books, seriously and systematically, and I discovered, with some awe, that the Communists had repeatedly warned the world of the impending economic crisis. Herbert Hoover's cheery campaign cry of a car in every garage and a chicken in every pot did not impress them. As a matter of fact their Central Committee at its October meeting in 1929 declared, after careful scrutiny of the national scene, that it saw "the clear features of an oncoming economic crisis which would shake the very foundations of the power of American imperialism."

The crash they foresaw came within days. For they had frequently written that the prosperity of the Twenties was built on sand; they pointed to the continued agricultural crisis, the considerable unemployment in coal, textile and other industries, and the fatal effects of overproduction caused by speedup and low wages. Profoundly impressed by their analyses based upon the principles of Karl Marx, I went to his books for further enlightenment: they spoke of the inevitable overproduction that results from the contradiction between owning industry privately and operating it socially. The insatiable appetite for the dividend created, periodically, a surfeit of commodities in this setup where the workingman could not buy back the goods he created. Economic glut caused human starvation and the drop in our stock market that wiped out, as with a wand, some $160,000,000,000 in paper values shook the entire capitalist world: some 5,700 banks failed in our country; and by 1933 some 17 millions of America's workers would be walking the desolate streets, jobless.

Though the tenement children seemed more scrawny, more ragged, than any I had ever seen, they played the immemorial games of childhood, pale of face, great of eye, played with that whole-hearted intensity that defied the craving within. Their elders moved in great gray caravans, it seemed to me, every morning to the employment offices that gave them scarce hope, and then to the relief offices, the only places where business flourished in that time. Many, evicted from the cold railroad flats, descended from the familiarity of the crowded slum to hopeless exile in the colonies of tin shacks then springing up in the shadows of the city, the cold hells they dubbed Hoovervilles. Yet, I marveled, that their culture, the appetites of their minds, remained alive. Nightly, speakers on soap-boxes talked endlessly and passionately to them of economics, politics, as if, by some legerdemain, words could fill stomachs. And the theaters, their prices drastically reduced, continued to play the Yiddish drama; no man's tongue shriveled with the hunger, for these were articulate, expostulating people who would not die silent amid empty cupboards. The life of the slum is infinitely more public than elsewhere. The red throbbing heart of the poor was as visible as the bleeding heart of Jesus that you often saw in the paintings exhibited in the stores where articles of religion were on sale for the Roman Catholic believers.

My room was on the top floor of a tenement house in the apartment of an old man, Aaron, and his wife, Sarah, who were members of the ILD. I had interviewed him one night for an article in the *Labor Defender* which I was now editing. "Come to my house," he said hospitably "we'll have a glass of tea and we'll talk." The simplicity and undercurrent of passion underlying his deliberate choice of words had drawn my attention at an ILD conference, and his face was one that captured you: long, reflective, seamed, his eyes a lucent gray, a crown of pure silver hair around a bald spot, he had the mien of an old Hebrew sage.

The apartment was pin-neat, though the floors were uncarpeted and the cold drafts seemed to came up through the wood's pores. But the walls took life from the cartoons pinned on them, drawings by working class artists whose names I was beginning to know well: Fred Ellis, Robert Minor, William Gropper, Hugo Gellert, whose workers seemed always to be giants in overalls, and whose bosses were always fat, in silk hats, pigmies of wealth. Their image of the worker as a kind of Gulliver captivated me, for nowhere else in the land, especially in these days when the worker, in the flesh was, like as not, approaching emaciation, reflected the confidence these folk had in their class. Poverty, misery, cold and hunger did not wither their dream, their concept, of the eternal rectitude of the workers' cause. In their mind's eye they saw him as he could be, or *is,* they would contend, I already knew, from my talks with the ILD members.

The cupboard may have been empty, but the bookshelves, I noted, were full: I took a few down from the shelves, well-worn novels of Jack London's, Maxim Gorky's, several of Mark Twain's, Sholom Aleichim, Marx' Capital, many pamphlets and slim books of working class songs and cartoons.

Aaron's wife, a small, dark woman who moved with the agility of a sparrow, sized me up silently. She thawed when she learned I worked at the ILD and I met their friends, men and women of the garment trades mostly, many of whom were Communists. Though they were pinched by the time's hardships, who was not in this day, they seemed always to have enough coin to buy the *Daily Worker,* and often, the *New York Times.* They were, like the others I was already encountering, astonishingly well-read, argumentative, their talk generously interspersed with quick laughter and friendly, if sharp, quips. Though food was certainly scarce (they seemed to exist on their tea, the bread and the potatoes) yet they sparked an electric energy and were incessantly on the go. Aaron, for example, swallowed his meager supper after his long day of work (for even in this time of unemployment he seemed somehow to find a day or two's work each week) and he was off for a meeting: his fraternal organization, or his Unemployed Council or his union or his ILD meeting or his Communist Party meeting, this conference, that. And though all about him men were forgetting how they looked and caring less, his dignity obliged him to dress neatly, brushing his single good suit carefully, and changing into it from his work clothes. Tall, spare, the aureole of fine silver hair well combed, he bore himself with the air of an ambassador.

At night I read the books Aaron thrust at me, and during the days I wrote for the *Labor Defender* and other periodicals on the left, most of which dealt with the unemployment of the time.

One blustery afternoon in February, I had occasion to seek Aaron out at the headquarters of the local Unemployed Council which were set up in an abandoned store. There they told me he was down the street, "putting the furniture back." Putting the furniture back was a phrase as commonplace as having a drink at the corner bar. A family down the block had been evicted from its quarters, a familiar sight these days; the marshals had piled the chairs and the tables, the bedsteads and iron pots on the street corner outside. Sometimes you would come upon an elderly woman sitting in a rocking chair, in her overcoat and hat for warmth, rocking and waiting. God knows for what, dispossessed of even the small corner of shelter she had known.

Down the street a score of men and women were industriously carrying furniture from the pavement up the front stoop into the house. The heads of dwellers in the adjoining houses poked through the windows, watching the scene solemnly, with an air that said there but for the grace of God go I. A child's voice piped up, "The cops, cheese it, the cops." A squad car sped up to the curb and halted at the scene. A policeman dourly shouldered his way through the men and women weighed down with tables and chairs who ignored him with a studied indifference. "Who's in charge here," the cop demanded and none among the men and women, carrying the furniture, answered. Aaron's lanky figure came down the stairs and he asked the policeman his business. "You in charge here?" the officer demanded.

"I am chairman of the local Unemployed Council," Aaron replied. "What is it I can do for you, captain?" There was an urbanity in his voice, though I detected a note of impatience as though the policeman's interruption had interfered with a commonplace but imperative civic operation.

The officer raised his voice authoritatively: the law was being broken and did you people know that? The men and women soberly continued up the stairs with the household goods. A middle-aged woman wearing a blue beret and who held one end of an old dresser said quietly, "Officer, would you mind stepping to a side, please?" The cop, startled, stepped aside and fastening his attention on Aaron whom he saw as the ringleader, blustered again that the law was being broken. Aaron ceremoniously put down the chair he carried. "Captain," he replied evenly, "I would suggest you ask the people if we're breaking the law." He looked up at the many faces in the tenement windows and the cop followed his gaze. What he saw in those faces unsettled him, it seemed to me, and casting a malignant glance at Aaron, he made for his prowl car, ducked into it and sped off to a chorusing jeer from the tenement windows.

I saw much of this in these days, but not all such episodes ended peaceably. Frequent was the sound of the crack of police-club over the skull of the folk who returned the furniture; and in a number of instances after the police had precipitated a conflict, their pistols spurted and men died. A man by the name of Steve Katovis was the first, and thirty thousand marched through the streets in his honor. A. B. Magil and I wrote a pamphlet on the tragedy, told of the Greek shepherd who came from Hellas with a heart-full of hope, to die in America because he believed no man, no child, should have a pavement as his home.

As the lines of the jobless grew longer, and the relief offices closed for want of municipal funds to feed, to some degree, the starving, the Unemployed Councils, supported by the Communist Party, designated March 6, 1930 as a day for the jobless to demonstrate on the public squares of the nation, to demand state and federal unemployment insurance that would be paid for by the employers, the state and the federal governments. "Work or Wages" their slogan declared: "Don't Starve—Fight!" A fury of official and newspaper denunciation rose. This was the European dole, a concept totally alien to the proud and free American, the newspapers cried, regarding the sale of apples on street corners more suitable to the genius of our countrymen; it, evidently, reflected the spirit of free and private enterprise, a calling similar to the transactions of J. P. Morgan and Co., differing only in the commodity sold.

An electric air of tension rose through the streets of New York. The police commissioner warned the Communists "to leave their women and children home March 6th," and the mayor prohibited the demonstration called for Union Square. President Hoover, who had faithfully been predicting the end of the depression in sixty days, suddenly summoned a national conference of employers and of labor leaders "to discuss unemployment."

I left my room early that morning, while Aaron and Sarah were preparing to go to the demonstration, and I headed for the Square. At Fifteenth Street, I passed many platoons of apprehensive police, half-hidden in the doorways of office buildings. Troops of mounted cops champed on the nearby pavements. As I turned the corner my heart leaped as my gaze encompassed multitudes who filled the Square from corner to corner; on they they came, endless brigades of the jobless, sweeping down from all the highways and hungry boroughs.

Policemen stood silhouetted on the roofs of buildings surrounding the square, the bright March sun glinted off the shotguns they brandished. None seemed to notice them, nor even to care, for on they came, singing, as though the very act of hauling their hunger into the public reaffirmed their dignity. Standing among the pressmen I saw the police commissioner, a celebrated dandy who had been loaned by John Wanamaker to the city. He wore a little pink boutonniere in his lapel and the hair of his temples was sleek beneath the polished derby. One of the reporters said, "The goddam fool's provoking them." The police official coldly refused this vast assembly of New Yorkers the right to march down Broadway to the City Hall. He had suffered a delegation chosen by the jobless to consult with him and he denied their request. The delegation was led by William Z. Foster, then the chairman of the Trade Union Unity League, and others were Robert Minor, the editor of the *Daily Worker,* Israel Amter, New York leader of the jobless, Harry Raymond, then an unemployed seaman and another jobless man named Lester.

Foster returned to the rostrum and silence fell upon the scene so that you could almost hear the heartbeat of 100,000 men and women; I heard the hoarse whistle of tugboats, and the distant honk of a horn. "Shall we march to City Hall?" Foster asked, raising his arm high. The affirmative roar startled the pigeons that went wheeling into the sky. Suddenly I heard the wild clatter of rearing hooves and I saw the horseshoes gleam over men's heads: a swarm of plainclothesmen separated from the crowd, swinging blackjacks. The March air groaned with the thud of nightsticks across human bone. The horsemen rode into the crowds, motorcycles of police joined them, and the great mass of unemployed seemed to break into segments, that closed up immediately, massing on the pavements and inching their way, inexorably, southward, toward City Hall. When I arrived there the police were patrolling every byway amid the slim maple trees whose spring buds were showing. I came in time to see the unemployed delegation, Foster and Minor and the others, standing on the municipal steps. A score of police fell upon the delegation and dragged them from the steps, into patrols, to prison.

The ILD had mobilized its branches through the country to represent those arrested, to supply bail and to issue statements to the newspapers. The numbers of those demonstrating began to come in by telephone: 100,000 in Detroit, that same number in New York, scores of thousands in other cities. By nightfall we knew that more than a million and a quarter had marched. How Americans had changed since General Jacob Coxey led his ragged army across the nation to Washington in the "panic of 1893," only to be dispersed on the White House Lawn. His noble ranks lacked the iron of discipline, organization, planfulness of these latter-day marchers.

This was the beginning of the historic counter-attack: hunger would not rampage, arrogant and unchecked. The demonstrations shook Washington, Albany, all the state capitals: unemployment insurance was a banner flung across the land. Men, for the first time, cried that the state's primary obligation was to feed its hungry millions when the wheels of industry came to a standstill. It was a turning point in our nation's history.

The crisis roared on in flood-tide when the dam is broken. Lines of ragged men wound round the nation's factories. Fourteen, fifteen, sixteen, and finally seventeen millions were without jobs, official statistics reluctantly admitted.

The editors of *Labor Unity,* the weekly organ of the Trade Union Unity League to which the Unemployed Councils were affiliated, asked me to travel across the country and write a series on the jobless. I promptly agreed, and packing a couple of clean shirts and pairs of socks in a satchel and Frederick Engels classic sociological study, *The Condition of the Working Class in England in 1844,* I shook hands with Aaron, and Sarah, who kissed me goodbye.

Next to me, on the bus, her face virtually hidden by her kerchief and turned-up collar, slept a woman of, I assumed, middle-age. The driver doused the lights as we came into Jersey and the woman, at one point where the bus stopped with a jerk, awoke and began to talk to me in the dark. Her voice trailed off as she told the familiar story of the day: her husband had gone away to hunt a job; after the first few letters in the first few months, he stopped writing. She had no knowledge of his whereabouts, assuming solely that he was wandering in pursuit of the job, and discouraged because he found none, abandoned his marriage and his family. Three children had already gone home to her folks on a farm near Columbus, Ohio; now she was coming home, penniless, the fare eating up the last few dollars she had.

She too had searched for work everywhere in New York, where she had lived the past ten years with her husband, a printer by trade. No, she could not blame him, she said, he had such pride, and no man is a man when he has no job, he would say. She saw no future, she had lost her man, "a good man, a good provider, never came home drunk," a good father to his children and now there was nothing and nobody, save her ageing folks who, God knows, had trouble enough of their own. What she would do when she came home? Who could tell? It was better to be dead than to live this way, mister. What is it, why does it need to be this way? How did it get this way? Why do some people have all, and others, nothing? What curse befell her? She was honest, a good mother, she had lived a good life with her husband, and now—what?

She spoke in a monologue, talked into the ear of a stranger in the dark on a bus careening across America. She never saw my face, nor I hers; her voice seemed disembodied, the voice of millions suffering as she suffered. She got off at Pittsburgh, as dawn was about to break, and for the first time I saw her face.

It was that of a woman no more than thirty, who had once been pretty, not long ago, but care had stolen the sparkle from her eye, and left deep lines about her mouth, taut now, when once, I could see, it had been merry. She said good-bye in a lacklustre voice, and as the bus pulled away she stood, uncertain at the curb, looking to the right and to the left, her suitcase in hand, a figure of bewilderment.

So much of America was bewildered, looking to the right and to the left. In the rich farmlands of southern Indiana I saw a scene that seemed to sum it up. A young, broad-shouldered farmer rattled along the road soberly driving a contraption born of the depression: a Ford sawed in two, the horse hitched to the rear half which had been fitted up with shafts, the machine-age reverting to the horse-and-buggy time, slipping back half a century. "No money for gas," the farmer said laconically, "but grass comes free. Least it did when I last looked." In Duluth, queen city at the head of the Lakes, as a signpost described her, I hunted up the organizer for the Unemployed Council, a local man who spoke of his city's pre-depression glories: Duluth sits at the edge of the great wheat belt; Duluth makes and ships steel; Duluth gathers to herself the dairy products of Minnesota.

And today, he said, today—no, he would not tell me the story, I must hear it for myself. He took my arm and led me along, the edge of Lake Superior, past handsome shops that catered to those few who were fortunately weathering the depression, and we came to the ramshackle part of the city where the Finns, the Negroes and the French Canadians lived. He knocked on the door of a shabby two-story frame house and a Finnish woman of 60 or so, wiping her hands on her apron, came to the door. He told her a protest demonstration would be held at City Hall the next day and would she come and speak, just tell her story. "We heard about it," he said, "and by God we expect to get something done."

The woman brushing loose strands of her faded flaxen hair into place invited us into the kitchen where a stove stood forlornly, unlit. She said her husband had gone off to Minneapolis seven months before, hunting work, but he found none. The few dollars he had been sending ceased coming, and now the city relief had ceased helping. "And now?" the organizer prompted. "And now there is nothing." The organizer said, looking away, that a mutual friend reported to the Unemployed Council that she had killed the pet dog for food. The woman's pale blue eyes surveyed us unblinking. "I got three children," she replied, "It was Oscar or them. We had nothing else for five days." The children were out, scrounging for food, she said, and pointed to a little wooden cross near the fence. "The young ones buried Oscar's bones," she said evenly, "He was a pet a long time."

Doubtless today's American would find this Duluth episode unimaginable, yet I encountered two more similar instances on my travels. Picture the moment however: unemployment rose so steeply and so fast that the municipalities—unaided by federal funds—found it impossible to keep pace. Relief offices, inadequate and heartlessly so at best, closed down in city after city, as mothers and fathers beat on their doors. Since no man sinks willingly to the pavement to starve when food is stacked on shelves all about him, what I encountered in Van Dyke Michigan, was inevitable. Americans knew that mountains of surplus grain were being deliberately burned in great bonfires; read that oranges were dumped into the sea in California. And they looked into the pallid faces of their children. So, in the Michigan town I saw a grim procession of some two hundred men, women and children march down the main street toward Six Mile Road. They bore placards that said: "Fools Starve—Men Fight," and "Our Children Are Hungry." They converged on an A.&P. store and dismantled it in a matter of minutes. A matron pulled down a stalk of bananas and flung it over her shoulder; two gaunt men hauled out a tub of mackerel; a child in pigtails hugged a ham while her mother piled boxes of Kellogg's cereals into a large basket, and her husband lugged a rump of beef to the door.

I spoke to a large, round-faced woman who stuffed a bologna, five loaves of bread and half a dozen cans of soup into a big sack. "Mr. Licht at the Welfare said he couldn't help us, mister. Well, we're a helping ourselves. Expect us to starve while there's food on the shelves?"

In Youngstown I sat in a large bare cement room while a gray-headed Negro spoke to the unemployed. "It's one thing," he said, his large, black fingers outstretched, "to starve when they ain't no vittles. But," as his fingers curled into a fist, "when stores is full, the Lord says we gotta do something." Cries of "Amen" went up through the room. "Boss man says to us," the Negro intoned, " 'Go on, workin'men, and stahve.' What we say to boss man?" A small white woman of German origin shouted, "If they won't give, we'll take." The meeting concluded in a march to City Hall where the mayor listened very respectfully, nodded his head vigorously, sympathetically, as they spoke, and conceded promptly to one of their demands: that five hundred men sleeping in the building housing the city incinerator be given cots in the precinct police station. And the mayor hastily said he would, that afternoon, see to it that appropriate funds would be supplied the relief offices.

In Chester, Pennsylvania, where vast plants belonging to the Sun Shipbulding and Drydock Company line the waterfront, as well as an assortment of other major industries, I listened to the Unemployed Council meeting in a long room above the river. The speaker, a Scot, was telling the audience, "So the little gairrl fainted in class. The teacher picked her up. 'What's wrong, Mary?' the teacher asked. The little gairrl shook her head, then whispered that she was hungry. 'Hungry?' the teacher said, 'Why you poor child, you go right home and eat!' The little gairrl said it was no use to go home. 'Today ain't my turrrn to eat,' she told the teacher, 'Today's my sister turrrn.' "

And so, in the midst of this saturnalia of hunger, the respect for the program of the Unemployed Councils exploded into a tangible political force overnight. Belief in the power of massed men burgeoned everywhere; March 6 had been a lightning bolt in the bleak American sky. The precepts avowed there crossed the land, by the grapevine, by leaflet, by the speeches of aroused men and women who rightfully deemed it insanity to condemn Americans to starvation while the abundance of our soil lay in locked warehouses. Members of Unemployed Councils united, pounded thrice to Washington, D. C., in national caravans, insisting that the government intervene against this man-made hunger. Social wisdom grew like grass in spring—and ultimately I saw the well-fed pass laws to provide unemployment insurance for Americans, eager, desperately eager, to work, but unable to find work because capitalism was found wanting.

I wrote many articles for *Labor Unity,* some for the monthly *New Masses* and I submitted one to the organ of the liberals, the *New Republic* which had carried some vivid pieces on the plight of the jobless. The editors of the *New Republic* invited me to their offices in Chelsea, where I came—after my journey through famished America. I respected its writers and critics as men of erudition and superior literary attainment. I was unprepared, however, for the—to me—elegance of its quarters, the thick Persian rug on a polished floor, the stained glass windows that gave it the sanctified air of a cloister. Half a dozen men, several in smoking jackets, stood at their ease, laughing, gay, carefree, or so it seemed to me, my nerves frayed by the sights of my journey.

One editor introduced himself as Edmund Wilson whose pieces of first-hand observation at scenes similar to those I witnessed had passion and a memorable literary quality. At his desk he asked me softly about the Unemployed Councils and their program, and he concluded with a question about their political goals, whether they "advocated revolution." I replied, nettled, that the councils of hungry men advocated survival, through the immediate redress of their well-established grievances. Of course, Communists among the jobless declared their belief that only socialism could ultimately cure this madness about which he had written so eloquently himself.

And then Wilson asked if I were a Communist. I replied that the question was a non-sequitur, that although I had no hesitance to discuss my political beliefs with him, I failed to see its revelance to an issue which should command the instant and joint attention of all civilized men. No, Wilson replied, his question was pertinent; if I were a Communist my report would inevitably be colored by my beliefs and would lack the objectivity his magazine required. "A larder, for instance," he smiled, "might be half empty. A Republican would describe it as almost full, a Communist might say it is almost empty, and a liberal would say, forgive me, that it is half full. The viewpoint is decisive." I thought of the woman in Duluth who ate her dog and I reminded Wilson of an old English proverb that says a full stomach cannot understand the empty one. He laughed, saying he might justly suspect that my views are Communistic. Anyway, my account appeared a few issues later and was titled," A Communist Looks At the Depression."

Afterward, I considered Wilson and contrasted the liberals to the Communists I had met. Wilson's sympathies lay with the America that was hungering; he wrote powerfully as a man whose heart was hurt by the sight of human waste, degradation amid plenty—herein he and the Marxists shared a community of view. The common path forked at a point where Wilson trod to the right: he believed that capitalism, managed by men of conscious humanity, could furnish our nation an abundance that would erase the shame of the depression. Communists, I felt, believed that men of good will and unquestioned ability could not steer a foundering ship, its rudder smashed, through the shoals of our contemporary economy. Men like Wilson—nobly intentioned as they might be—could only misguide the hungry. Those respectable vandals who burned wheat scoffed at the pleas of the hungry; and the hungry could scarcely nourish their children on the merits of Wilson's prose. Communists, as I understood them, were convinced that the mighty retreat only when a greater might confronts them, and that the political potential of organized and determined men was that great might. Wilson—the gentle adherent of capitalism—feared, at bottom, the creation of that counterposing might and confused it with a summons to revolution.

I thought afterward of a scene near Pontiac, Mich., that I should have recounted to him. An old farmer, whose father had walked across the Appalachians to settle on this plot of land, invited me to his house for some elderberry wine while we talked of the Unemployed Councils. When we finished speaking, the grizzled old man pointed to the sill over his door. A big shotgun hung suspended there. "When the Unemployed Councils are ready," he said with a meaningful smile, "I'll take *that* down." He was not needed for this *political* action, he said deprecatingly, others could do that as well and better. But he could shoot straight. No, I repeated, the Unemployed Councils do not propose to settle matters with *that,* gesturing toward the gun. "That's what's wrong with them," he grumbled. And he spoke of neighboring farmers who had been mortgaged off the land their families had owned and worked for a century. "Good, hardworking farmers," he said, thoughtfully, "and now the city bank's got their land." Not him, he shook his head, not him: he would fight it out, bullet for bullet, if they ever tried that on him.

Yes, there were Americans to the "left" of the Unemployed Councils Edmund Wilson missed on his travels.

6

Some Tattered Scholars

The New Republic regarded me as a Communist, but my old Hebrew seer, Aaron, knew better. "Well," he asked, peering at me thoughtfully through his spectacles, "why *aren't* you a Communist?" I could not answer that question, not immediately. My past had left a scar tissue, a subtle, stubborn distrust of ideas which men purported to be gospel truth. I believed the real was as slippery and as uncertain as quicksilver when you lay your finger on it, apt to scatter into a hundred pieces.

Communists, like Aaron, I saw, had an abiding belief, a trust, a conviction that the world could change and the men on it could change it. True, I shared the crusade of which they were the core, to help America's workingmen, my class, survive. It seemed to me that the Marxist alone had the answer to the agony of the times. I saw none else advocating rational answers that would restore this land to sanity. The liberals expounded the difference between a full larder and a half-empty one. But they did not march with the hungry, or beat on the doors of legislative halls; the Communists did, and it was necessary. My impulses were primarily humanitarian—really akin to those of Wilson's. I held with the Communists that the well-fed must shoulder the responsibility to provide bread for those who had none. A man need not be a Marxist to understand that.

As the months rolled on I saw that our people were less hungry because Communists existed in America. They offered hope on this earth, as religion offered it in a remote Heaven. But they dedicated themselves to a fight for it here and now. I saw that the Communists asked no profit for themselves, accepted scorn and hatred and physical injury to promote the welfare of their fellow-men.

But I did not know, nor could I understand, why the Communists alone appeared to have the apt answer and the brave deed. Aaron contended that Marxists saw farther than other men because they stood on the eminence of a philosophy, a social science, which held that truth was knowable, that man could illumine the dark and chart a direction though it.

Naturally I sought to understand that science, that philosophy. Marxists, like Aaron, diligently plied me with books and pamphlets which I read, as well as their newspapers, the *Daily Worker,* and the literary magazine, the *New Masses.* I found, after a time, that this movement, maligned and misunderstood, was a kind of poor man's university. All about me I discovered men and women, virtually in rags, in need of three square meals a day, who studied with an ardor I rarely encountered at college. Mark Hopkins, I believe, said a university could be a student and a teacher seated on a log. The new universities had their campus in the cold rooms of working class neighborhoods where men and women pored over books, scholars in rags. "And why don't you join a study group?" Aaron asked one night. "Even a college man can learn," he smiled.

I joined. A dozen workingmen and workingwomen came through a drizzle carrying books, handling them with a reverence that I felt was actually religious. Covertly I contemplated these proletarian scholars, their scuffed shoes, their worn coats and the glow in their faces. A stalwart man of twenty-five introduced himself as the teacher. "It doesn't matter how little schooling we've had," he said softly. "These are working class books and the working class can understand them." I discovered that most of these students had five or six years of formal education, some less, and yet they came to study after a hard day's work, or a hard day seeking work.

We pored over books of philosophy, political economy, pamphlets on matters that were at the core of our time. They talked of Hegel and Feuerbach, Marx and Lenin. They were not dismayed by formidable terms like dialectical materialism, surplus value, absolute and relative impoverishment. I realized the faults of my education at Penn for not once, in my years there, had I even heard these terms. Gradually, I began to marvel at the Marxist philosophy as I read on into the dawn hours—I sensed why it held men. It inspired hope by destroying illusion.

Yes, history came clear and I saw the indisseverable relation between the social, the economic, the political. I traded Plato for Hegel, Socrates for Marx, and I was the gainer. I saw that these Marxist thinkers were men of towering dimension, but most meaningful to me was the realization that they stood as giants because they plumbed the innermost truth of their time and they built upon that; they were nurtured by the same social forces which created the working class and they affiliated their lives to the class destined to embrace all of humanity. I believe I understood why Marx and Engels said nearly a century before, that "The history of all hitherto existing society is the history of class struggles." The years of my own life spelled that out for me, and I understood then why workingmen come more quickly to grasp the essentials of Marxism than those of other classes. I concluded that Marxists were justified in their confidence, for their faith, unlike that of my friends who worshipped God, had roots in reason, in science, not in mythology. And for the first time in my life I gained a sense of certainty, a sense of history. Mankind could, and would, as Engels said, march from the Kingdom of Necessity into the Realm of Freedom—Socialism. All else, he wrote, was "pre-history." Others strove to understand the world: Marxists sought to change it. The passionate yet scientific humanism of these books, their essential optimism and joyous belief in life was oxygen in these dark and stifling days.

My bookshelves soon became heavy with volumes and pamphlets that explored the course of history in the France of 1789, 1830, 1848, 1871; of our own nation of 1776, and 1861; of Russia in 1905 and 1917. I discovered that many men in my own land had had a dream of socialism, and stubbornly pursued their belief through lifetimes of hardship and imprisonment: such a man was the Eugene Debs of my boyhood.

I discovered later, that Robert Owen, the Utopian Socialist, a precursor of the scientific socialism that Marx and Engels founded, came to our land in 1825 and received an ovation when he spoke of socialism before both houses of Congress with President John Quincy Adams in the chair. And Horace Greeley and Charles Dana had no hesitance to employ Dr. Karl Marx as the European correspondent for the old *Tribune* during the crucial years from 1851 to the outbreak of the Civil War. Staid old Samuel Gompers, one of the founders of the American Federation of Labor originally foresaw a socialist commonwealth as the best of all possible worlds for labor; and he once desperately sought Engels' advice to help him solve an inner labor dispute here that involved the crusade for the eight-hour day.

I learned that the socialist idea gained such headway here in the latter years of the Nineteenth Century that men like William Dean Howells, editor of the *Atlantic Monthly,* the author of *The Rise of Silas Lapham*—close friend of Emerson and Longfellow and Thoreau—died a socialist; and that by 1912 its partisans won nearly a million votes at the polls for Debs, as president, as again they did in 1920, when their candidate sat in a penitentiary cell because he opposed war. I saw that the socialist idea had roots in all lands, in mine as well, and that no alien brand could be stamped upon its forehead anywhere in the world.

If the American Bellamy's *Looking Backward* envisaged, in 1888, a fraternal commonwealth in which all workingmen would own the nation's wealth—a book that had a massive sale here—I chanced to come upon a time when a nation of the world was known as the Union of Socialist Soviet Republics. What was happening there? My bookshelves soon acquired the works of Beatrice and Sidney Webb, who visited that land as enemies and came away as friends: of the Soviet writers themselves—Gladkov, Alexei Tolstoy, Sholokhov. And I read all of Lenin's works I could find. I could almost see that endless and mysterious land which only a few years ago was the home of the "dark masses" who lived by the chant of black-garbed priests; I saw the onion-shaped spires of the Greek Orthodox Church rising from the snows and the steppes, and understood the poverty Gorky painted, (I had sensed much of it from my earlier readings of Chekhov, Turgeniev, Tolstoy, Dostoievsky). John Reed, the American from Oregon, Walter Lippmann's classmate at Harvard, enabled me to understand the ten days that shook the world in November. Lenin's writings had a transcendent effect, and I understood how the slogan of Peace, Bread and Land could bring the decisive strata of a hungering, war-weary and disillusioned nation to adopt the socialist solution. I pored over every day's budget of news from that land as Walter Duranty wrote it in the *New York Times,* and as I came to find it in the *Daily Worker.* The folk of that land, I decided, had chosen an unalterable course to advance the possibilities of the world's peace. For I saw that socialism could not, by its nature, promote wars for aggrandizement or for the enslavement of the unarmed and impoverished colonials of the world.

So what I read, but primarily what I saw in life, in action, of the Communists I met (added to what I knew of my own capitalist world before I encountered Communists), persuaded me that the cause was just, its victory was inevitable as the leaves of spring. I came toward them originally from humanitarian purposes, for I had no stomach for politics, having seen enough in my home town to last me a lifetime. But theirs appeared to be politics of a different brand: no quest was this for boodle. It had the essential purity of the Golden Rule, and if its mode was militant so was that of a Carpenter who whiplashed moneylenders from a Jerusalem temple. So I accepted the dictum of Lincoln Steffens who, from Russia, wrote that he had seen the future and it works. I believed him. And I believed that my patriotism was truest if I advocated the ultimate transformation of our society to one free of classes, where all were truly equal and all would cooperate for the advancement of mankind. For, if I believed that socialism was a stage higher in humanity's status, and if I stayed silent because of possible penalties pioneers must pay, then I was a betrayer of my patriotism.

It was a heady joy to realize that I lived in the age of the turning point. Hence I rejected the newspaper accounts written about Soviet Russia, regarded them as products of "lie factories," as someone termed them, for I knew what publishers wanted in their papers. I would not believe the iniquities of socialism they described, and which obsessed them.

Nor was I so naive to assume that the road to Utopia could be as straight as that of an arrow to a bull's-eye. I had read enough of our own Revolutionary War to know the Tories; of our Civil War to know the Copperheads. Each age has its Copperheads. The Marxists said no class relinquishes its possessions and privileges without fiercest conflict. So it had been in the French Revolution, so in ours, so in our South; when I read of "excesses and crimes" committed daily in the first socialist republic, I judged them as I would the accounts in our papers of America's trade unions.

7

My March Through Georgia

I SAT LATE one night working at the ILD offices, along with another man, Richard B. Moore, a tall, slim Negro orator who had a magnetic quality of speech. I was editing the *Labor Defender,* whose previous editor James S. Allen had gone to live in the South where he edited the *Southern Worker,* a Communist tabloid newspaper, and where he collected material to write his pioneering books on the economic and political substructure that supports the oppression of America's Negroes.

A Western Union messenger delivered a telegram which said that nine Negro boys were "taken from a freight train at Paint Rock, Alabama, near Scottsboro, threatened with lynch frame-up on rape charges." At midnight Moore telephoned Joseph Brodsky, the ILD's leading lawyer who, a few minutes afterward, charged into our office, a roly-poly man with a pair of bright, searching eyes. He summoned the ILD officers, and together they mapped the first moves to help the innocent sons of the South.

The key to win, the ILD, and its supporters, exhorted their members and all others who would listen, lay in what they called "mass pressure"—the organized, political outcry of millions. William L. Patterson, also a lawyer, the first Negro political leader with whom I worked, and who was then the ILD's head, radiated a confidence that the boys could be saved. But it would not happen unless the blacks and whites of the nation cooperated. A disturbing fear nagged at me that that cooperation could not be realized in time. Too well I remembered the race riots in my home town when whites stalked Negroes to kill in the streets.

My newly-acquired Marxist convictions insisted that unity could be won; my experienced associates were confident, yet I had my doubts.

One day I agreed to speak on the case in Red Bank, N. J., at a meeting to be held in a Negro church. The town lay in the heart of territory where the KKK burned crosses thirty feet high at convocations several years before. I learned that the Negro parishioners had been threatened, but they had determined to hold their meeting.

I arrived in a rustic tree-lined town, and found some 700 men and women, all Negroes, inside the church, virtually the town's entire colored population. As the meeting opened a white man in a seersucker suit strode up the aisle to the platform, motioned to the minister, with a crook of the finger, to say that he wished to speak for the Americanization Committee of the local Legion post. The minister replied courteously that the list of speakers was closed but he would gladly make room for anyone favoring the cause of the Scottsboro boys. The man nodded and leaped on the stage. When he spoke, he turned to the flag, saluted it, pivoted to the audience. His people, he said, respected the colored folk as law-abiding citizens. What happened in Scottsboro seemed to be a miscarriage of justice which he was certain the courts would rectify. But, he said, his voice turning curt and hard, "aliens in America's midst" make capital of such cases. Their sole aim is to fan hatred between the races, set each man's hand against his neighbor's, and his Post knows who they are. "They are on this platform," he ended dramatically. And he returned to his chair.

The air turned tense, electric when the minister called on me. I outlined the facts of the case, its patent frame-up quality, gave my evidence for believing so, and I related it to the general oppression of the Negro millions who were "chained to the soil by brute force and the denial of their Constitutional guarantees." I said the innocents would never die if Labor and all fair-minded whites supported the Negro cause. I cautioned them against reposing confidence in the Alabama courts which represented the mind and interests of the landowners. Who, I asked, had heard of one Southern court that convicted one single Klansman?

As I spoke, the man in the seersucker, rose and strode toward me, his eyes blazing. "You Red bastard," he muttered as he stood before me, and he raised his fist. As it rose the assemblage of 700 rose with it, silently, but with an undeniable purport. The man, glancing sidewise, caught the impact of 700 pairs of eyes focussed on his fist. Ludicrously, he stared up at his own clenched hand, his eyes returning to the audience, and then his arm came down slowly, reluctantly, and the audience, as slowly, and as reluctantly, settled back in the seats. His face frozen in a mask of scorn, he marched down the aisle and out of the door.

The decorum of the temple was possibly disturbed by the audible jubilation at his departure, but a few minutes later, a Negro who had remained outside as sentinel, passed word in that a band of whites was gathering a block away. When it came time for me to leave, the entire congregation, seven hundred strong, women as well as men, escorted me through the streets to the railroad station; only an armored tank could have pierced the protection of that human wall. A dozen of the most stalwart rode with me to Newark, to guard against any chance that the fellow may have telephoned his henchmen up the line.

I arrived in New York, agog with triumph. The display of understanding and fraternity of black men for a white exhilarated me. The white opponents to the meeting had totalled no more than thirty, the Negro minister said when I boarded the train, it was nothing to worry about. The episode served to dispel the doubts assailing me, for here in Red Bank I believed I had seen that which is "nascent"—the new that was being born—displacing that which is "moribund"—the old that was dying—an expression from my Marxist readings which impressed me indelibly. It seemed to be the epitome, to me, of the Marxist attitude toward reality. They endeavored to discover and define truth in a world of perpetual change, and I believed that they were right: the truth can be attained only be distinguishing the new from the old, and recognizing those components of the old which cling to the new.

I had no illusions about my adventure in the small Jersey town. It was the exceptional, even though it represented the new. And what I had witnessed there was not so rare in by-gone days: the history of the Abolitionists was studded with instances of a joint effort between white and Negro: John Brown and Frederick Douglass were symbols of that. The early Reconstruction days, as I learned from books like James S. Allen's, revealed that. But then grim aspects of the old were restored a dozen years after the Civil War in the code of the nightriding Klan, spawned, as it was, by the recalcitrant gentry. And sanctioned, as it was, by the treacherous alliance of the Republican bankers of the North and the defeated landowners of the South who signed their private peace pact in President Hayes' day. A war of attrition followed, a subtle and an open terror, that robbed the Negroes of the hard-won rights the 13th, 14th and 15th Amendments guaranteed them.

A new slavery was born that displaced the chattel form; and millions of Southern Negroes lived as virtual serfs in the fertile crescent of the Black Belt that curved from Virginia to the Gulf of Mexico. And in those farmlands plowed primarily to cotton, where more Negroes lived than whites, the terror to cow them was greatest.

And so, as the ILD and the Communists argued, we saw the Scottsboro case: many similar atrocities exploded in the lovely southern land. Desperate sharecroppers of Camp Hill, Ala., banding into a union against the hunger fending them in, were shot down in their meeting place. And so, news came North that a young Negro named Angelo Herndon was sentenced to twenty years on a Georgia chaingang because he was heroic enough to lead a procession of two hundred unemployed men and women, whites as well as Negroes, to the Atlanta municipal building to ask for some alleviation of the widespread hunger.

I read the Georgia law under which he was tried, convicted and sentenced: it had been written into that state's books a full century before, in 1831, and its preamble said enough: "Any person convicted of the defense of insurrection of slaves shall be punished with death, or if the jury recommend to mercy, confined to the penitentiary for a term of not less than five years or more than twenty years."

The jury had regarded itself as mercifully Christian when it recommended mercy—20 years. Herndon, the son of a Tennessee coal miner, a tall, handsome studious youth, had left home after his father's death to find work in Gadsden, Alabama. His path crossed that of the Unemployed Councils, he became acquainted with Communists, began to read their literature, and shortly thereafter, became one of them. Displaying the zeal of exceptional youth, he volunteered the organization of the jobless, was arrested time and again, chased by a mob intent on lynching him, and finally, came the Atlanta conviction. They kept him in Fulton Tower, a notorious Georgia prison, where his honesty and courage gained the loyalty of the prisoners about him. The

ILD carried his case to the higher courts, and, after two years of arduous legal effort—and "mass pressure"—he came out on bail. I was at the uproarious celebration honoring his release when he came up to New York to speak for the ILD; several thousand persons at Pennsylvania station carried him triumphantly on their shoulders. But the joy was short-lived: after he addressed mass meetings throughout the country, the Appellate Court of Georgia ruled against him, cancelling his bail and demanded his return to Fulton Tower. A columnist in the *Pittsburgh Courier* advised him publicly to jump bail: the young man carefully considered his course and declared publicly that he would return so that the issues of his case would be aired before the courts and the nation. "Fool!" some journalists sneered, one newspaper carrying a cartoon of a small figure standing outside the towering gates of a Georgia prison, the caption asking, "Little Man, What Now?"

A hero, others said, and they were many. At the ILD offices one of the attorneys suggested, and I agreed to it, that I accompany him back to Atlanta and write a series of articles. The Klan had threatened to "get" Herndon when he stepped off the train in Atlanta, thereby terminating "the Red's propaganda plot." The ILD suggested that "I stick close" to Herndon, "just in case." Although they believed the Klan would probably not dare to fulfill its threat because the case had become known to the world—demonstrations for his freedom had been held in various European capitals—still. . . .

I sat next to Herndon on the train and when we changed to Jim Crow cars in Washington, I insisted that I remain with him. White passengers were not allowed to travel in the cars "reserved" for Negroes, but I pulled my collar high and sat on the window side. The conductor passed us by. We sat up all night, talking, and I prevailed on him to relate the story of his life. It was extraordinary and yet I should not have been surprised. He revealed his passionate determination to study, this lad who had not had five years of formal schooling, and to learn of the world which opened to him when he began reading the Marxist periodicals and books. "It was like going up an old muddy road," he said, "and suddenly coming to a big shining palace."

He described his two years in Fulton Tower and the encouragement he found in letters that came to him from many lands of the world. "I read these letters and I said to myself, 'Angelo, you are going to be free.' So fired was he by his certainty that he packed his bag to be in readiness. "It made me feel better just to look at it packed." Chief jailer Holland came to his cell and saw his bag. "Unpack, boy," he said. "You ain't goin' nowhere." The jailer poked his finger through the bars, saying, "Ham and Eggs, you are sure plumb crazy." He had dubbed Herndon "Ham and Eggs" because he had received hundreds of telegrams from Americans who had learned, from the *Daily Worker,* that the prisoner's food was mouldy, and some protestors suggested that the prison authorities give Herndon ham and eggs. The jailer often brought Herndon the *Daily Worker,* which he had deliberately torn in strips, and he regarded it as hilarious when the prisoner silently, without anger, lay the strips on the prison floor and pieced them together. The jailer would call his assistants to enjoy the sight and all stood laughing wildly as Herndon, sprawled on all fours, read the newspaper. Then the news came Herndon had confidently awaited, that bail was won. The jailer came and stood outside the cell as the young Negro prepared to leave. "You'll wish you'd stayed here where it's nice and cozy," he said, and when Herndon smiled, the enraged jailer exploded: "Ham and Eggs, you're nothing but a bad nigger, a goddam black Red." When Herndon walked down the steps outside he looked back and saw the faces of prisoners at the windows. They waved and shouted "Angelo, don't you come back no more." The jailer stood atop the stairs, jangling his keys, "Next time you come," he said, "and sure as God is on high, you're coming back, you will come for good."

Now Angelo was coming back.

I jotted notes for my first article and wrote: "The train carrying Angelo Herndon back to a Georgia chain-gang had four golden bars running all around the streamlined locomotive and the first Pullman car was named Rotary Club. It was one of the fastest trains in the world and it tore down the Atlantic Coast as though demons were pursuing it; the siren kept sounding through the fog every few minutes in a low mournful wail—through Delaware, Virginia, the Carolinas and Georgia."

When we arrived in Atlanta I glanced apprehensively around

for the Klan, but the kleagles evidently had reconsidered. I said nothing to Herndon nor did he mention it though I was certain he knew of the threat. We hurried through the streets to the home of a Scottsboro mother whose address was given us at the ILD. A withered woman of 55-odd, shoulders bent by years of scrubbing floors, she looked hard at Herndon. "Bless you, it is Angelo," she cried, kissing him and she took us in like prodigal sons. She ran about in an ecstasy, rustling up food. After dark four friends she had summoned came, and they sat stiffly trying their best not to stare at Herndon, their eyes brilliant as they gazed at him. The Scottsboro mother, eager to ease his last hours, played the little gramaphone in the pin-neat parlor. She searched for something cheerful among the twenty-year old records but they were all blues: the Backwater Blues and the Deadcat Blues, the Birmingham Gambling Blues and the Mean Woman Blues, the latter saying:

Blues got me drinkin'
Trouble got me thinkin'
And it's gonna carry me to my grave. . . .
It's mean for a woman to be drinkin'
When she ain't got a dollar
To meet the rent man.

It was Saturday night and the prowl car patrolled the dark streets: we talked in lowered voices behind the drawn blinds. They persuaded Herndon to sing and in a tender, youthful tenor he sang a song he had learned in Fulton Tower, "their theme song," he called it:

Look a-yonder, yonder
Hard-boiled sun is turnin over
It's comin' down, O Lawd,
It's comin' down.

Give me, give me a cool drink of water
Before I die, O Lawd
Before I die.
I don't want no
Corn bread, peas and molasses
At supper time.
No—at supper time.

Every mail day—mail day
I get a letter
Son, come home, O son, son come home.

How can I go, mother
Shot gun and pistols
All around me
To blow me down, O Lawd, to blow me down.

So the forlorn merry-making went on well past midnight when the guests crept away in the night between rounds of the prowl car; and, before dawn, the Scottsboro mother fried some chicken and fish and baked some hot corn muffins. God only knows where she found some drops of red wine. "Eat and drink, Angelo," she said, stroking his face as she left to scrub floors somewhere in town.

Angelo played a few more records, we washed the breakfast dishes and about noon we went to the Atlanta prison. He strode up the high stairs, in a firm, youthful tread, suitcase in hand, the big doors closed behind him and I stood motionless on the pavement across the street a long time. I began to walk, aimlessly, fast, walked for hours through the streets, hating my tears: I remembered he had had none when he went up the stairs.

I wrote my dispatch in the Western Union office and handed it to the operator, a young blonde woman: she read it, glanced at me strangely, then bent over her machine, banging away silently. I stayed until she finished, to be certain this story of Angelo Herndon's homecoming to prison would get out to the world.

I decided to seek an interview with the notorious governor of George, Eugene Talmadge, "Our Gene," whose red-galluses, "wool-hat" jargon and Confederate mind had received considerable publicity in the North. The state building was an imposing mansion of Corinthian pillars, a high dome, and an air of ancient magnificence which must have been mighty impressive in Jeff Davis' time. The Governor's secretary, a young comely woman chewing gum, sat in the anteroom reading *Astrology* magazine, a Crab and Scorpion on the cover. She asked me to wait a moment, among the gaunt, tobacco-chewing men in overalls who awaited audience with their governor. Finally I was ushered into the great man's quarters. A small, dark man wearing a blue serge suit sat behind a big glass-topped desk, the state seal of Georgia above him. His shrewd, black eyes behind big horn-rimmed glasses surveyed me as he held out his hand. I had told the secretary I was here from the New York press to cover a current convention of prison wardens that had convened in Atlanta. And the Governor, who addressed them the previous day, greeted me warmly, asking if I had heard his speech (which had praised the state's penal system of chain-gangs as humanitarian and healthful, affording the prisoners fresh air and exercise). I murmured that it was a remarkable speech and he grinned, well satisfied.

A hulking six-footer sat silent in a corner of the room, his elbows on his knees, his eyes focussed steadily on me like a great cat surveying its prey. "The Commissioner of Highways," the Governor said. The figure made some appropriate noise, part snarl and part grunt, and I made my own estimate of his job. After all Huey Long had just been assassinated in Louisiana and Our Gene said, as though he divined my thought, "I reckoned you-all ought a been down to N'awleans on that assassination." Good ol' Huey, he said, his voice dropping as he told how they drew lots to murder ol' Huey and that there Dr. Weiss got the short one. Ol' Huey was an honest and a brave man, a fine pal, but his ideas of guvment were opposite to his, Gene's. Ol' Huey believed in topheavy guvment while he, Gene, faithful to Jeffersonian democracy, thought that guvment best that guvvened least. Huey was a 20th century Caesar, too great for his time. "He bestrode us like a Colossus," Talmadge said, asking if I remembered my Shakespeare, and betraying his own Harvard education which he sedulously camouflaged by assuming his broad, down-home dialect.

"Every man's got his Cassius, his lean and hungry Cassius with that mean eye. And if a man's smart, not too trusting like ol' Huey was, he gits his Cassius fust." The Governor glanced toward his Commissioner of Highways. "Right, chief?" The hulk stirred in assent. But then, Talmadge droned on, when a man's time comes, nothing he can do can halt it, neither bodyguard nor suit of armor. The Angel of Death will not be denied, for he walks the byways of earth and peers at all men, great or small. He, Gene, has no bodyguard for he does not fear death. When his time comes he will go to his Maker, unafraid, with clean hands.

I managed to steer the conversation to the purposes of my interview and began a question on the Negroes of Georgia, but the Governor interrupted before I finished. "Course the Nigras merit better than they been gitting," he snapped. "Been gittin' better than they got." We folks up North didn't realize that we had set the South back a century by the war between the States. Gene said his people were still suffering from the Carpet-baggin' days when the Nigras ran wild and no Caucasian life was safe. Only time could heal the wounds, but they were healing. "Take the Nigras outta work. Why they gits equal bounty, same as whites. If some damn Nawtherners didn't come down stirrin' up trouble, all would be well in Dixie."

I hoped he was leading up to Herndon and I had my pencil poised, but he stopped short, obliging me to mention the case. "Herndon case?" he asked, blankly, cautious suddenly, treading easy. "Oh, that Black Commune-ist," he exclaimed as though he had dredged the depths of memory and it came back to him, "tell the truth, Ah don't rightly know the merits for Ah ain't follud it. Heap a crime's going on and no guvnah can follow 'em all." I replied that there had been a great deal of talk about the Herndon case up North, and abroad. He remained silent. I then ventured a comment on the insurrection law of 1831 and asked his own opinion of it. Well, he replied carefully, staring at me, he would not have written that law himself, but it *is* constitutional, and he was sworn to observe the constitution, both state, as well as federal, and he was bound by it. I finally asked him what he would do in the Herndon case and he replied that he could not commit himself, retreating from his pose of ignorance.

"Ah understand it mought come up befo' me shortly and Ah'll have to render a decision. Ruther not say much now." Had he received many telegrams and letters? "Some," he replied, becoming increasingly monosyllabic. I knew I was treading on marshy ground and I debated whether to continue for I planned to stay in Georgia several more days. The Governor rose and paced the room, turning to stare out the great bay window that opened on the broad plaza below. He pivoted on me suddenly, a lean finger pointing outside. "See those streets, suh? They'd be piled with corpses like haystacks, the gutters would run blood, if I let Nigras like Herndon run loose. If that Nigra is what they say he is and is stirring up general hell, preachin' equality, he will stay in jail until his black hide rots." If there were others like him, preaching revolution, the Governor would give every Caucasian a shotgun and tell him to use it as conscience dictates.

The hulk in the corner shifted his bulk and rose abruptly. Alarmed by the Governor's explosion, yet elated that he had confessed his innermost bias, I quickly slid to another topic and praised his speech at the warden's convention as honest and plainspoken. I suggested that it would be beneficial if I could visit the chain-gangs he had described as "salutary to health and character," and his eyes gleamed. Of course, he said, he would arrange it. He always welcomed all honest Northern newspapermen so that they could spread the truth about Georgia. Too many scalawags were running around the North maligning his state and his penal system. He was referring, I knew, to the public scandal that flared when some trapped prisoners, chained inside a cage on wheels, burned to death.

A book had recently appeared called *I Am a Fugitive From a Georgia Chain-Gang* that unveiled the barbarism of the setup. And John L. Spivak had brought another book out, called *Georgia Nigger,* which carried damning photographs of Georgia's penal system.

As I rose, the Governor shook hands again, smiling benignly, and asked, deprecatingly, as though in passing, if I would delete "that part I said about giving every man a shotgun and all, that was off the record." I could use the remainder as I saw fit, for Gene Talmadge welcomes the truth. I will see with my own eyes that false witnesses had deluded the North, and I know what the Scriptures say about bearin' false witness.

A big, shiny Lincoln awaited me, and a prison official drove me to a chain-gang that labored about fifteen miles out of Atlanta. As we approached my heart beat hard, for there, under a burning sun, I saw a sight that must shock all Northern eyes: black men in striped prison clothes were grading a road, their picks swinging in unison as they kept time to the beat of a melancholy work-song. A lanky guard in a big black hat, a huge rifle over his shoulder, slouched nearby in the shade. He had evidently been briefed with care: Oh, sho', the prisoners always gain weight on these gangs, the food and the fresh air being so "salubrious." Most of them had the venereal disease when they come in, he said, looking me straight in the eyes, "but we cures them." The chain-gang system had additional virtues, it saved the country close to a million in road work this past year. Yes, suh, the chain-gang's a blessing for them and the state.

Later, my guide conducted me to a kennel of bloodhounds where the keeper, a short, sallow man, hefted one of the dogs and stroked it tenderly. "This one's the best damn man-tracker we ever had," he said, lifting its long, flapping ears.

Later we came to something that stopped me dead: the weird structure of the stocks, which flashed old Salem and its witch hunters onto my mind. I stared hard, and my guide glanced at me, puzzled. "Nothin' but a ordinary ol' stock," he explained. They didn't keep prisoners in them more than a few minutes until their contrariness was over. "Never mo' than an hour at a time." When I asked if I might try it he laughed incredulously. "Fust time ah heard a man ask for it." But if that was my desire, okay, he would satisfy it. I climbed into the stock, slipped my legs through the lower holes, as he directed, my arms in the upper, and he shifted the lever. My body swung up from the earth, leaving me hanging in space. The weight of my body strained at the ligaments of my wrists and my ankles and I could clearly imagine the condition of a man who hung here for the eternity of an hour. The warden shifted the lever after a few moments and I struggled free, rubbing my aching wrists, silent.

Back in his office at Fulton Tower, the official greeted a bustling visitor from downstate. "Mr. J. P. McCleskey," he said, courteously, "meet a gentleman from New York." Mr. McCleskey, well-proportioned, his cheeks an apple-red and his eyes a bright blue, had been in charge of chain-gangs going on seventeen years, he said, a pride in his tone, and we talked about corporal punishment a while. "Ain't none now," the official said, "none save the stocks. Cut the lash out years ago."

"The lash," Mr. McCleskey said nostalgically, "the lash, that, suh, was the most humane punishment there ever was."

The other placed his hand gently on Mr. McCleskey's knee. "I don't quite agree with you there, my friend," he said affectionately. "The stock's much more suitable." Mr. McCleskey dissented, laughing. "That's what makes hoss races," he said. "You got a right to your opinion, and I got a right to mine."

His friend was similarly obstinate. "Stocks," he repeated, "stocks is the best punishment ever invented." But apple-cheeked

Mr. McCleskey was a man who stood by his convictions: "The lash," he argued, "two, three licks with it and I never did have any more trouble for a month or mo' in my gangs."

I have reflected on the bromide that truth is stranger than fiction. Were I not witness to this macabre colloquy, had I read it in another's account, I would probably have scoffed, incredulous. The two men conducted their little disagreement with such an air of sweet reasonableness that they might well have been two housewives debating a superior way of baking biscuits. I could only conclude that these two exponents of the Southern morality regarded the Negro as something less than human. I have since heard friends, at hunting season, debate the merits of various rifles to bring down deer.

Mr. McCleskey and his friend may well have been responsible family men, kindly to their children and considerate of their wives—though I found that hard to envisage at that moment—but the matter of inflicting bodily pain, torture, upon Negroes was a matter outside the range of their code, their morality. These were technical matters, and had no relation to humanity.

I have traveled South a number of times since, during the Second World War when I lived with sharecroppers; to Brevard County, in Florida's orange groves, in 1951, to write of the murder of two NAACP martyrs, Harry T. Moore and Mrs. Moore, killed by a bomb on Christmas Eve while men sang carols extolling the birth of the Prince of Peace; latterly, in 1956 I watched a screaming mob in the Kentucky town of Henderson rampage across the lawn of an elementary school to prevent six Negro children less than eight years of age from entering; and always I remembered the Governor of Georgia's outburst and the gruesome colloquy of the two prison officials. Then it was that I sensed the deadly virulence of the Southern disease which blighted the moral health of so many in Dixie a century after a million sons of our nation died at Antietam and Gettysburg and Bull's Run. The blight could last as long as the present southern economy which perpetrates it. I wrote that I understood Booker T. Washington who remarked that if you wish to keep a man in the gutter you have got to get down there yourself.

On the train coming North the signposts of backwoods Southern towns flashed by: Mina, Lawrenceville, Calhoun Falls and, in deep night, I saw, under the arc lights on lonely station platforms bales of cotton awaiting freight cars. By the railroad platforms I saw the carts drawn by long-eared mules driven by Negro sharecroppers in patched overalls and ragged straw hats. In the sad, lonely night the outlines of the Marxist case came clear—the South was virtually a colony of the Northern corporations: the southern governors were the pro-consuls of a native imperialism. The concealments of the North were naked and visible in the South. I understood Governor Talmadge well: he donned the "wool-hat" to pose as a son of his people but beneath his homely top-piece worked a keen mind, honed to the requirements of profit. His deification of the Nordic was an ancient hoax to retain the loyalty of the poor whites and to crush the possible resistance of the poor Negroes.

So I wrote in my first article describing this journey: "It's all tied up together: to understand the Herndon case you must understand Georgia: Georgia is the South and the South means cotton; and cotton means a Negro people in semi-colonial oppression. Hence the chain-gangs and the Winchesters and the bloodhounds and Governor Eugene Talmadge."

I wrote of Herndon—and Georgia—many times until the Supreme Court ruled in his favor, in 1937, after multitudes, here and abroad, declared themselves for his freedom.

8

I Help Found a Magazine

ONE DAY, SHORTLY afterward, I walked into the drab and noisy newsroom of the *Daily Worker* and encountered, behind a desk littered with books, a dark, lean man about my age, whose high forehead, scanty brown hair and sunken, ascetic eyes seemed familiar. I remembered. He was A. B. Magil, a classmate of mine at Penn. Though I scarcely knew him at college, I recalled well his lyric poetry that had appeared in *Junto,* the campus literary magazine. I remembered him drifting across the green in my senior year, dreamy and contemplative, the image, I thought then, of The Poet. He had achieved renown when he won a national intercollegiate award for his poetry. He remembered me too, and we laughed as he quoted that old line from old Moliere: *"Que diable faites vous dans cette galere?"* —What the deuce are you doing in that galley? Yes, what? We found ourselves, graduates of Drexel's and Biddle's University, in the ranks of the proletarian Marxists. Abe said we had another Penn man at our side, Sol Auerbach, the philosophy instructor, whose pen name was James S. Allen.

I accompanied Magil to a meeting of the John Reed Club, an association of writers and artists who, in their majority, held the Marxist philosophy as the key to truth, to reality. No few foremost American novelists and painters of today owe their first, fresh stimulus to this club—men and women like Nelson Algren, Richard Wright, Meridel Le Sueur, who were profoundly influenced by the older socialist adherents like Michael Gold, Hugo Gellert, William Gropper, Fred Ellis, Lydia Gibson Minor. . . . The John Reed Club was later to merge into the League of American Writers whose members included Malcolm Cowley, Matthew Josephson, John Steinbeck, John Howard Lawson, and many similar—the foremost group of its kind in that day. The John Reed Club had adopted the name of the American writer—Harvard '10, the class that also produced

Walter Lippmann and Heywood Broun. Reed's superb reporting brought him national fame while he was yet in his twenties and he died, at 33, a Communist, one of the founders of the American movement. I had read his principal work, *Ten Days That Shook the World* which I considered an epic.

That winter I listened often to passionate disputations on literature in a big blowy loft on Sixth Avenue that was heated by a pot-bellied stove; its fire died in the small hours of the night while the disputants raged hotly on. Here I met Mike Gold, a young, square-built, handsome man with a shock of jet-black hair, a firm chin, dark luminous eyes, who spoke with a blunt and often poetic eloquence. His words had the passion of his book *Jews Without Money,* and his poem "Strange Funeral in Braddock"—a proletarian son, he was, of Walt Whitman. "Life shapes literature," I heard him say that first night, "but life in turn is also shaped by it." I regarded him closely, and with affection, for he had, as editor of the monthly *New Masses,* written me after I submitted a short story describing life in my town, "As sure as God made little green apples," he said, "you can write."

At the Public Library the day after I heard Mike, I read his celebrated review of 1930, in the *New Republic,* where he asked Thornton Wilder, author of *The Bridge of San Luis Rey*: ". . . Is this the style to express America? Is this the speech of a pioneer continent? Will this discreet French drawing room hold all the blood, horror, and hope of the world's new empire? Is this the language of the intoxicated Emerson? Or the clean, rugged Thoreau or vast Whitman? Where are the modern streets of New York, Chicago, and New Orleans in these little novels? Where are the cotton mills, and the murder or Ella May and her songs? Where are the child slaves of the beet fields? Where are the stockbroker suicides, the labor racketeers, or passion and death of the coal miners? Where are Babbitt, Jimmy Higgins and Anita Loos' Blonde? Is Mr. Wilder a Swede or a Greek or an American? No stranger would know from the books he has written."

Mike, a prophet out of the slums, summoned America to write of America, in all its power and tragedy and glory. His words disturbed, and stirred me, as they inspired countless others of the working class. I wrote half a dozen stories and articles which his magazine published and, one day in 1934, the editors invited me to a meeting. The publication was on the verge of closing and a group of writers and artists were to discuss the means of saving it. I considered the magazine a bright lantern in the dark of America's night, and I came. Writers and artists being what they were, we resolved to rescue the monthly by transforming it into a weekly, a solution which startled sensible men who adhere to the customary rules of cost-accounting. "If you can't keep a monthly afloat, how in the name of God do you expect to maintain a weekly?" the worldly asked, misunderstanding the exquisite dialectic of the matter. The answer seemed as clear to me as the day. Great questions of life and death hovered across the nation, demanding answers. The monthly magazine had a remoteness, it lacked the immediate topical, and, those of us who agreed with the transformation to a weekly, argued that if the literary were subordinated —in space—to the political, its resurrection was at hand.

The magazine, founded in 1911, had always been, dominantly, an organ of arts and letters; that was its glory and many of the nation's finest artists and writers were inspired by it, for it published the first works of a generation. It died during the first World War because it opposed the conflict; resurrected as *The Liberator,* it later became the monthly *New Masses.* And now it needed a new reincarnation. It should direct its appeal to advanced workingmen as well as to the harrassed students and literati, and for that its emphasis must be journalistic—to descend into the stormy arena where the day's battles were raging. Its writers must carry their notebooks and pencils to the surging picket-lines, to the worried farmsides, to the smoldering South, and write—each week—of the current strife.

I agreed to be one of the four working editors to fashion it as the times required. A large, echoing bare room with a single window looking out on the backyards of New York was our office; we outfitted it with several second-hand desks and went to work.

We decided that a budget of $10,000 would be enough to launch us, but as our publication date approached, we discovered we had less than $1,000 in the till. Characteristically we were not troubled by that. The Muse, like the Lord, will find a way. After endless dispute we decided upon a thirty-two page magazine, patterned in general after the *New Republic,* undeterred by the fact that the liberal magazine was liberally endowed by

Mrs. Willard Straight, the widow of a Morgan partner. We worked in a white-hot zeal; soliciting the known and unknown for articles, exposes, short stories, poetry, cartoons, illustrations, criticism. We searched for new writers, anonymous sons of workers, who were, we insisted, knocking out poetry, short stories, novels somewhere in terra incognita. Not all of us were Marxists, and those who were knew precious little of its doctrine. But we saw eye to eye about tyranny and starvation: that bond held.

The first week of January 1934 we sponsored a meeting at the New School for Social Research to greet the new magazine: Henri Barbusse, the French novelist, author of *Under Fire,* who crossed the Atlantic to crusade against fascism and war, was our main speaker. Fatally ill, coughing his life blood as he stood on the platform, his dark luminous eyes glowed with irrepressible life, as he cried, "Literature must become valorous!" He spread his long arms as though to embrace us all, and summon us to the good fight.

The meeting was a moral success, but after deducting expenses we were still $8,000 short. The business manager groaned and moaned; he was licked. He had pleaded with the printer, cajoled, threatened, stormed, but the fiend would not permit a single copy to roll from the presses until we delivered another thousand dollars Friday afternoon at six. For some reason I cannot to this day understand, I was chosen by the other editors to go to New Jersey and solicit that thousand from a well-to-do reader of the monthly. "Our last chance," the business manager pleaded. I left the office with the heartfelt benedictions of my colleagues, then, in the hall, remembered that I lacked fare for the journey and rushed back in. The editors emptied their pockets and we raised enough in coins for the journey out, but not back. "If you don't get it," the managing editor said dourly, "it won't be necessary to come back."

Our potential benefactor was a tall, severe-faced man with a stubble of greying hair, who listened gravely as I spoke. When I concluded he drew a checkbook from his desk and made out a draft for $1,500 while my eyes bulged. Handing it to me he said tartly, "It is a sorry sight to see editors gad about on money business." In the future, he advised, let business managers manage, and writers write. I agreed with a fervor he understood. He was an admirer of the old *Masses* since its foundation in 1911, and in the interim he had become, as he said, a pigmy capitalist, "about so big," raising his forefinger an inch above his thumb. But he had maintained his faith in Marxism, in socialism, and we could, he said, return to solicit his help.

Suddenly I remembered the impatient printer: the office was doubtless in a dither of expectation. I explained and ran. Half way down the block I stopped dead, reaching frantically in my pockets. I had only five cents left after the bus trip here. A nickel and a check for $1,500. I stood frozen in my quandary. I certainly could not return to our benefactor and ask him to make it $1,500.78. At the nearest drugstore I spent the nickel to phone the office collect. There was an exultant shout as I explained. Yes, I would hitch-hike back and arrive in several hours, in time to meet the printer's deadline. I thumbed my way back to the city on a truck while the check for $1,500 scorched my pocket.

So the first issue appeared. We sat up that night turning the pages. My first impression stabbed my heart: nothing is so brutal as a page of virgin type, the words reaching at you like talons. Manuscripts that glowed with a brilliant light turned lack-lustre in print. The writing was raw, unfinished, even mawkish, I felt, but on the tenth or twelfth reading I saw that the passion transcended the crudity: the fiery lustre of truth shone through. We had the main thing, the answers for the time, a crusading fervor even though it was unpolished.

The issue caught on phenomenally. It contained the first of a series giving the low-down on native fascists who had begun to goose-step across America. Written by John L. Spivak, a reporter who had no fear and less tact, the style bordered on the sensational. The style was the man: Spivak moved on the enemy with a D'Artagnan-like insouciance: he had a way of walking in on the fascists, forearmed with damning evidence he had already collected, and, throwing them into consternation by the facts he already knew, he wrung further damaging admissions from them. By the time they regained their wits, he had his story. I knew our Brahmins would denounce his sensationalism, but I was sure most readers would applaud. They clamored for more.

A gauge to our success was the fury of the attack which came not only from Hearst; dignified Raymond Moley, editor of the magazine *Today,* ridiculed us, deftly misquoted us to give his readers the impression that we called for "the bullet" to settle political debate. The *Saturday Evening Post* denounced us in a full-page editorial as "men of mystery" hiding behind pseudonyms.

Overnight our office became a Mecca in the wilderness. The mailman brought enough letters to fill three pages of small, six-point type. We printed the most eloquent in a special department called "Letters from America." In comparison to the rest of the press, they seemed like correspondence from an unexplored continent. A young writer traveling to Pittsburgh wrote, "Steel Towns Are Preparing," and he quoted a striker: "I ain't et nothing but milk and bread all last year. I can't go on like this. I'd rather starve on the picketline." The writer's name was Albert Maltz, the novelist whose short stories and novels, like *Underground Stream*, the *Cross and the Arrow*, became known to millions throughout the world. His staunch advocacy of truth brought him a year's prison in the latter Forties as one of the Hollywood Ten.

Hundreds of letters like his came every week. The magazine caught on. America's stuff was in its pages.

The good editor is father and mother: warm, helpful, considerate, critical, demanding, selfless, patient, and slow to wrath. He must also—on our magazine certainly—be a captain of industry, a merchant prince. He must organize that most mercurial of all men—the writer, the artist and simultaneously he must know how to sell their wares, and raise the moneys for them. Indeed, unless he learned to balance a budget, his entire venture would cave in on him like the Mississippi Bubble. Nor may I omit the qualities of the statesman, or at least, the politician, and he could learn from Machiavelli: to be able to reject articles by writers whose good will you wanted to retain. Naturally the possession and exercise of all these excellent qualities left me no margin of time to write, or to travel to the points where history was squalling like a new-born babe, demanding attention. I longed to be footloose, on the road . . . to savor cities, the skies, the lives of our citizens. Outside my four walls rolled a land of terrible beauty and here I was, imprisoned by my work as editor. Not that the routine was dull: it had its cycle of buoyant life, its conflicts and its deep satisfaction, not the least of which were the many people who knocked at our doors.

One day a spectre materialized before my desk. At a slight

knock I looked up to see a man with a goatee, a pair of piercing black eyes and a brilliant smile. The apparition wore a black coat, a flowing red tie and an antique hat that sat on the top of his big head. He needed only a cape to swirl and the Nineties would have been recaptured in his person. Five feet high or so, his body seemed built around his lustrous eyes. He introduced himself—Lincoln Steffens, and I took his hand reverently, feeling that it was history's hand I held. The little man's years cut across almost half of our nation's history: his *Autobiography* told me that. He knew the Forty-Niners in his California childhood; he had been a youth during the Reconstruction; a spectacular reporter hated and respected by those he caught on his pen; Teddy Roosevelt scorned him as a "muckraker" because he had his go at the high-placed crooks of industry, finance and politics; Woodrow Wilson, as well as J. B. McNamara, the heroic labor leader, listened to his counsel which could be wrong but could scarcely be ignored.

He sat down and thumbed through several recent issues of *New Masses* that lay on my desk. He had been following the magazine, he said, in a voice that had not lost its resonance. "I wish the grave would stop calling," he smiled. "If I were younger I would come in with you." The perennial reporter, he asked many searching questions, about our plans, our "perspective." I obliged, and he replied, yes, reporting is the life blood of a magazine. I expected this superlative reporter to say that, I responded.

"But now I am a man in the preterite tense," he said laughing. "Remember your preterite? Past action completed. I have been a muckraker." His small, delicate hands twisted around the ivory head of his cane. "Muckraking was needed, then. And now. Rake muck as long as the world has muck. But now you need to do more." The American who had gone to the first country of socialism and who reported that the future he had seen "works," continued: "No, muckraking is not enough. Long long ago I knew that, but I never got to know much more then. Later I learned but it was too late. You did a good job of muckraking in your Georgia pieces, Talmadge, the chain gangs, but, you know, to expose is only half the job. I never got to the other half. You're lucky. There's a compass now. I never had one. Reporting must have direction, purpose, the other half."

Best, he said, he found my description of Herndon's heroism, my account of the Scottsboro mother who had taken us in and honored Herndon in the only way she had. It reminded him, he said, of Anatole France's story of the penniless juggler in Notre Dame's cathedral performing his act before the Virgin Mary in lieu of a cash donation. "And you implied these people's can't be beat. That's the Herndon story. That you must show and you are showing it."

"In a way," he mused, a note of sorrow in his words, "you fellows have it easier. You've got the greatest story in the world to tell—the Communist story." He got on to a discourse about liberals and Communists. "Marxists may not like this, but I say we, the liberals, held the front before you came along, before your movement was born. It's your turn now. We couldn't win. You can." He advised me not to scorn the liberals, not to brush them off. There were many dodoes among them, like himself. But no Communist comes full-grown from Minerva's head. "Mankind is born conservative," he smiled, stroking his goatee, "and most of it dies conservative. That's how it's been since time began. But tomorrow is up to you, your movement. Those who begin to question—there are always questioners—begin as liberals. A man who asks questions is a liberal. When he fails to get satisfactory answers he may slink back into conservatism; if he gets them he becomes a radical. If he really understands them, he becomes a Communist. Get that, and you'll put out a magazine that can change the liberal to a Communist. Isn't that what you're after?"

It was, yes, I said hesitantly. "But don't write for Marxists. Write for people you want to get to be Marxists."

"And for people who will never become Marxists," I added, "who may never take socialism but who will join with us for the day."

"Of course," he said, "the united front. Scratch a septuagenarian and you find a sectarian. I try not to be. That's why I came to give you my two cents worth of advice. Sometimes I'm afraid you're too far out in front of your readers, the besetting sin of radicals. You take too much for granted. Never forget you're writing to men asking questions and they're asking questions about you—the fellow presuming to answer them. Tell it straight, simple and clear. They'll know you're not talking through your hat."

He wanted to hear more about Herndon—really no fear as he sat writing those letters on the train? And when he went up the stairs to that prison, Fulton Tower? No, none that he showed, I answered. "Well," he mused, "that's what Marxism does, I suppose. Tom Mooney and Billings seemed to show no fear either, but they had the idea too, or ideas akin to it. They believed. A doubting man fears. Don't forget its the age—the Marxist age, the Enlightenment of the 20th Century." He promised to write for the magazine if he had energy and time, and he departed as he had come, drifting out of the door, cane, eyes and all.

Many pilgrims came to Mecca, to offer advice or to seek it, or simply to talk. Some remained, to become stalwarts who worked for the magazine later, no few becoming writers whose names are known today to the nation and to the world. And there were the artists, blessed men, whose eyes seemed to pierce walls as well as hypocrisy and cant.

Art Young, for example, a roly-poly man, asked blunt questions and squinted at you humorously if your reply hedged, but his humor was as sharp as the spear of Bayard the Chevalier. I had loved him since I first saw his drawings, the two slum kids looking up at the stars and one saying, "Jeez, Mame, as thick as bedbugs"; and the weary, sweated Irish housewife berating her exhausted husband home from work with, "Me sweating over this hot stove all day long and you working in a nice, cool sewer." This was the old warrior who fell asleep when he was on trial for his life as one of the indicted *Masses* editors during World War I. Now, in the last years of his life he lived alone in his small house near Danbury where the townspeople loved and respected him. Like most artists he read the magazine picture-wise, turning from cartoon to cartoon, illustration to illustration, leaving, as he said, the "reading stuff" for bedtime since so many articles had beneficial effects on his insomnia. He was nonetheless well-informed, a brooder, and often he came to talk about this event or that, murmuring his gentle but tart assessments of men.

Once when he was ill I came to see him in his room at the hotel where he lived alone. I regarded him as a man of profound loneliness originally, but I discovered that his mind was inhabited by memories of men and women of his past whom he had outlived: nor did age exile him from his contemporaries. The charwoman, the elevator operator, the children on the block knew him as he knew them, their confidant to whom they brought their woes, large and small, realizing that a respectful and affectionate ear awaited them. The day I came he sat at the window where the sun streamed in, his head flung back, his mouth wide open. "The sun is the healer," he explained and he had invited its rays in "to warm his tonsils which had been aching."

He opened a bottle of wine and we spoke of many things, including the Marxist movement. His best years, he said, were in it, and he knew the leaders of the old Socialist Party "too well." His knowledge of them had brought him to the Communists. He could not abide hypocrisy, arrogance and selfish ambition that was satisfied at the expense of others, and in this case, men and women who claimed the good of humanity as their ambition. "You call such people opportunists," he said. "They will be found everywhere, even among Communist leaders." He conceded, he said, the emoluments were scantier there, but men being what they are, the law of averages certified that the beast of selfishness—"that ol' devil, Ego"—roamed even among the most trusted of Marxists.

Yet he could never become disillusioned, he said, for his eyes were wide open since childhood. He had studied radicals since he covered, as illustrator, the trial of the Haymarket Martyrs, back in 1886. But he had kept his eye on No. 1, he said, which in his case, did not mean himself, but the people. The idea of socialism was the best and truest thing he had known in all his life, and he had the great good fortune to have survived to see the establishment of the first socialist country in the world. "I make no bones in saying I don't understand everything going on there. Much is mysterious to me, and some things disturb me." But he was certain, he wagged his big head, that wrong would be made right; so long as the peasants worked their own land and the workingmen their own machines, so long as their sons and daughters had the advantage of books, of learning, it would turn out all right.

He had continued to read the periodicals of the Socialist Party, and he was aware of the charges made in each issue against socialism in Russia. Doubtless some of them were true, but he had read enough elsewhere to know that great things were happening there. "Five Year Plans, industrialization, look at their movies, Potemkin, Chapayev, all the rest of it, universal education," and since those who indicted the USSR never recognized the successes, he could not accept their estimates of the failures. He had heard much criticism of their art; maybe it wasn't the way he would do it, still, the arts correspond to the level and tastes of a people. "After all, Norman Rockwell of the *Saturday Evening Post* is our favorite artist—among the millions—and what they are doing over there is not much different. If they want to call that socialist realism, that's their business. I dare say that's about what the people love most—at this stage of the game. I doubt if they would go for Picasso, Monet, the Cubists and all. Neither would ours, and we have the century and a half, since 1776, over them." I found his observations forever stimulating, fresh, perhaps because they corresponded so much to my own impressions. Of all our artists and writers who came to our office, I loved old Art best.

Gropper strolled into the office every Friday, with his portfolio of drawings, leaving a full page for us as regularly as a milkman brings his bottles and with scarcely more fanfare. His mordant drawings had genius; this was a bulldog of an artist whose teeth, once they lodged in the carcass of his victim, sank deep and stayed forever. Reluctant to waste time reading, he seemed to catch the truth out of the air, impatient as he was to read words; and often when I visited him in his workshop, the radio blared, all day long, and he seemed to absorb the news by osmosis. His was the powerful art of long and smoldering hatreds that could only startle you, for his eyes had the serenest glance, his smile was captivating, and he told stories like a bard, with a deliciously sly humor. His drawings belied the amiability of his public personality; in them raged guerilla war against sham and poverty, and so seared his fierce painting hand that I recall no single tree, for example, in his paintings that was not crippled, stunted, black. His eye saw no green leaf on a pleasant bough: in his paintings no birds sing.

And Glintenkamp with his merry, crinkled smile and booming voice, a bear of a man, big of shoulder and head, whose tender drawings and landscapes revealed his love of life and nature. The many humorous cartoonists, curiously pixieish in their manner, came with a blitheness which masked a keen and unforgetting eye. The artists, the cartoonists, seemed somehow, a breed different from writers: the artists had the longer view, saw the universal in the particular more clearly. Theirs was a world of the eternal verities. The daily fits and starts of politics scarcely concerned them: they kept their sights on distant, but bright, horizons.

Our pages carried the writings of the world's foremost authors and journalists: Louis Aragon and Gabriel Peri, from France; Aragon, the poet and novelist, now the editor of *Lettres Francaise,* who wrote four books of poetry and a novel while he organized some 40,000 professionals into the Resistance during the Nazi occupation; and Peri, the foreign editor of *L'Humanite,* who was to become the chairman of the Foreign Relations Committee of the French Chamber of Deputies before his execution in a Gestapo death-cell, and who commented, in his last will and testament, on his editorial relation with the *New Masses;* there was Martin Anderson Nexö, of Denmark, the genial author of *Pelle the Conqueror* and *Ditte;* Ralph Fox, the gifted British critic who lost his life defending Madrid several years later, and John Strachey who lost his interest in us when he became a Cabinet minister of Great Britain; Sean O'Casey, the playwright regarded as the successor to George Bernard Shaw; Heinrich Mann, Bertholt Brecht, and many other refugees from Nazi Germany; the Russian novelists, Maxim Gorky, Ilya Ehrenburg and Sholokhov; and these are but a small sample. A few Americans whose pieces, stories and poems we published were Steffens, Genevieve Taggard, Ernest Hemingway, Erskine Caldwell, Richard Wright, Ralph Ellison, Langston Hughes, Thomas Wolfe, Dorothy Parker and Theodore Dreiser; and these too are but a sampling.

Our relations with them varied: some wrote an article or two, a story or two, and we never, or rarely, saw them; others, like Dreiser, maintained the intimacy of close friends, brothers-in-arms, so to speak. For when Dreiser wrote a diatribe against rapacious publishers with whom he dealt, and referred to the Jewish origin of some, Mike Gold responded with a piece called "Dreiser, That Gun Is Loaded." For Dreiser had so written his article that it had unquestionable overtones of anti-Semitism. He came to our office, a lumbering bear of a man to argue the point and we spent the greater part of an afternoon trying to persuade him of his error. He had barged in, blustering indignantly, certain of his innocence. "They are sharpers, these publishers" and he had only "incidentally" mentioned that they happened to be Jews. We did not question his facts, but argued that non-Jews as well as Jews in the publishing trade cut corners and are guilty, like all entrepreneurs of capitalism, of mulcting their fellowmen.

Alexander Trachtenberg, the publisher, who had never lost his interest in *New Masses* since his days on the old *Masses,* had come to the meeting and he reminded Dreiser that Lenin had written of the Jews, and had assailed anti-Semitism, that legacy of the Tsar. Dreiser asked to see the article, which was duly given him. After pondering it well, he wrote a piece for *New Masses* expressing his agreement with Lenin and retracting his original statement.

He was, of all writers, and possibly of all men I have known, the most impressive. I had met him first during a strike in Pennsylvania's coal fields, in 1931, and shortly afterward, in the fierce miners strike of Harlan, Ky. Two strikers had been murdered by the Pennsylvania Coal and Iron police, and Dreiser invited to the scene by William Z. Foster hastened to aid the miners as best he could. The strike was led by the Trade Union Unity League, headed by Foster who came, personally, as is his wont, to the arena of battle.

When I had first come to see Dreiser, in Pittsburgh's Seventh Avenue Hotel, he welcomed me as a representative of the ILD, and invited me to his room where he sat in a musty, old armchair by the fourth floor window, and recalled that he occupied this same room when he got his first job as a newspaper reporter. He had sat here, after the deadlines, when he returned home, looking down on the street late at night, watching the passersby and speculating on their destination. Were they hurrying to a rendezvous with a sweetheart, or home to a waiting wife and children, or to a bar to drink with cronies? What was in their heads? Who were they? And why? In this room, he said, he first began to write as novelist. And he drifted on to describe his experiences in the Soviet Union whence he had recently returned and had written his book *Dreiser Looks at Russia.* He regarded the life in that land as augury for the future. Surcease from economic fears would enable men to be men, fully, not marginally, as we are under capitalism.

Yet, he said, returning to a theme that troubled him all his days as novelist, not even a perfected socialism will ensure mankind's tranquillity. "There is what we call romantic love," he said, ruefully. "Even under socialism Jack will love Jill and Jill will love Jim." "That," he smiled, "can cause havoc. And nothing the Politbureau can say can alter it."

Man was born to die, and, the more we love life the more we abhor death, and nothing the Politbureau can say will alter *that*. The advance of science will double or even treble man's life span but will never conquer death. However, he laughed, and this was after 4 A.M., and a quart of whiskey, the quality of such unhappiness is infinitely superior to the misery of mankind today. The loss of a love is not degrading; the loss of a job may well be, and often is. To come to the close of a fruitful life is a death infinitely preferable to that which comes to most men today who live, as Thoreau said, "lives of quiet desperation."

The next morning Dreiser learned that one of the local leaders of the coal miners was kidnapped by company deputies; I accompanied him in his wrathful search for the missing man. I will always remember the towering, wall-eyed figure, clad in a white Palm Beach suit, a vast straw hat on his big head, brandishing his cane in the coal company offices and demanding the immediate return of the victim. The guilty officials who probably had never heard his name, were startled by this apparition, this Angel of Wrath, and apprehensive that some Senator of liberal inclinations, or worse, a do-good relative of the company's owner, had appeared to plague them, promptly released the miner. When the three of us returned to Pittsburgh, in a hired car, Dreiser chuckled through the valleys saying that the life of the boss is so full of bluff that only a greater bluff can cow him. His concern for the miner was so transparently genuine, so earnest, that my heart warmed whenever, in the future, the incident came to mind.

"I hope Bill Foster will like this," he said, boyishly, for of all men on this earth he had met, he told me, Foster was "the most saintly, the most Christ-like." The great novelist would relish the approbation of the man he conceived as Jesus since he first saw him as leader of the great steel strike back in 1919. And Dreiser, inspired by Foster and other Communists he came to know, joined the Communist Party the year of his death; "the logic of my life," he wrote, had led him to it.

Yes, they were beautiful men and women who came knocking on the doors of the *New Masses,* which they regarded as their conscience.

9

No Strike Is Ever Lost

I DO NOT RECALL any strike, since I was a child carrying lunch to my father in the factory, that I did not side with the workers. The record is unbroken. Marxists call that "class consciousness," the realization that you are of the class of workingmen, and that its aspirations are sacred. Even before I came to the working class movement, I regarded the picketline as holy, the scab as loathesome and the employer as the irrevocable foe.

I have tramped the pavements more times than I can count, bearing placards, and I have described many strikes in my writings; peculiarly, one most lasting in my memory is that of a strike that was lost, the first I covered for the *New Masses*.

I was on the streets of New York when the city's hackies left their wheels and began to walk—all 40,000 of them, early in 1934. The hackie in his shabby coat and shapeless cap was the skipper of a wheeled landboat, but who lacked even the dubious status of a barge captain. The police regarded him as their prey, photographed his face, took his thumbprints, hung his picture in the car like the posters of bank robbers you see in the post offices. Yet he drove his cab twelve, fourteen hours a day, earning a pittance these days, little more, if as much, as fifteen, eighteen dollars a week. Entangled in the web of a notorious New York company union, he rebelled; and I saw his traditional arch-individualism melt overnight. The street gamin, on wheels, caught the infectious spirit of American labor as it stormed into its counter-attack.

Unaccustomed to strike, he was, at the outset, a latter-day Luddite, the early hand-weaver who blindly struck at the power looms that robbed him of his livelihood. The hackies, on the first day, encountering a scab-taxi, hove to enthusiastically, tipped the car over, and in some instances on Broadway, the most reckless flicked lit matches into the spilled gasoline which made a blaze that paled the lights over the marquees.

The managing editor of the magazine— the morning after the spectacular blazes—assigned me the story and I was glad to take it. Reporting was my dish, the highways my workshop. Where, I thought, could an American study the human fauna better than as a writer for *New Masses?* I wrote what I saw, what I thought, and they printed it as I wrote it. I cherished the tradition of reporting that was so uniquely ours, dating from John Reed's powerful writing in the *Masses,* and later the *Liberator.* Reed's *Ten Days That Shook the World* seemed to fuse in a magic tapestry the arts of poetry, drama, history. I had also read the Czech Marxist, Egon Erwin Kisch, a swashbuckling genius of a reporter who formulated an impressive philosophy for his craft. A good reporter must, he wrote, realize that life's sole certainty is change, and that every fact has an evolution, a beginning and an end. He began with Heraclitus, and concluded with Hegel and Marx, to the effect that truth was a synthesis that resulted from the clash of counterposing forces, thesis and antithesis. The good reporter needed what he called logical fantasy," an orderly imagination which could combine these elements into narration that moved the reader. I read how he strolled into a swanky jewelry shop in Berlin and watched a dowager buy an expensive pearl. The lady barely interested him but the pearl did: what, he asked himself, gave this smooth and tiny bauble such value that it cost a fortune in marks that a workingman could not earn after a year's hard work? The question carried Kisch to the South Sea isles where he lived among the pearl fishermen, dove into the shark-infested seas with them, traced that bauble to its oyster, followed it to the gem merchant, to the shipper, to the Amsterdam cutter and polisher and back to the swanky shop. And when he had it down on paper you knew the precious stuff enwrapped in that pearl: the hazardous lives of distant fishermen, the weary toil of many ships' crews under hot skies, the haggling in many languages of pot-bellied Occidental traders—invisible veins of life's blood ran through the pearl that was no larger than a tear. To me that reporting had the magic of art and of science.

I marched with the hackies, talked with them in the chill dawns of early spring, listened and watched, squatting with them on my haunches around a flaming salamander, heard the tales of their lives, their union, their strike and their leaders—and I felt that I was coming to the verge of knowing them, and what I already knew appalled me. They worked half the clock round but fell behind each week, were carrying their meager possessions one by one to the pawnbroker to pay their debt to the grocer, the landlord, the doctor.

I made friends with a short, snubnosed hackie whose tangy Brooklynese had to be heard to be believed. He told a parable, resting on his heels as a distant bell tolled three, and the moon, a yellow ball, hung from the tower of Rockefeller Center. The others listened attentively as the words slipped from the crooked corner of his big mouth:

"So you rides the streets all day long and at five o'clock you look at the meter and what do you see? A soldier!" The imagery of these unschooled men, this word "soldier," $1, that martinet of a digit which dictates the hackies' life! "My God," he continued, "I gotta make t'ree more bucks before I turn in. So I cruises around and round, I gets desperate and I opens the door and says to the woild, 'Come on in, anybody.' And who walks in but a ghost. So I says, 'Where to, Mr. Ghost?' and the ghost says 'Drive around Central Park.' So I drives the ghost around Central Park til the meter hits four bucks. Then I decide I better ask for the fare. Then the ghost says he's broke. So I t'row the ghost out and I come back to the garage. I shell out t'ree bucks of my own so they don't give me the air. When I gets home the wife says 'Where's the dough?' I tells her I give it to the company to keep the job. Then she says 'Keep the job hell. You're keeping the company. Well, jerk, take your pick. Who you gonna keep? Me or the company?' So, jerks,' he concluded, rising to his full height of five feet four and gazing ironically around the circle of his listeners, "Well, who we gonna keep, the wife or the company?"

They joined in wry laughter, lit cigarettes that glowed in the dark about the shadowy fortress of a great Yellow Cab garage. My guide, the storyteller, named Louie Cheznar, was assigned by the union to inspect the picketlines. Meticulously, he checked, in a small black notebook, the numbers picketing, their names, and had a cheerful word for all. When he came to a company garage he peeped inside the big doors and at one, he turned, whispering ecstatically: "Look at 'em, two hundred and fifty of 'em crowding the walls." Within, row on row of golden cabs stretched a full block, phalanxes of empty cars, eerie with that emptiness of machinery when the human is gone. The wonder of it overwhelmed Louie. "The beauty part of it is," he said oracularly, "we're making history for the whole woild. The eyes of the woild is on us, the New York hackies." Said it with the air of Napoleon in Egypt telling his grenadiers, "Soldiers, from these Pyramids forty centuries look down on you."

As we walked Louis told of the hackie's life: the years of enforced association with night-life underworld characters, the pimps, the whores, the greedy cops, the meager pay, the slavish hours. . . . I knew that the union was foreign to his experience, and yet overnight, he displayed a discipline, a profound spirit of community with his fellow-strikers; how quickly the best in man manifests itself when he is no longer one man alone. I felt his pride in the strike; proud, he was, that they were facing the companies and the Chicago gangsters—the fellows wit' the soft hats driving the cars.

We entered Germania Hall, one of the strike headquarters, as a very dark Negro stood on the dais, speaking for the Negro strikers of Harlem. I was aware of an old enmity between the whites and Negroes, and now the black man was saying, "Boys, when you tell us you're with us, mean it. We been rooked and robbed since 1865. If you mean it you will truly get the sweetest bunch of fighters in the world." The shabby caps began to fly through the air, Louie's among them. "See," Louie turned to me exultantly, "put that in: the nigger is wit' us, it's black and white from now on."

At central strike headquarters, our next destination, we found bedlam, men in dispute, laughing, cursing, mounds of leaflets littering the floor, and a massive youth called Pondsie, big of shoulder and chest, in a bright green sweater, was saying hoarsely: "So we got up a delegation after these Reds invited us to come and make a collection speech at their convention at the Coliseum. We walks in and them Reds stand up, and start singing, about a whole million of them. Man, the Reds was singing songs for us!" The others were listening very carefully. "We walks up to the platform and they throws the spotlight on us. When they come to the end of the song, they give us the Communist salute." His left fist, a huge chunk of knuckle and bone, went up in a short uppercut. In this time Communists, like the Republicans in Spain, raised their right fists in salute: Pondsie, being left-handed, could be forgiven his error. "That's what the Red salute is," he said, looking about the room, "the left-hook." The others tried the salute and so did Louie. "Then," the Green Sweater continued, "they holds a collection for the strike. Man, they rake the coin in wit' dishes on broomsticks and they give it all to us, every damn cent of it." One hackie slight and hollow-eyed, with a shock of jet black hair, a palm cross in his lapel (it was Palm Sunday) threw a left hook into the air, shouting, "Left hook, left hook! If them lefties is wit' us, I'm wit' em." And Louie was shouting with the others, honoring the Lefties.

But the Chicago gunmen with the soft hats, the jowly men who sat in the front office, proved too mighty for Louie Cheznar, the strike was lost. Two weeks later, Louie got off his feet again, back behind the wheel, twisting that ironic smile on his face again. For a day he had a glimpse of the power that was his. But he lost. Well, chalk it up to experience, it was fun, chum, while it lasted, next time. . . .

Louie never heard of Carl Sandburg, and perhaps he would not have agreed, but I thought of the Chicago bard's poem:

> *"No strike is ever lost": an old cry*
> *heard before the strike begins and heard long after, and*
> *"No strike is ever lost": either a thought or an instinct*
> *equivalent to "Give me liberty or give me death."*
> *On the horizon a cloud no larger than a man's hand rolls*
> *larger and darker when masses of people*
> *begin saying, "Any kind of death is better than this kind*
> *of life."*

Several days after my story appeared, a solid, handsome young man with an aureole of blondish hair above a high forehead called on me at the office.

The name, he said, is Clifford Odets, and with a boyish grin, described himself as "an indigent actor and an aspiring playwright." My taxi piece had inspired him, he said, to try to do a play about the strike. Would I tell him more about the hackies? Believing with Mike Gold that the magazine must nurture every young writer, I consented, and that evening we talked into the morning hours at his room where he had invited me for dinner and a bottle of chianti. A bust of Beethoven hung over the door and I remarked on it. Yes, he smiled, he wrote best when he had Beethoven's music on the victrola. It happens that Beethoven is my favorite composer and I have spent many an odd hour at the keyboard trying to get the hang of his sonatas, especially the *Largo* which has in it the wonder of planets revolving in their orbits. We spoke a long time about Beethoven, the genius, and finally got down to Louie Cheznar, the hackie.

Some months later in January 1935, I sat enchanted watching Odets' play, *Waiting for Lefty,* that opened at the Civic Repertory Theater. It had won the joint *New Masses*—New Theater contest. The Group Theater presented it with passion and brilliance, actors and actresses, famous today played Louie Cheznar and his pals. *Waiting for Lefty* became a sensation and within six months workingmen were cheering Odets' version of Louie Cheznar in cities across the continent. Many of the well-heeled, as well as the shabby, came. *Lefty* won the George Pierce Baker cup at the Yale Drama Tournament in April, in New Haven; Yale, Harvard, Johns Hopkins, Michigan State, Syracuse University, put it on; in Chicago a middle-aged taxi-driver played the leading role; in Milwaukee the Retail Clerks Union staged it; in Peoria dirt-farmers, the unemployed, admitted free, rose to cheer like madmen at the curtain's fall. Odets had caught a moment of history, their history. Efforts to halt the play failed and the folk of Boston insisted on seeing it despite a virtuous Roxbury judge who said: "I don't care if the world is collapsing, Roxbury will stay pure."

The story, as Odets told it, was superlatively simple: his scenes flashed back into the starved lives of the strikers who were waiting at their union hall for their leader Lefty, who never shows up. A character dubbed MAN cried out a moment before the curtain descends, "They found Lefty behind the car barns with a bullet in his head."

Today many critics (and lamentably, its author) recoil at the bare explicit statement of the plot, at the super-charged poetry in the speech of its characters: like Agate, who shouted, facing the audience when he learned Lefty's fate: "Hear it boys, hear it? Hell, listen to me! Coast to coast! HELLO AMERICA. HELLO. WE'RE STORM BIRDS OF THE WORKING CLASS. WORKERS OF

THE WORLD . . . OUR BONES AND BLOOD! And when we die they'll know what we did to make a new world! Christ, cut us up to little pieces. We'll die for what is right, put fruit trees where our ashes are!" Then as the curtain is slowly descending he turns to the audience, crying, "Well, what's the answer?"

The script of the play concludes:

> ALL: STRIKE!
> AGATE: LOUDER!
> ALL: STRIKE!
> AGATE AND OTHERS on Stage, AGAIN!
> ALL: STRIKE, STRIKE! STRIKE ! ! !

No, the artist then, did not fear to end his sentences in exclamation points, this was no time for the private, couch-sick confidence. History, full lunged, roared: everywhere, as though a nation of workingmen heard Agate's curtain-call proclamation, they were striking. I packed my bag, time and time again, traveling here, to the general strike in Terre Haute, then to the department store clerk strikes in Pittsburgh, strikes which culminated in the tidal wave of sit-downs that altered the political and economic life of our nation.

Sit-downs—what a homely word to describe one of the most meaningful movements in American history. All times, I suspect, choose the commonplace expression to dub their great moments, as though man seeks always to get on familiar terms with history: a Boston "tea party" preceded an American Revolution. In any event, the term, sit-down, was no parlor expression to President Emeritus A. Lawrence Lowell, of Harvard: he summoned the press to his Back Bay home and notified the nation that the valid term for "sit-down" was "revolution." In a way he was right, although Stella and Marie and Tommy and Kaintuck whom I interviewed in the storm of Detroit sit-downs would scarcely agree. Stella, for example, said she sat-down for the thirty-seven days at White Owl against those giant cockroaches that kept falling from the ceiling on her curly head, and to get her union recognized in the bargain. Marie, fingering the crucifix at her throat, said she had two babies at home and the wages couldn't feed them; Tommy said—well, I am getting ahead of my story.

It was at the block-long, red-brick plant that sprawled like a medieval fortress, and where 11,000 men were sitting-down, that I saw the shape of our American future. Sentries of the union, wearing UAW buttons on their overseas caps, as jauntily as Jacobins wore the red cockade a century and a half earlier, stood vigilantly on guard. The bright flush of youth was in their cheeks, they were stalwart of shoulder and chest, chosen, obviously, for the possible emergency. Banteringly, they asked me for my credentials when I asked permission to enter the plant for my story. I noted the glint of suspicion, though they continued to smile brightly. I knew they had been maligned by all the newspapers, and they could spare no love for one of my profession. When they looked up from my note of introduction, and said, grinning, "Well, that's different: the *Worker*," I was elated.

They turned me over to a guide, Kaintuck, a lanky, red-faced youngster of twenty-two whose corn-colored hair rose to a cowlick and whose words had the soft Dixie slur. He'd come North three years before, he said, talking readily, for he had observed the sentries welcome me. No, he had never seen my paper, he wasn't much for reading, but if those hombres at the gate say it's okay, it's okay with him. No, he'd never belonged to a union before, onliest thing he'd ever joined was the K.K.K. Noting my surprise, he grinned, well, that was before he saw that the kleagles were out for a fast buck, and when he saw that, he got out of those damn bedsheets fast.

Inside the plant the lavender-hued neon bulbs discolored the faces of men, but did not mask the rollicking rough-house humor, and, as I soon discovered, the confident discipline of embattled men. The great factory floor was spotless, not a curl of waste lay underfoot amid the uncompleted tonneaus of cars on the belt that froze when the strike signal sounded. The plant was home, now, *their* home, and they kept it clean, like conscientious housewives.

Their experience as trade unionists was minimal, or even nil, yet, overnight, they won their degree as unionists. They displayed the genius of American labor for swift and impromptu organization. Overnight they banded into a self-imposed government by committee: one committee guarded the gates, as I saw; another scouted the neighborhood grocery stores for donations of food; another, of their wives, on the outside, to cook. There were committees for law and order within the plant;

financial committees helped families tide the hard time; publicity committees wrote leaflets and press releases; and beyond all, was the central strike strategy committee.

As I moved among the strikers, their humor, irrepressible in adversity, captivated me: the quip, the wise-crack, the folksay was everywhere. They hung placards over their narrow cots lined neatly row on row, that said "The Statler," or "The Detroiter," ironic comment on the accommodations where automobile springs served them as bed springs. I came upon the men roaring a parody of the current Tin Pan Alley song, "Pennies from Heaven," which they changed to "Dollars from Hudson." Young blades sported beards which they vowed not to shave until the strike was won. Mechanics undertook the thespian's art, wrote and acted out skits lampooning the company union, while their audience, seated on the floors, roared.

Yet they were in deadly earnest: this was the humor of men going to battle. For Kaintuck brought me to the corner where they mimeographed the union paper and a dozen men crowded around us, insisting that Kaintuck read it. He demurred, but agreed finally, and, striking a pose like a ham Shakespearean actor he read the editorial in a shaky baritone which grew steady and sober: "We are only two weeks ahead of starvation on the job," he began. The editorial described the Cadillac Square demonstration the previous week as the greatest in Detroit's history. "These massed thousands," he read, savoring the words in his Southern drawl, "were not asking for a mansion, while others live in a rented shack. They were not demanding thousand dollar cases of champagne while some poor kids can't buy an ice cream cone. But they were demanding what they actually earned, a decent annual living wage, with job security." With a flourish Kaintuck turned to his audience, with a verse concluding the editorial: "In these words of the immortal Bobby Burns, the poet of the poor:

'Not for a coach and four, with a trained attendant,
But for the glorious privilege of being independent.'"

The men yelled, cheered and clapped him on the back. "That's tellin' 'em, Kaintuck," and an elderly, gray-headed striker intoned, "Amen, amen."

White Owl I visited the next morning as the bronze bells

of Detroit's churches tolled. This was Easter Sunday, the cigar-makers, girls and women dominantly, were in the thirty-seventh day of their sitdown. The sentries were young women in Easter finery; one wore a frock of delicate green, the other pink, and though they had a gossamer beauty their manner was business-like, briskly stern, as they asked for credentials. Like the men at Hudson, they welcomed me when they saw the name of my paper, ushered me inside, suddenly like undergraduates at commencement exercises. Here, too, the floors gleamed spotlessly, they had routed the cockroaches and all was orderly, even gay: A large room on the second floor was transformed into a "beauty parlor" and a dozen strikers started when I entered, their hair done up in metal strips for curling. A young woman arrived, carrying her three-months old baby which her husband had just brought in for her to see, the first time in a week, and girls in metal strips crowded round to coo over the infant.

Yet, the day before, they had barricaded the factory doors with boxes, chairs, when word came that the mayor of Detroit had decided to evict all sitdowners by force, as he had the strikers at the R. C. Dun plant. These girls, the day before Easter, had resolved unanimously, at a hasty meeting, to fight for every floor of the building, "fight them on the roof if need be," the shop chairlady said. "We got ourselves big sticks and we went to sleep holding them in readiness." She told me the Big Brothers, the boys from UAW, had sped to the factory in a motor caravan "at zero hour" and piled into the plant. Thereupon the cops thought better of it and the girls wearing crucifixes held their cigar fortress. They were ready to do battle in the name of Jesus and the CIO.

That night at a cafeteria I talked to Tommy Dixon, one of the Big Brothers, a Minute Man, captain of the strikers' shock troops who wore green berets and armbands and who sped to any danger spot. Thirty years old, as American as Johnny Appleseed, his cheeks a high color, his eyes a bright blue, he spoke with a quiet confidence. When I said I came from the *Daily Worker* and the *New Masses,* he warmed up appreciably, grinned, extended his hand and said he had been reading the *Daily* for eight years. I do not know if he was a member of the Communist Party. But the familiar word "unity," came from his lips frequently, and he spoke cogently of the left-wing's part in these sitdowns, of the many instances where Communists and their supporters, in the Trade Union Unity League, organized skeleton organizations which led department strikes that were dress rehearsals, in effect, for this decisive engagement. After the successful sit-down against General Motors at Flint, the Communists and their supporters believed the whole industry was ready. They should know, he said, for their associates like Wyndham Mortimer and Robert Travis led the Flint strike on to success. "Flint was the kingpin. Pull it, and the rest had to happen—providing there was good leadership." Evidently good leadership was at hand. The first recruits to the UAW—after tireless, infinitely careful work, under the noses of the goons and company spies everywhere—forged nuclei of the most far-sighted men in the plants. That started something which snowballed, he said, "when the objective situation was favorable." I then assumed that he was a Communist, for this was the unmistakable idiom of a man who knew the literature of Marxism.

The previous November, he continued, Labor elected FDR president, and Murphy, Governor of Michigan. Labor's mandate could not be ignored. State power, he said, always lined up with the employers in the past, but it shrank today, for obvious political reasons, from calling out the Army or the National Guard. Michigan's workingmen, certain no attack would come from the state, went into action with confidence. The sitdowners at Flint notified Governor Murphy that they would stay on inside until their justified demands were met. If the company called its plug-uglies, and if they killed any strikers in the necessary resistance, the Governor's hands would have blood on them. So the Army and the Guard did not come in, bayonets fixed. And the Michigan workers realized, as they never had before, he said, the explicit relationship between politics, that is political action, and the economic action, the strike. "We used both weapons," Dixon smiled radiantly, "like a two-gun cowboy."

So he sketched the background to the strike. "But I haven't finished," he said, raising a forefinger like a professor delivering a lecture. "Another reason we won is due to the principles of the CIO." For this he credited William Z. Foster's ideas of industrial unionism and militant tactics. And why, I asked, did the strikes assume the form of the sitdown, and not the older, more orthodox method? "Glad you asked me that," he said. Americans noted the success of the French workers when they sat down in Paris against the Michelin tire company. And Dixon, in mien the workingman you could meet in a thousand union halls, spoke on the international community of labor. Today working class ideas, he said, crossed oceans. "After all, if scientists study and learn from each other, why can't workers?" He remarked that a scientist in London, and another in distant Moscow, had independently discovered the element oxygen, and simultaneously. So it was with the sitdowns. "America learned from Europe." (I recognized the concepts I had encountered at my Marxist study classes.)

As he spoke he glanced at his wrist watch and abruptly excused himself, hastened to the nearest telephone booth, and after a call, returned. "The girls down at Square D are calling," he said rapidly. They had word that the cops would raid the plant unless it was evacuated by two o'clock. And tear-gas would certainly be used. "Got to move along," Dixon said cheerfully, extending his hand; then he darted from the restaurant a plain, stocky figure, broad in the shoulder, an Atlas of today. A few minutes later I saw him in his car, the klaxon sounding like the horn of Gabriel. His car led a file of fifteen others to the besieged girls at Square D.; the girls who had just returned from Easter prayers, were awaiting zero hour again.

And waiting for their Big Brothers, the Minute Men. Yes, waiting for Lefty, who was not, as Odets saw him, dead behind the car barn.

10

Newsmen and a Newspaper

THE TIDE OF strikes swirled into the arid precincts of the newsroom, that holy of holies of individualism, and newspapermen went on the march. I hold Card No. 9702, issued by the American Newspaper Guild, November of 1934; one day, upon my return to New York, my Guild chapter notified me that the *Amsterdam News,* a Negro newspaper in Harlem, was on strike. Heywood Broun would lead the pickets that afternoon: could I come?

No newspaperman, harking from that time, can speak Broun's name without respect, or, like those of us who helped found the Guild or were among its first members, without reverence. I had read his column in the *New York World* for years: its limpid, vivid, witty style won him a large and faithful audience; his passion for social justice conquered that audience's heart. His crusade for Sacco and Vanzetti brought the publisher's axe down on him, but he had not surrendered; he was a man of great heart and abundant talent, a crusader.

I was on the Harlem picketline half an hour, taking my turn in the winter's gale with the Negro strikers who let neither rain nor snow keep them from their appointed rounds, when a taxicab came up and out of it unrolled the great, bulky figure, his crown fringed by a mass of curly hair, his eyes small and keen, his chins astonishing in size, his torso, a barrel. All of him was so distinctive that I felt only a cartoonist could have created him. We cheered as he lumbered on, through the frowning cops, grabbed a placard and took his place in line.

Always, before he came, the Black Maria would charge up to the pavement, the cops would shove the strikers inside, and off we went to the precinct police station. But the police authority feared to lay a hand on him, shrinking from his pen and his popularity, and though Broun strove, time and again, to be arrested, the police warily refused to give him satisfaction.

Though they would not lock him up, he sped down to the precinct headquarters after the police rounded up their prey, inquiring about the bail, gadding about so ponderously that the blue-coats were disconcerted at their job. Broun greeted each arrested picket with the warmth and urbanity he might a new member of his famous company of wits at the Hotel Algonquin. My first encounter with Broun was in the police station. Later, he told me he read the *New Masses* regularly and regarded it worthy of its predecessors, the *Liberator* and the old *Masses*. In fact, he had arrived at his liberalism, he said, from the pages of the old *Masses,* shortly after he left Harvard and its famous class of 1910.

Broun invited me to his hotel room one day to talk about Marxism. I came, at the rather rare hour of nine A.M. on his suggestion; he entered the room in slippers and a scant night-robe, his eyes smiling. He got down to business at once. He was considering becoming a Marxist—or a Catholic, and with a laugh, he said he was studying dialectical materialism and St. Thomas Aquinas simultaneously. "A course in comparative religion," he grinned. His was a curious dilemma—"Should I go to Karl Marx or Jesus Christ?" I replied the two were really not mutually exclusive. But, he replied, "not Christ's reward, the Kingdom of Heaven." Communism got you the hard end of a police club, Catholicism offers you an eternal seat at God's right hand. And he did not know whether he was man enough to agree that virtue is its own reward. Then, lightly, but quickly, as though he had some pre-vision that he expected his Maker to call him soon (suspecting evidently that his heart had been overtaxed), he said Death was a matter of some considerable interest to him. He confessed to small patience and less time to plow through the works of Marx and Engels but what he read impressed him mightily—"on temporal matters." Most answers to the dilemmas of this sorry world were there: but he was a mystic, in fact, he craved for a Hereafter and perhaps the Scriptures would win out. He had the need to know the origin of life, and there Marxism did not satisfy him. Aquinas was better on that score, and so perhaps he might choose Catholicism. Broun died, a convert to Catholicism, at the age of 50.

I am certain he will be remembered always as a gallant man of the pen, one of the foremost in American journalism and I am proud to be, in a major sense, his disciple. I know he loved and respected his fellow craftsmen, not only for what they were, but much more for what they could be. More than any single man he won for them the measure of dignity they now enjoy, which, he would be first to say, is but a paltry beginning.

Sometime in the autumn of 1935 the editors of the *Daily Worker* invited me to join their staff. They had decided to publish a Sunday edition, in the tradition of Sunday newspapers —varied features of popular interest, a review of the week's major news, a woman's department, a sport's section, comic strips, columns on health, the potpourri the American reader gets when he plunks down his dime—in those days—for his Sabbath day-of-rest reading and entertainment. Naturally the budget was small and severely limited: most of the writing, the drawings, the lay-outs would perforce, be done by volunteer talent. But within the range of the sums available (the dimes and dollars that came willingly from workingmen throughout the land) could we duplicate a reasonable working class facsimile of a capitalist Sunday newspaper? If I believed that I could, would I accept the editorship of that edition?

I thought the matter over carefully, and concluded that the time was propitious. Though we could not offer the reader the five pounds of Sunday entertainment the commercial newspapers offered, we could, I felt, give enough to make it worthwhile to a significant number of readers. My travels convinced me that questions, new, challenging, knocked around in the heads of millions, questions the established papers could not and would not answer. These questions had a significance, a scope that compared to the most decisive that ever bedeviled our privileged classes. For the first time in our history, in this day of the New Deal, of renascent Labor, most Americans agreed that the State had the central responsibility for its citizens's economic welfare.

Herbert Hoover had denied that, and his fellow-Americans cast him from their midst, a political leper who could not, for a generation, step foot in the White House. His cherished concept perished in the Hoovervilles.

Giant questions swept America like cyclones. The time was ripe for a Marxist newspaper of the sort the editors envisaged.

A popular newspaper for workingmen whose minds grappled with political and economic quandaries no generation hitherto had faced. This is not to imply that Americans had not confronted such questions before: the turn of the century and the two decades afterward saw a sweep of socialist ideas that gave nearly a million votes to Eugene V. Debs in 1912 and in 1920, true. But the depression of 1929 dwarfed all crises since the Civil War: 1873, 1893, 1907, 1913, 1921, and nullified the claim of capitalism that it would give Americans an eternal age of prosperity. The golden haze that lay over the land in the Twenties disappeared in 1929; and the naked American eye saw the starved vistas of the Thirties.

If, in equivalent times, America had a socialist press, like the *Appeal to Reason* that reached editions of over a million, and scores of regional periodicals, could not these times maintain a *Sunday Worker?*

After several days' consideration and consultation with friends of journalistic and labor experience, I agreed to undertake it. It was indeed a challenge and though I preferred to write, I was persuaded that to edit—at such a moment—must take precedence over my own inclinations.

Within months we mustered around the paper a hundred men and women who volunteered their various gifts—writers, cartoonists, critics, columnists, doctors, and even some aviators who conducted a column on aeronautics for the young which they named "Jimmy Collins Eaglets," to honor a doughty test pilot who had become a Communist some months before he rocketed to death in a plane which fell apart.

The first issue came off the press, early January 1936, and it was exhilarating and humbling to know that hundreds of ardent workingmen and workingwomen stood at the freight stations of railroads in Pittsburgh, in Detroit, in Chicago, in a score of industrial cities, awaiting the precious cargo which they sold from door to door in working class neighborhoods.

We even had a four-page rotogravure section. The circulation passed 100,000 within two months. The readers responded warmly although some expressed concern over comics, sports pages and various features which were scarcely "class-angled." My philosophy of journalism collided with those who recoiled at the space and money devoted to writings about baseball, prize-fighters, Hollywood. A trade union leader of courage and unquestionable worth, expressed his horror over a front page devoted to a photograph of Shirley Temple, the child movie star, whose dimples and curls looked up at you under the heavy masthead of the *Worker*. "How can you squander workers' money with such a picture when miners' children are starving in the coalfields of Pennsylvania?" he cried. Taken aback, I replied that the paper, in sum, described the life of the working class. It could not be indicted for ignoring the brutal realities of our day. But, I argued, most Americans are reared in a tradition of Sunday newspaper journalism, and we could not afford to ignore that, nor should we. Many a family saved quarters and half-dollars to see films starring Shirley Temple. And so it was when they bought a Sunday newspaper. Our success depended upon recognizing and satisfying their tastes. Give them the movie star on the cover: they would, as they should, encounter the class struggle inside.

My argument was not spectacularly successful. Though most Communist leaders and active members wanted Shirley Temple, the hard-bitten recalcitrants did not surrender easily; they ignored the contention that we could be as keen politically as our minds and program allowed, without surrendering the popular touch. The paper continued most of its innovations, but "sectarian" pressures unavoidably limited its appeal to a wider audience.

This experience blunted my own editorial ardor but did not kill it. I concluded that a perpetual tug-of-war existed within working class movements as they spiralled upward inevitably; old ways, old habits, impeded the new, the necessary. I saw men of fine talents, chafing at these lags and inadequacies, grow disillusioned, and drift away. I argued with several brilliant cartoonists among our volunteers, who asked how I could "swallow" this stuff. *They* could not. I explained it as I saw it: a working class movement, even the most advanced, is no island unto itself. It exists within its prevailing capitalism, and it cannot proceed, pure and unblemished, to its destination. Communists, like all members of the human race, have their failings: God knows, I had mine and they theirs. Could we expect unanimity, conformity, on any matter? Should we? We must stand our ground, champion our views, and if we did not succeed, we must still see first things first. First was the main direction of the Marxist movement: its philosophy, its goals, and its adherents, even those with whom we quarreled, surpassed, in their totality, any other aggregate of Americans in intention, will and performance. I pointed to the advances which American Marxists, in considerable measure, inspired: the Wagner Act and its guarantees to labor, the establishment of social and unemployment insurance, the steady, if all too slow advance in Negro rights; and, first and foremost, their steadfast championship of a world at peace.

I convinced some volunteers: others I could not. The blunt fact of bureaucracy, which unquestionably accounted for most of the paper's hindrances, repelled them. It blurred their vision, and they parted, unhappily, some to become well-paid servitors, finally, of Hearst's King Features, knocking out a laugh-cartoon daily, harnessing their talents to the publisher's will for the dividend. Though I blamed them then, I cannot fully do so now after a score of years and no little experience. I believe now that bureaucratic practices were significantly responsible for their loss even though I know that some, failing to acquire a solid knowledge of Marxism and a conscious adherence to its ideals (despite the shortcomings of some of its practitioners), would doubtless have yielded to the lure of the fleshpots. Yet even these, in their majority, did not become foes of socialism. The idea will not die in them, for it sank deep into their tissue and blood. The ranch house in Connecticut may compensate for the loss of the dream but I doubt it. I met some, years later, and I detected a regret, a wistfulness for the days when they gave their talents for men and women and children they might never see, but whose fate they identified as their own. They traded crusades; the one for the dollar could never be as satisfying as the one for humanity.

But outweighing all these considerations, which are largely personal, was this essential fact: a newspaper was born, a workingman's newspaper, which is, in our America, a kind of miracle. True, it happened to be the week-end edition of a daily paper, but it had, in considerable degree, a life of its own, and a circulation thrice the size of the every-day edition.

Now the paper has been called, among other choice appellations, the best-known and the least read journal in America. This is not quite true on either count: certainly the latter observation was unjust in this time of which I am writing. I had occasion to study the circulation tape to ascertain where the paper was going. There was heady wonder in the fact that we were reaching into 1,200 cities, towns and hamlets, including the south's Black Belt.

It must be said that our readers were, in a large way, unlike those of any other newspaper. Ours, generally, constituted the soul of a community—the most public-spirited, the most intellectually eager, the movers and the shakers of men. They read not merely for pleasure (though they did not scorn that) but to know, in order to do.

If they were workingmen (which, in their majority they were) their fellows in the unions sought them out for their counsel, their leadership. If Negro, as many were, they were the most self-sacrificing and knowledgeable of their community, whether in Chicago's South Side or in Chambers County, Alabama. If they were intellectuals, their minds were the most fruitful of their fraternity, be they of Hollywood, or Broadway, or the campus. I say this knowing that the reader may suspect me of bias, and there is no way to prove my case precisely. I can only say that I travelled among our readers, East, West, South, North, came to understand them well, their works, their standing in their communities: I know whereof I speak.

The paper was as vital to most of our readers as the bread they ate and the shelter above them. For many, like the sharecroppers of the South, read it at the risk of their livelihoods, and possibly, of their lives. They set aside their nickels, dimes and dollars to secure the paper's existence.

When I say "miracle" to describe the paper's existence I have in mind the fact that the great trade unions which had several hundred times as many members than we had readers, were unable until recently, to float a daily newspaper. The quality of dedication, of total commitment to the cause of our readers made the difference. And so our journal helped enhance the effectiveness of many thousands in the social and economic crusades of the time. It captured, in important respects, the best qualities of its predecessors, *The Appeal to Reason,* Frederick Douglass' *North Star,* Garrison's *Liberator.* I say that pleading no special journalistic eminence for ourselves as editors, but because, in greatest part, the *Worker* was a product of the breath-taking times—whch swelled the ranks of labor, and of its vanguard elements, the Marxists. Those times brought us the most eager and gifted of the land.

What many of us lacked in experience we compensated for in enthusiasm, energy and, most important of all, we had a political line geared to the time. The ideas our columns contained happened to be closer to reality, to sager counsel, than that of all other newspapers.

After all, their aspiration was money: *ours,* the welfare of men. And so our paper significantly helped America's workingmen to found the CIO which brought new life and new millions into the labor movement.

11

Center of the World

WHILE NEW YORKERS sang carols to peace that frosty Christmas day of 1936 twenty-six Americans boarded a ship in lower Manhattan. We did not know, at the *Worker,* that Americans were joining the International Brigades to help the cause of Republican Spain. We learned that later when the lists of the dead came through.

There was John Scott, the Englishman who had come on our staff a year before. Red-cheeked, tall, he spoke with the easy worldliness of the European intellectual. He had a gift of many languages, a knowledge of many lands, a scholar who had seen much and traveled much in his twenty-seven years—to Africa, to Asia. When I drew him out he talked brilliantly in a curious nasal monotone about Shakespeare, Bacon, Donne, Chaucer, his favorite authors. Or about Goethe, Schiller, Balzac, Tolstoy. Often I saw him, late at night after the paper had gone to press, sitting at his desk under the green lamp, a heap of books stacked on its corner. After July 18, he talked often of Spain's politics, its culture, of Goya, Velazquez, Cervantes, Unamuno. And then one day, he was gone.

By the time we learned of his death on a Spanish battlefield we knew that many a good man had left, unannounced, slipping out of our lives. Our Government had stamped all passports "Not Valid For Spain," and all who went, stole away, in secret, like fugitives.

The image of Spain haunted me. I hammered away at the typewriter trying desperately to describe the grandeur of its resistance. I tore up sheet after sheet, the right words didn't come. I, all of us, followed the war bulletins avidly. We had printed the call of the Spanish Republican Government for volunteers. Bombs, the Loyalists said, are not falling in London and Washington because they are dropping in Madrid and Valencia. Spain's frontlines were ours, our paper said.

The November 7, 1936, issue of *Mundo Obrero,* the Communist daily newspaper in Madrid, had an extraordinary effect on me. The great type in red ink on the front page said:

ALL OUT TO THE BARRICADES . . .
THE ENEMY IS ACROSS THE RIVER.

Yet, in this same edition, on page two, in the upper right-hand corner, I saw a quarter page advertisement: "Charlie Chaplin at the Rialto, in Modern Times." That advertisement seemed to be the epitome of Madrid's heroism: the insistence upon life as bombs fell and shells dropped on the streets. I read how the Communists of Madrid had built the famous Quinto Regimiento, the Fifth Regiment, in the very first days, asking for a thousand volunteers and within four weeks had 70,000. The other parties, too, overnight improvised their volunteer armies, the *milicias,* from among their followers who went out into the streets, untrained for war, barehanded virtually, and stopped Franco at the gates. A large picture of *La Pasionaria*—Dolores Ibarruri—daughter of the Asturian miners had beneath it, as caption, the words she had first uttered that went around the world, "Spaniards—It is better to die on your feet than to live on your knees."

To be in Madrid now, it seemed to me, was to be in the Paris of 1789, the Washington of 1864, the Moscow of 1917. And one day I spoke to the editors. Yes, they said, the paper did need a man in Spain to cover the war. Yes, if I wanted to go they would be glad to send me. And so, overnight, I bade my wife and children goodbye and I was on the ocean liner to Spain.

One day in Paris, just long enough to buy the tickets to Valencia. The next day I stood on Spanish soil. The train had scarcely pulled out of the dark tunnel in the Pyrenees, at Port Bou, when I heard a long wail of a siren and saw men and women break into a run. A border guard, a small, lithe, tanned Spaniard in a blue uniform resembling overalls, fell to one knee, aimed his rifle and fired at the sky. The civilians ran at a dogtrot, like figures in a slow-motion film to the *refugio.* I followed them and stood at the mouth of the refuge, in the tunnel bored into the Pyrenees, and stared up at the blue Mediterranean sky to see a plane, like a graceful dragonfly, spiral off and away.

I heard a great hollow boom nearby and a woman convulsively covered the head of the child she held.

Though I had written about it, now, as I *saw* it, this first time, my head under the bombs, I experienced a sense of grotesque unreality, felt a sort of macabre insanity, that in this year of 1937, men were dropping dynamite and steel upon the heads of other men. When the all-clear sounded, I emerged from the tunnel to see a tall, lean brown man rise from the ground. He wore a Republican uniform that bore the insignia of the medical corps. He stared angrily at the sky, and a soldier of 19, a heavy gun slung across his back, brushed mud from the shoulders of the medico. The doctor's face seemed familiar, long, narrow, intense, one eyelid drooping and suddenly I remembered. He was Dr. Arnold Donawa, a Negro dentist of Harlem who had been a leading figure at Howard University's medical school. I had not known he was a volunteer and I ran to him and grasped his hand. Speaking as though he had just seen me the day before, he said bitterly: "That damn bomb almost got the ambulance! There's nothing in the whole army like this ambulance and it almost got it." *It* was a gift from the Republic's friends in the United States, *it* was fully equipped with the latest gear, and the doctor reverently wiped some specks of mud from the shining fender. He bade me goodbye, climbed into the driver's seat, his lean face glowing, and pulled away, the young soldier waving at him as the car moved toward the coast highway. My first glimpse of Spain was about as I had pictured it would be, and I jotted a few words into my notebook: "Is it symbolic that the first American volunteer I met as I crossed the border is a Negro? And a white Republican soldier brushed the mud from his uniform."

I made the journey to Valencia on a train so crammed with refugees, men, women and children, that I stood all the way: the train inched through a sparkling countryside of white villages and green farms. Valencia was then the capital, and I thought I had never seen so beautiful a city where palm trees grew on the broad avenues amid white, towering buildings. The main plaza teemed with people, talking, gesticulating, laughing. A fountain played among marble statues in the lovely central square. Crowds stood at the glittering counters of the bazaars set up beneath the great stone porticos that had shaded them from the tropical sun for five hundred years. Women hawked the brilliantly red Valencian roses and overhead, among the white buildings, towered a big sign in which a great hand pointed north: "The Front," it said, "is 64 Kilometers Away."

I hunted up Robert Minor, the Communist leader who had come as a war correspondent for a number of Marxist newspapers in the states. He swept into the dark foyer of his hotel, the Inglaterra, a monument of a man, his great bald head gleaming, his bright smallish eyes sparkling beneath the craggy forehead with its two heaped tufts of eyebrows. "You come at the right time," he said, throwing his arms around me in the Spanish *embrazo.* The Fifteenth Brigade, the Lincolns, had just captured two key towns in the Aragon mountains, Quinto and Belchite. It was a tremendous victory, he exulted. But the losses were heavy and he was at that moment about to leave for the front. I must go with him. We drove for thirty-six hours, through pine-covered highlands, across tawny plains, through the "silent villages" of Cervantes and we found the men in an olive grove, the cannon booming a few miles to the east where the fascists were counter-attacking.

A tall, young man in his late twenties, shy of manner, his blue eyes warm, introduced himself. He was Captain Robert Merriman, the chief of staff. Merriman had taught economics at the University of California and he was one of the first Americans to arrive in Spain. He brought me to the soldiers who sat in the shade of the grove, weary men, unshaven, fresh out of battle. My interview with them was extraordinary: they scarcely permitted me a moment to ask a question. *They* were asking the questions. A short, broad-shouldered man with a tin plate of steaming beans in his hands, *garbanzos,* asked how his UAW local at Flint was doing. Another soldier, tall and lean, about 35 years of age, grilled me about the National Maritime Union and the CIO. A bright-eyed youth of twenty-two, slim, slight, asked in unmistakeable Brooklynese how soon would Washington lift the embargo on arms to the Republic. The questions came fast, political questions in the main that reflected their awareness of the war's meaning. Not all the questions were of politics: a youngster no more than nineteen, with a cowlick of sandy hair that rose like a crest on his crown, asked earnestly whether I thought the Giants had a chance this year: another inquired about Joe Louis. Was he in good condition and would he kayo that goddam Nazi Schmeling?

A dark figure came out of the shadows and asked sepulchrally whether it was true that that bastard Joe North was here. I turned to look into the unshaven face of a haggard man of thirty, blue eyes bloodshot in a bald head, his high forehead furrowed in wrinkles. "I'm Alvah Bessie," he said, "Remember?" I remembered. He had been on the staff of the *Brooklyn Eagle* and had written pieces for the *New Masses* on the theater. He grinned as he recalled how he had come to our offices a year ago to raise a rumpus about the favorable review of a play he thought "lousy." He reminded me of it. "Well, I'm just the same cranky old bastard," he said. He asked about the plays on Broadway this season, about some mutual friends and then, suddenly embarrassed, he thrust several letters toward me wrapped carefully in heavy string. They were to his two young sons whom he wrote regularly, once a week. "Mail them," he smiled, "and I'll love you forever." He flashed a snapshot from a battered wallet and I looked at two laughing youngsters of about eight and ten, in chin-high jerseys. A soldier nearby clapped his hands to his eyes. "If I see those two brats again," he groaned, "I'll shoot their father dead."

Through the night the soldiers talked and when they finished they wrapped themselves in their ponchos and went to sleep on the ground beneath the olive branches. I lay among them staring up at the Spanish stars. On a mound nearby, a sentry leaned on his gun, a tangle of barbed wire behind him against those stars. I thought of their stories told simply, gruffly even; nobody had used the sonorous words Humanity, Justice, Democracy. That was understood: theirs was the monosyllabic speech of war. And here they lay, men of war, yesterday's civilians, dreaming of home as once the Colonials from Massachusetts dreamed of the white frame houses and green village squares, of a woman's smile and a child's laugh.

After I returned to Valencia I hastened to the Censor's office with my bulging notebook to cable my story. I knew so many parents of these boys, so many of their sweethearts, who waited for word.

The victory at Belchite was big news; any victory, no matter how small, was big news, for daily, hourly, the Franco radio predicted the collapse of the Loyalist Government, and all too many newspapers at home trumpeted the propaganda. It had its baneful purpose, of course, was designed to counteract the possibility that the embargo might be lifted. For obviously, no Government would consider altering its policy toward the Republic if its days were numbered.

The press office lay in a vast stone building on Calle Cortes: a bomb had shorn away the adjoining house; you could see the pictures still hanging from the walls, the pattern of the wallpaper. Newspapermen from virtually every country of the world sat tapping away at their typewriters in the Censura's office. Senor Rubio, the chief censor, was a short, heavy man wearing smoked glasses, who had a somber air and his welcome was tepid. "The *Daily Worker?*" he repeated as I introduced myself. "Of New York? A daily newspaper?" He did not know, he said coldly, if his office had made provisions for me to send press cables. I had been assured, back in New York, that it had. No, he knew nothing of it. If I wished to send my articles by airmail, that was of course, satisfactory to him. But cable was another matter, "a matter of many pesetas." Yes, the Government had agreed to send cables gratis for certain newspapers that were friends of the Republic and that could not afford the costs, but the budget for that purpose had recently been reduced. However, he said in a sudden burst of generosity, he would allow the *Daily Worker* 500 words by cable per week.

"Five hundred words a week!" I echoed blankly. That was scarcely a column in our pages: my first story, on Belchite, was at least three thousand words. I adopted my most persuasive air to tell Senor Rubio that many thousands of our readers had doubtless read of Belchite's fall in newspapers that opposed lifting the embargo and they knew that the Lincolns were in the action. They were awaiting word—these friends and relatives of the volunteers, "Doubtless," he replied, "but not only Americans are worrying about their sons." However, he would see. He took my story and disappeared into another room for an hour. He re-appeared to tell me morosely that they had decided to send the full story this time, as a special occasion, but they could not allow my paper unlimited cable rights. Later perhaps, after the proper authorities had considered it, but not now. I thanked him for his gracious permission to send this story, but he was adamant about the allotment of 500 words "for the time being."

That was calamitous. It was nothing. And if I sent my dispatches airmail the office would receive them in a week or two. No sooner, I ascertained. That meant I could only send feature stories, or analytical pieces that could be published any time, we called it "time copy," scarcely the fare for a daily newspaper. I was woe-struck by the irony. Here I was at the center of the world and I was virtually gagged. How could I convey the grandeur of this war in 500 words a week? I walked from the office with a sinking heart. Didn't Senor Rubio understand that the *Daily Worker* was the most consistent friend of the Republic in all the United States? I inquired about him and learned that he was a member of the right wing of the Popular Front whose sympathies would be less than ardent for a Communist newspaper. Of course, the Government must watch over every peseta, but the United States was key to lifting the embargo, key to the Republic's fate, and wasn't this being centimo-wise and peseta-foolish?

I thought the matter over very carefully that night as I lay in my bed. This was the Popular Front of which the Communists were a single component and they did not ask nor did they expect special privileges or consideration. I must persuade the good senor, or whoever else was responsible, that my paper was worthy of greater support. The following day I brought Senor Rubio an armful of copies of the *Worker* and explained its central position in the American labor movement for aid to Spain. I read to him passionately from the many editorials which we published, almost every day, arguing against the embargo and explaining the Popular Front. Furthermore, my paper had a greater portion of its readers who were members of the International Brigade than any other in the United States, and more, I was certain, were coming. One of its staff, John Scott, had already died here in battle. I used every argument I knew. Senior R wore smoked glasses and I could not ascertain whether my arguments were making headway. "We will see," he concluded, and there the matter stood. I passed enviously through the office among the correspondents of the other newspapers who sat clicking away at their typewriters, sending what seemed to me, limitless stories—and by cable.

I spoke to Bob Minor about my dilemma. I had not come here to write feature stories about the war: I came to cover the front daily. I would prefer to join the Brigade and do my stint with gunfire. No, Bob replied: others had come for that purpose; as a good soldier I must stand at my station, which was journalism. He predicted that I would win the coveted cable space if I sent air-mail stories for the time being, about the home-front, accounts that would go beneath the surface and would spell out the realities of the Republic's problems: its production needs, its political setup, how the Popular Front functions. That may not be spot news, but it was as important at the moment as news about the front. For nobody could understand the Front unless they understand what is happening in the rear. No, he for one would oppose my enlistment in the Internationals. I had come to *write* about the war, he said, and I must remain to write about it. If I did not get my cable rights within six weeks, he said, he might change his mind, and he persuaded me to try it for that length of time.

I soon came to know the trade unions, the schools, the factories of Sagunto where the Government manufactured the small arms it could for its armies. I learned the life of Valencia, the capital, became friends with Communists, Anarchists, Republicans, saw how they worked, how they lived, what they ate, how their families lived under the bombs.

The news from the North was bad. Mussolini's generals issued exultant communiques predicting the fall of the entire Biscay coast within ten days. Il Duce's armored divisions swept inexorably on, from two directions, east and west, forcing the Republicans into the last stronghold, the port of Gijon. They were in a hopeless sack, but they fought on, shotgun and grenade, against tank and Caproni.

The atmosphere in the Censura was tense: the censors, customarily cheerful, as a matter of policy, were now subdued. My nemesis Senor Rubio was transferred from the office and Constancia de la Mora was now in charge: a tall, handsome woman of the Madrid nobility who had broken with her father who was a Franco supporter. She was as gracious and spirited as Senor Rubio had been curt and melancholy. It made no difference to her whether my newspaper was Communist or not, she said, so long as it was a friend of the Republic. She had read it and she knew its worth. She would look into the matter of my cable allotment. "Five hundred words a week," she scoffed. "Ridiculous." I promptly fell in love with her.

The next day she came silently into the room, her dark eyes troubled, the brilliant smile gone and she took me aside to whisper: "The news is terrible. Thousands of our troops will be trapped in Gijon. There is no escape save by sea. And Franco's two big gunboats, the *Baleares* and *Canarias* are patrolling the coast." She asked me to hold the news to myself. "I have confidence in you," she said warmly. "I read your cables myself. The other newspapermen would make big headlines of it." Defeat was bad enough, but the danger here was massacre. If only, she mused, we could persuade a delegation of British members of Parliament, liberals, to be in Gijon when the fascists entered. Their presence might restrain the enemy. She suggested I indicate the need for such a group. The Government, of course, could not admit the certainty of disaster there. My cabled story, that day, sounded the alarm.

After I had dispatched my story, I sat thumbing through the files of foreign newspapers, brooding on the question of rousing America, France, Britain to the danger. This was sheerly a matter of humanity that transcended politics. The lives of a million Republicans, soldiers, their wives and children were trapped. The appeal to the world should be humanitarian, arousing solicitude for the civilians as well as the soldiers. And yes, perhaps the presence of notables could curb the fascists as their presence at the Leipzig trial of Dimitrov had curbed Goering.

As I read the papers, my eye caught an item in a French paper, the *Depeche de Toulouse,* a sad wisp of a report from Gijon. It was captioned, "By Cable." An open cable, an open cable, the thought tumbled about in my mind and an idea crystallized. If even one newspaperman on the side of the Loyalists could be at hand as the fascists approached the outskirts, he might get word out that could perhaps be that final additional push to generate an international protest and bring a delegation to hamper the enemy's bloodlust. I showed Constancia the item. "That cable was sent by a civilian," she said sadly. "All newspapermen have gone." "Could a newspaperman get through?" I asked. She shook her head wearily. No, the city was entirely cut off by land, and the *Baleares* and *Canarias* cut it off by sea.

I asked if contact could be made by plane. Her face brightened: her husband was General Hidalgo de Cisneros, head of the Republican air force and she knew something about planes. "Of course," she replied, grabbing my arm. "I would try it," I said, my heart pounding. "It might be of some help to get that delegation." She ran off to consult her superiors, and returned in several hours, asking how soon I could leave. "Now." The documents were ready in an hour. A plane would take me to Toulouse, from there I could go down to Biarritz, St. Jean de Luz, Bayonne, any of the French towns along the Bay of Biscay where I would find Republican consuls. They would try to slip me across the water, at night, into Gijon.

The plane flew over the icy Pyrenees, the pilot searching the horizons for enemy craft. It was an outside chance, I thought, surveying the grandeur of the peaks, glinting emerald, gold, green in a vista of fantastic beauty. An outside chance but nothing dare be ignored.

The Republican consul at Toulouse hastened me on to Biarritz: the consul there, a small squat man with shrewd black eyes spread his hands. "The last plane was shot down yesterday." No, no Republican craft dared try it by sea: it was suicide.

Accidentally, I learned from him that the American Ambassador, Claude Bowers, the historian, had left Spain and set up his embassy in a villa at St. Jean de Luz. I decided to appeal to the American ambassador himself. Bowers sat at his desk in a chateau perched high on a hilltop. An odd man, he sat wearing a black derby, smoking a cigar. I knew one of his books, on Jefferson and Hamilton, a good book, and I knew he had some sympathy for the Loyalist cause. I explained my purpose quickly as he puffed serenely away, contemplating the rings of smoke he blew. When I finished he said, "Yesterday I ordered two Americans, stranded in Gijon, to leave, took them off in one of our gunboats. I could not allow you in, sir, I cannot take that responsibility for your life." I replied that the lives of a million Spaniards were at stake. "You can't save them," he said curtly. If he let me in it might provoke some kind of incident. The Non-Intervention Committee. . . . He remained adamant. "We have done what we can," he said deliberately. "The President's 'Quarantine the Aggressor' speech in Chicago is as far as we can go now." I pleaded that my stories from Gijon might induce a delegation to be on hand when the fascists entered and avoid a certain massacre. He rose and turned his back on me, stared out of the window, the absurd derby on his head. "Son," he said in a suddenly kindly tone, turning toward me, "I can understand what you want, but believe me, it is hopeless. I cannot take the responsibility."

Defeated, I walked down the steep hill to St. Jean de Luz and entered a cafe where I downed a cognac or two and tried to figure this out. The Republican consuls said it was hopeless: the American ambassador washed his hands of it. What now? A newsboy passed hawking his wares and I noticed that one of his papers was *"Arriba Espana,"* a Franco organ. So they were selling his stuff openly, here across the border of democratic France, and there was no copy of the Republican papers so far as I could see. The Franco sheet said, in big headlines "GIJON WILL BE OURS SOON." A half-page photograph of the Generalissimo dominated the front page. I tossed the paper away, determined to try again.

Well, I would try Bayonne, some twenty miles to the north, see the last Republican consul on this coast. He was a tall, slim man, impeccably dressed, who stared sadly at me as I spoke. The French coast guard's vigilance added to Franco's gunboats, made my plan impossible, he replied. He said the Republicans had a vessel docked up the river that ran through Bayonne, but it was interned. It could, he mused, as though to himself, get me over to Gijon in no time, after dark, could slip past the *Baleares,* but the French had their eye on it. The French premier, Senor Blum, he said, "that great anti-fascist," was meticulously observing every syllable of every paragraph in the Non-Intervention Agreement precisely as Franco hoped he would. "It is strange behavior for a Socialist, no?" he concluded bitterly. He poured me a consoling draft of cognac and we parted. I went out into the Basque street. As I walked it struck me that the consul may have had another motive in telling me of the interned Republican cutter. Was he saying, go see the sailors, but don't involve me? I clutched at the straw.

I almost ran to the waterfront and stood on a little quay along the river that opens into the big bay, scanning the hundreds of little, bright-colored craft docked along the sides, hunting a ship with a Republican flag. After a few moments I heard someone say, with a laugh, nearby, *"Hombre, que tal?"* It was Spanish! I turned to see a lithe, dark young man in a beret and espadrilles who was thumping a friend on the back in the Spanish fashion. He spoke to a sailor in uniform whose little hat wore the name of a Spanish craft. Maybe he was from the interned cutter. His voluble Castilian rolled too fast for my ear and I wracked my brain. Suppose they were Franco Spaniards. Hell, so what, and impulsively I turned to them, introduced myself as an American correspondent who had just come from Spain and I watched their faces intently. "What part of Spain," the sailor asked cautiously. "Valencia." His face betrayed, almost imperceptibly, a smile. Good, I thought; so far so good. The other interrupted. "What kind of newspaper is yours?" The answer was safe now, I felt, for the other had revealed his loyalty and I replied, *"Periodico obrerista"*—a worker's paper. *"Quel partido?"* the sailor asked. What party? *"Comunista,"* I replied. They glanced at each other and I pulled my *hoja de ruta* from my pocket, my government credential, signed by Juan Negrin. They read it carefully, turned it over once or twice, and then the sailor turned to me, a grin on his face, extending his hand. Breathlessly, I explained my purpose.

The sailor took my arm and we went off, to his ship, a small low cutter that mounted a small-bore cannon on the foredeck. In the messroom, crowded with the full complement of the crew, a dozen men, they discussed me pro and con. Several shouted eagerly let's go, but one of the older men insisted on consulting the captain. They ran for him and returned with a solidly built man of fifty, who listened intently, and then, his face averted, shook his head: No, he had strict orders to avoid, at all costs, an international incident. And that was that.

The sailors grimly accompanied me down the gangplank. The one I had met first took me aside after the others waved a sorry goodbye. He whispered that I follow him and he led me through the maze of craft, across row-boats, piles of ropes, to the end of the quay where he stood scanning the harbor. He whistled, suddenly, to a man on a battered motorboat, a stocky red-faced fisherman of fifty. The man hove to, climbed up, and listened, his small, blue eyes darting quickly from the sailor's face to mine. "Tell him to be here at exactly seven this evening," he replied, giving me a long, slow stare from head to foot.

At precisely seven I stood on the quay. The fisherman helped me into his motorboat, puttered with the machine: it sputtered, caught on, and off we went. As we jockeyed into midstream he pointed at the horizon: a great, gray cloud lay thick on the waters, and he shrugged his shoulders. The gleaming city grew distant, the ragged peaks of the Pyrenees rose on the horizon.

"Comunista?" he asked, breaking the long silence. I nodded. He gestured toward the horizon, toward Gijon. *"Malo,"* he said. "Things are bad." The boat sped on, the water became choppier, the sky grew darker, and clouds were scudding low. The fisherman sat, hand on the tiller, his narrowed gaze scanning the horizon, and he glanced at the sky often. It was turning pitch black and I could scarcely make out the face of my companion. Suddenly a big wave smacked against the boat, the little craft tilted dangerously and I held tight to the side. Waves began to splash across the gunwales, into the boat. I heard a curse from the fore and I felt the boat turn slowly. We were heading back, I realized, my heart sinking. He maneuvered into the harbor, up the little river, carefully fastened the ship for the stormy night and extended his hand to help me up the ladder of the quay. He stood a moment under the dim arclight, staring hard at me. "We would have gone down," he said softly, then, abruptly he bade me leave the waterfront quick. "Be here tomorrow evening, at seven." He sauntered off without looking back.

I walked to the center of town, shivering, soaked to the skin, as disconsolate as I had ever been in my life. Near a movie house, under the bright lights, I bought a copy of the evening newspaper. I stared at the headline. "GIJON FALLS." I drew a deep breath, looked around at the people passing on the street, a young man strolled by with a girl at his side, a woman hurried on carrying a long loaf of bread, a gendarme in a blue cape directed traffic. I stood and looked out across the Bay of Biscay, toward the west, toward Gijon, and I wept.

Back in Valencia, Constancia greeted me and I saw by her face that she knew my story. Yes, Biscay had fallen but the bitter cup of Spain was not yet full. While I was away, she said, word came from Washington that Roosevelt had lifted the embargo. She had almost collapsed with joy. The censors were dancing on the tables, she said, and she telephoned Negrin. "Wrong," Negrin replied. "Roosevelt had almost come to the point but the archbishops walked in." That was as near to success as the Republic came: the embargo was never lifted, and history has written the result.

12

Gathering of Heroes

I DESCRIBE my mission to Gijon in some detail, as you see, and you must forgive me. My need to tell it is related to my desire to be *of* these volunteers, not merely *for* them. I had seen many an American go to his death and I knew, as correspondent, that I would probably survive, and a sense of guilt welled up in me whenever I spoke with them before they went into battle. Though I had no reservations concerning the importance of my work here, I recoiled from the fact that I had a relatively safe post, when other men went voluntarily into the no-man's land where death walked. So, beyond the over-riding fact that I believed in the need for the mission to Gijon, I felt equally that *I* must be the one to undertake it. I well realized that the chances for survival, once I got into the besieged city, were not good, not even-steven. But I felt compelled to face that gamble so that if I came back alive, I could meet the Volunteers as a peer. *I* had volunteered too, as they had. If my mission failed, it was due to no fault of mine. But I needed that assignment to salve my dignity—for myself: to be at one with them.

Theirs was a holy confraternity: I had sensed that in their attitudes toward all other men. Though they did not comport themselves as martyrs—far from it—they had no arrogance of righteousness, either covert or open: I knew that, overwhelmingly, they sensed their affiliation to the future, knew that the currents of a bright tomorrow ran in their lives. They were building it, not slowly, not piecemeal, as most others dedicated to a cause build, by the slow and steady application of their powers and talents. These had a *total* dedication, offering, in their outstretched hands all that they owned and that could be taken by a single clutch of Fate's hand, their youth, their body, mind, soul—their life. Mankind senses this and has always revered, as its favorite sons and daughters, the volunteers prepared to sacrifice themselves for other men's liberty. So we worship the memory of Marquis de Lafayette, of John Brown, of Sojourner Truth.

After my mission to Gijon, about which I told no one, I felt, in my own heart, that I belonged to the Volunteers, the International Brigades, truly.

My cable problem solved, I was now able to roam the fronts; I stood in the ancient Moorish arches of Teruel when the Republicans recaptured that mountain city; mounted the parapets in the trenches about University City, visited the battlelines around Alicante where the soil turns red and the surrounding hills, bare and orange-colored, seemed like man's earth before man came; I interviewed the Republican generals, Modesto, Lister, the many others, but most of all I sought out the Americans. I made my way through Catalonia to the Ebro when Franco mounted his offensive against Valencia with the objective of cutting the Republic in two. Virtually every correspondent sped to the Valencia lines, but I had noticed that the long caravans of trucks carried rowboats—under tarpaulin—to the Ebro river, and I suspected that the Republic was preparing a counter-thrust to relieve the southern pressure.

My hunch was right and I was on the Ebro banks when the loyalist armies astonished the world by their daring tactic: successfully, under the cover of dark, they crossed the wide river, virtually under the armed cliffs of the enemy. Peter Kerrigan, correspondent for the London *Daily Worker* and I crossed with the troops that scampered up the heights held by the powerfully armed, but bewildered enemy, and pushed on seventeen kilometers to Gandesa. I wrote my dispatch on a stone wall held only an hour before by the enemy and a runner sped it to Barcelona where the Censura cabled it to my paper for that evening's edition—the first to arrive in America. I lay in the slit trenches along the Ebro banks when the furious Capronis, Junkers, Messerschmitts roared through the skies, bombing and machine-gunning the pontoon bridges thrown across the river during the night.

Somehow, though several times bombs landed so near us that we were deluged with showers of sand, I was certain no bomb had my number; the exhilaration of the crossing, the consequent delight of loyalist partisans everywhere throughout the world—plus my grant from the Republic to be able to cable what I wanted to cable—all these happy circumstances gave me the certainty of survival. This was simply no time to die.

But wherever I traveled in Spain I saw valor and death walk arm in arm. Men you knew, talked to you and joked with you one day, of everything under the sun, speaking dreamily of their sweethearts and the families they would raise, the work they would undertake, and the next time you heard of them they were dead. Dave Doran, Bob Merriman, Jim Lardner, Aaron Lopow, Arnold Reed, a former editor of the *New Masses,* a brilliant young man whose sense of dedication surpassed that of almost anyone I had ever known: all dead. There were the Britishers, too, like young, zestful David Guest, whose book on dialectical materialism which he wrote at twenty-four revealed a mind that could be described as that of genius. Dr. J. B. S. Haldane, the scientist, came often to the front, a tall, broad-shouldered figure in khaki cap and heavy overcoat, a friend of Dr. Negrin. When he heard of Guest's death, his British reserve broke, and he wept. The British sacrificed some of the most sterling of their youth: Fox, the novelist and critic, Cauldwell, the poet, Guest and a number of others who would, had they lived, have become foremost figures in the intellectual life of their time.

I spent many days with William Rust, the young British Communist leader, who returned to become the editor of the London *Daily Worker*—a lusty, laughing, keen-minded, fearless man—the epitome of the Communist close to the ordinary man from whom he came and whose aspirations he understood, perhaps better than any I had ever met, who died at the age of 45, the victim of his boundless energies. Harry Pollitt came often to the fronts (I met Clement Attlee when he turned up to give his benediction to a company of Britons that took his name), encountered Britons, Frenchmen, Germans, Latin-Americans, North Americans, the bravest spirits of all lands, who came to Spain like pilgrims to the Holy Land, compelled, in this instance, by the tug of reason, not of mysticism.

For Republican Spain, as I saw it, was in its day the quintessence of Humanity's cause. It embodied the Enlightenment, the Renaissance, the aspirations of France's 1789 and America's 1776. Uniquely, it illustrated, within its narrow compass of geography—a land area not much more than New York state—the distilled history of the Western World since Torquemada.

You could recognize the terror of the Inquisition when you spoke with the captured Navarrese prisoners, the fanatical Requetes, who crossed themselves when they spoke to you, considering you as the Anti-Christ, as one of them said to me, staring coldly and defiantly into the eyes of his captors, as though he were in the clutches of Satan and he would not be swerved from his allegiance to the Father, Son and Holy Ghost. Yet on the other side, science, learning, flourished. The Republicans, overnight, transformed the bookstores into temples, and I saw the weary *miliciano,* home for a brief leave from the fronts, thumb reverently through the bright, inexpensive editions of Cervantes, Tolstoy, Dreiser, Balzac, Shakespeare. The bookstores were forever crowded, like the churches had been at mass. I was impressed by the fact that the bullfight, about which an entire mystical literature has been written to illustrate the primitive atavism that lurked in the "dark soul" of Spain, was outlawed by the Republic as a barbaric sport, and nobody turned a hair.

Here, in Loyalist Spain, one could virtually see the awesome workings of the delayed Enlightenment. Its image to me lay in the delight I saw in a peasant's face when he turned to me, in the mud of the trenches where the Government had conducted classes against illiteracy, and handing me a postcard on which he had just scrawled a few sentences, said: "Now I am a man. I can write." Caliban had turned Ariel, here in Republican Spain.

Had I not been a Marxist before, Spain would have made me one. For even in the time I was there, I saw the Communist Party grow tenfold from some 30,000 members to 300,000. And—despite all propaganda to the contrary—I saw they asked no preferment, save the right to fight and die for the Popular Front, for a Spain, free, independent, governed by the will of its majority. And that will, at that moment, was not for a socialist government, but for a way of life that corresponded, by and large, to the New Deal of our land. The Communists abided by that will. Indefatigably they opposed the traitorous intrigues and subversive preachments of the POUM, the Trotskyist formation which assailed the goals of the Popular Front by their vociferous insistence upon an immediate socialism. When the anarchists vented their classic hatred of the Church by closing its doors and, in no few cases, burning the temples of Christianity, the

Communists sought to curb them, and sent delegations to the Minister of the Interior proposing that the churches be opened.

The image of the Communist here? I could never forget Dolores Ibarruri, whom I came to see when I was in Madrid. She rose from her desk when I entered her office, a small bare white room with a single desk above which hung the red, gold and purple of the Republic. Tall, erect, with the olive face of Spain, she was an Iberian Juno, her shining black hair swept back from her serene forehead. *Mucho mujer,* she was, much woman, as the Spaniards say, a woman of captivating femininity. A moment after I had introduced myself, she apologized and asked if I would allow her a moment of indulgence. "Come," she smiled and I followed her into an adjoining room. She held a postcard written by her daughter of ten, she said, who had, with thousands of other Republican children been evacuated to the Soviet Union. "It is remarkable," she cried happily, "it is a postcard and a victrola record at the same time." She showed me the card: a scene of children in a summer camp in the Crimea where the hills sloped to the sea. In the center was a hole like that of a phonograph record. She put it on a victrola and after a few scratching noises we heard a small piping voice say, in Spanish: *"Querida mama"*—dear mama—"I am here in the Pioneer camp and I long for you. All the Russian children love us and they send you their love. Mama, they call you 'the great Pasionaria.' They hold meetings for Spain and yesterday I made a speech." Pasionaria, her eyes brilliant, said softly, "Yesterday my baby made a speech." Outside, in University City, the stutter of machine-guns sounded.

We returned to her desk and she turned thoughtfully to the business at hand: to answer the questions of an American correspondent. The fond mother spoke now as the leader of a Party, without transition of manner, of mood. Cogently, simply, she talked of the imperatives for victory: the coalescence of Communists and Socialists into one united party of the proletariat which could be the core of the war effort, the reorganization of the national economy to achieve a higher productivity, the construction of a solid network of fortifications on all the battlelines along the coast, outside the cities. "Spain," she said, standing by the photograph of her two children, "must rely fundamentally on her own strength. That strength she has. The war will not be won by one man, or one party, but by the entire people."

Later that evening I ran into Ernest Hemingway at the Censura. He thumped my back, a grizzly bear of a man with a week's growth on his face, and invited me to drop by his hotel room at the Florida. We had covered the fronts together often, and once, returning from the Ebro battleline, May Day of 1938, we slowed down on the winding mountain road behind a truckload of singing youngsters, who raised their right fists in the Republican greeting. Lovely they were, their olive faces glinting in the bright sun, singing the songs of the Republic, of the working class, and Hemingway commented on their beauty. Herbert Matthews, of the *New York Times* was at the wheel, and even he, somber and taciturn, seemed moved. Suddenly, as the truck rounded a sharp bend, the driver lost control and it somersaulted before our eyes, the scene of gaiety changed to horror as bodies lay bleeding on the ground. Matthews jammed the brakes on, we leaped out; I can never recall where Hemingway found a medicine kit, but he was on his knees bandaging the injured and solacing them. We worked away together, the blood of the dying on our hands.

I noticed that Matthews strode among the bodies, bending down, not to help, but to interview the dying, jotting notes in a little notebook. After all, he was first and foremost, "a *Times* man," and deadlines to even the most humane of *Times* men, were more urgent than death or life. To every man his loyalties. Hemingway started at the sight: "You sonofabitch," he roared, "get out or I'll kill you." After this I felt a regard for him, a warmth, which has lasted to this day, for, I felt, thinking about it afterward, I had seen the real man; despite his tough-guy pose, here was a humanist, a partisan of humanity.

Shortly after dusk, the Nazi battery on Mt. Garabitas banging away in its mechanical rhythm like riveting guns, I came to his room on the fifth floor, at an angle to the street. "The shells come from there," he said, gesturing to the north. "I'm in the northeast, in a corner. It's like this," he said, and he dropped his chin beneath his shoulder, striking a boxing pose. "They can't get me, see? Try it." He thrust his chin out, then ducked safely as I made a pass at him. "See?" he said, delighted. So much about him was exuberantly adolescent and you felt, somehow, like an elder uncle. Ordinarily I shy from the expression of wilful boyishness in a grown man, but I could not with him. It *became* him.

After the third drink, he began to laud the Lincoln Brigade, their courage about which he had frequently written. And then, eyeing me, he said, suddenly, "I like Communists when they're soldiers: when they're priests, I hate them." "Priests?" I repeated, startled. "Yes, priests, the commissars who hand down the papal bulls," he glared. I reminded him that he once confessed he had never read a word of Marx, or ever truly knew a Communist. "That air of authority your leaders wear, like cassocks," he insisted. Evidently one drink too many roused his belligerency, and he muttered words like dialectical materialism, surplus value, rate of profit, dictatorship of the proletariat, as though he were trying to provoke me by reciting a litany; a comical yet sorry performance.

It struck me suddenly that he belonged to the anarchists whose loyalty to the murky ideas of Bakunin clouded their world outlook, their judgment of history. "Anarchy is the highest form of order," their posters said, and Hemingway would agree with that. We wrangled, and he repeated his declaration—that Communists are good soldiers, but dangerous when they are priests, snatching for authority. I replied coldly that the authority, the leadership of Communists was a matter of choice, of election, that they had grown to their status of political affluence here, as elsewhere, for the very reasons that he assessed wrongly. His categories "soldiers," "priests" made no sense, for the Communist was good as a soldier precisely because he had the qualities he attributed to him as priest; a good fighting man because he had conviction, purpose.

Hemingway paced the room. "Conviction," he shouted suddenly, "conviction with a capital C. Fatherland with a capital F. Goddamn the capital letters." The big shots since Pharaoh had used capital letters to bamboozle jerks like me. No, I shouted, the question boils down to who uses those words, for what, for whom. When Franco cries *Arriba Espana* at the end of his harangues, what does he mean? Juan March, the millionaire smuggler, the Duke of Alba, their wealth, Catalan textile, Asturian coal. To the Republicans, *Espana* means the farmer, the miner, the people, the Spanish tradition, Goya, Cervantes, Lorca. He stood eyeing me, for all the world like a grizzly bear, his long arms at his side, his unshaven chin thrust forward.

Then, characteristically, he laughed suddenly, reached for the decanter of whiskey. "Hell," he said, "I believe you're one of them, the god-damn bishops. Here, *mi padre,* a libation."

Then, he struck the pose of a pug, hunched his shoulders, flicked at his nose with his thumb, and pranced lightly around the room, jabbing and thrusting, ducking the blows of an imaginary opponent, dancing, it seemed, into the one philosophy he trusted, the argument of the fist: sock, sock, take it Man, take it. I watched him, fascinated: how this man of heart and talent had remained primordially ignorant of the cardinal facts of man's history, the struggle of classes and the shaping of people in that struggle. For him, a man had it or he hadn't; character was built-in from birth, a matter of genes, hormones, *cojones.* And alone, a man carried his destiny to his death. In the early Thirties when the United States hungered he had groped for a philosophy in his novel *To Have and Have Not.* It had concluded with the hero's dying gasp, "One man alone . . . cannot. . . ." But the gold flowed back into the tills, the wheels began to turn again and his search petered out. He danced about until sweat covered his bearded face. Then glacing in a mirror, he disrobed, rubbed himself furiously with a towel. "I keep trim that way," he laughed, "to fight the commissars. I suppose you stay fit memorizing a chapter of *Das Kapital.*" Mockingly, he made the sign of the cross.

I have often brooded over this memory: why could he not see in Communists what I saw as clear as a peak in the Pyrenees? Doubtless he had encountered the bureaucrat among Communists, the air of smug rectitude, or arrogance or impatience with those whose viewpoints differed. I had met these too, God knows, and had perhaps too readily sloughed off their irksome reality, the injury that they did. I had shrugged them off, abiding by the partisan axiom that they may be sonsofbitches, but they're our sonsofbitches. Men like Hemingway had no inclination to be charitable.

Zola once said, "Truth is not a simple, easily handled object that can be shown in the hollow of a hand and can at will be put into the hands of others like a pebble or an apple." Hemingway's quest for truth often led him astray, especially when he equated a movement of men, a crusade for humanity, with unsatisfying individuals he had met. In *The Bell,* Hemingway defames various Communists, including the heroic La Pasionaria because she sent her two endangered and ill-nourished children to sanctuary in the Soviet Union. (The son was later to die in battle against the Nazis during World War II.) But the lives of many thousands of children, of all political parties of the Popular Front, were treasured in the Soviet Union, which invited them gladly. No, Hemingway, the perceptive artist, did not see the truth wholly, for reasons which include those I mention here, as well as others which the space of this book does not allow me to detail. After all, an exponent (artist or not) of the capitalist idea cannot leap out of his skin, transcend his prejudices against those who envisage an opposite social order. Every man is captive of his own past, and Hemingway, wilfully ignorant of the Marxist philosophy, could not judge its qualities, or the ways and souls of its adherents. He loved the Volunteers because courage on a battlefield is as visible to the eyes as a Mauser: you clamber over the top and advance into the criss-cross of bullets—if you break and run, panic-stricken, you are a bad soldier. The moralities of the political battle are not always readily understood: its goals are often obscured by a thousand considerations, especially if they exist in the mind of a man opposed to your politics.

Yet, saying this, I think of that Hemingway, essentially, whom I saw succor the dying that May Day of 1938. I have read his writings, before Spain, and afterward, and I hold that his motivation is a love for humanity even though he errs, I believe, in his judgment of that growing portion of humanity that is transforming the world according to a credo Hemingway himself would accept: do unto others as ye would have them do unto you. He may never come to hold with socialism but I believe that he will some day understand its intention and its validity. He may not be able to read the sketchy blueprints, but when he will see the gleaming palaces, he will describe them with the magic that is his.

After sixteen months I came home, in October of 1938. I returned with my brave wife, who had come four months earlier, and worked to help the orphaned children of Spain. It had been a dreadful wrench for her to leave our own two children even though Clarina Michelson was caring for them at her home in Connecticut. Clarina, a valiant crusader herself, kin of Nancy Hanks, Abe Lincoln's mother, had encouraged my wife to go, assuring her that the children would want for no care during her absence. Only the sacred cause of Spain could persuade her, for she believed that men and women across the Pyrenees were dying for the future of our own children, as well as theirs. And so a generation of Americans believed who came of age, politically, inspired by Republican Spain.

Upon my arrival home, the Veterans of the Lincoln Brigade proposed that I tour the country, with one of their most valiant members, Fred Keller, a raw-boned American whose exploits during the Ebro battles were the subject of memorable cables to the *New York Times* by Matthews as well as Hemingway. We spoke in a score of cities, before university students and faculties. To have been in Spain was a passport to the respectful attention of most Americans. I saw the tell-tale gleam in their eyes as I spoke of the Internationals.

In many cities I spoke to fathers and mothers of volunteers. Twelve hundred of the 3,000 who crossed the Pyrenees would never make the journey home. Often I heard the grief-stricken question, "Did you see my son?" I recalled those that I could and every word was a boon beyond price to their parents. I felt an awful responsibility as I spoke with these plain folk. What could I say? Death is an axiom every man learns and sometimes the axioms can suffice the survivors. I reiterated that a just war is never lost and no life given in it is ever lost: those who died offered tomorrows up in their image. If Republican Spain would go down, the precepts of the dead would inspire multitudes to enlist in a just and timeless cause. We knew who had betrayed the Volunteers and we knew, too, that the time of the betrayers was running out. Not tomorrow, perhaps, but as sure as these mothers, these fathers, had memories of their sons, so sure would we be that the world will be in the image of their sons.

I returned home from my journey across the country to work again at the *New Masses*. In February of 1939 I edited a special edition on the anniversary of the Popular Front victory of three years before (three years that had the weight of three centuries!) I cabled Hemingway for a piece, and he wrote, from Cuba, where he now lived:

"The dead sleep cold in Spain tonight and they will sleep cold all this winter as the earth sleeps with them. But in the spring the rain will come to make the earth kind again. The wind will blow soft over the hills from the south. The black trees will come to life with small green leaves and there will be blossoms on the apple trees along the Jarama River. This spring the dead will feel the earth beginning to live again. For our dead are a part of the earth of Spain now and the earth of Spain can never die. Each winter it will seem to die and each spring it will come alive again. Our dead will live with it forever.

Just as the earth can never die, neither will those who have ever been free return to slavery. The peasants who work the earth where our dead lie know what these dead died for. There was time during the war for men to learn these things, and there is forever for them to remember them in.

Our dead live in the hearts and the minds of the Spanish peasants, of the Spanish workers, of all the good simple honest people who believed in and fought for the Spanish Republic. And as long as all our dead live in the Spanish earth, and they will live as long as the earth lives, no system of tyranny ever will prevail in Spain.

The fascists may spread over the land, blasting their way with weight of metal brought them from other countries. They may advance aided by traitors and by cowards. They may destroy cities and villages and try to hold the people in slavery. But you cannot hold any people in slavery.

The Spanish people will rise again as they have always risen before tyranny.

The dead do not need to rise. They are a part of the earth now and the earth can never be conquered. For the earth endureth forever. It will outlive all systems of tyranny.

Those who have entered it honorably, and no men ever entered earth more honorably than those who died in Spain, already have achieved immortality."

13

To the Brink and Over

A GENERATION OF Americans came of age in the time of Promethean Spain which, like the legendary titan, gave fire to mankind. For them the closing days of 1938 were bloodied by the fatal wounds of the Republic. Most of us hoped against hope, yet I knew that titanic morale that is empty-handed, deprived of modern arms, would not prevail against endless armadas of Messerschmitts, Capronis, Junkers, tanks, cannon—and, not the least of the enemy's weapons—international betrayal. No, political morality in today's world is not enough.

But so long as a single spark glowed in the republican campfires below the Pyrenees you carried on to rouse a national outcry, summoning all friends of Spain to wake the lethargic from slumber. After Catalonia fell I wrote a pamphlet *Why Spain Can Still Win.* My desperate voice pleaded with every reader to exhort our Government to abandon the suicidal embargo. For defeat, even at this eleventh hour, was not written in the stars: the heartland of the Republic still beat. Madrid, Valencia, Alicante, Cartagena, the capital of 8,000,000 undefeated Spaniards, still stood. An army of 700,000 tested soldiers remained in the field praying for arms to come. Catalonia fell only because a deluge of steel pushed the Loyalists, foot by foot, back to Le Perthus and Port Bou on the French frontier: the proportion of material, Negrin told the world, was ten to one. The armies of the Popular Front waged a superhuman rearguard war in Catalonia, protecting the refugees in exodus until they reached the French frontier, thousands of them bearing their children in their arms. I reminded our readers that Napoleon invaded Spain in 1808 and drove the Spanish government into a patch of Andalusia far smaller that the land the present government held. Relations among the nations shifted during the time of the Spanish resistance and Napoleon's mighty grenadiers retreated ignobly in 1813.

To help Republican Spain, even at this late hour, I pleaded, advanced our national interest as well as that of all democratic nations: the sovereignty of France was undoubtedly in peril, I wrote; Czechoslovakia already lay dismembered.

I followed that pamphlet with another, *Men in the Ranks —the Story of Twelve Americans in Spain,* to which Ernest Hemingway wrote a foreword. In it I quoted the loyalist newspaper *Dia Grafica* of Barcelona, which cried on the very eve of disaster: "To save the dignity of the human species, men raised themselves to the rank of gods." Yes, some spark of the superhuman glowed in every anti-fascist's heart.

I recognized its glow in the answers to an editorial question the magazine asked: "What," we wrote to scores of the world's foremost writers, "are you doing to fight fascism?" To one degree or another the replies resembled that of the eminent British scientist, J. B. S. Haldane whom I had met half a dozen times in Spain, that ponderous, mustachioed figure well over six foot three in height, broad-framed and deep-chested, who trudged the fronts in his hob-nail boots and tall, wool cap, grumbling, in his ironic English understatement, to conceal his grief. His reply to our question was blunt, direct and astounding. He had delivered 102 speeches against Franco and fascism that year, published three books, a 20,000-word pamphlet, taught biology to workers at the Marx House every Thursday night, wrote a weekly column on science in the London *Daily Worker,* and completed more scientific papers during the twelve-month than any previous year of his career. But he admitted, dryly, that he did lack the time to putter in his garden. Haldane attributed these phenomenal labors to his discovery and his acceptance of Marxism. "To sum up," he concluded, "I am trying to convince my countrymen that every patriot must be anti-fascist, and that every efficient anti-fascist must be a Marxist."

Many who were not of the Marxist persuasion answered similarly, regretting simultaneously that they were not "doing enough." So Dorothy Parker replied, that lovely and witty lady whom I first met during an air-raid in Spain, weeping on the sidewalk outside her hotel as she watched children scurrying like pigeons under the bombs. She could not, her reply said, brook those writers she met upon her return from Madrid who sat in smug and fatal isolation in their studies puffing their pipes of indifference. "Oh, well," one fatuously told her, she reported,

"I'm content to stay in my ivory tower," to which she commented that "its only window looks out on the fascist side."

The image of the resistance, and of the Marxist's part in it, stirred the admiration of many creative men regardless of their philosophies. Vincent Sheean, for example, the gifted author of *Personal History* whom I met frequently at the fronts, wrote about "the immortal blazing glory of Madrid" when, "two and a half years ago the workers took arms and defended themselves against the combined forces of the fascist alliance. . . . For this the Communists must be thanked." Others who replied to our question included Sir Stafford Cripps, Erskine Caldwell, Paul de Kruif, Martin Anderson-Nexo, C. Day Lewis, Elliott Paul, Irwin Shaw. Clearly, I felt, they considered the magazine a tribune of their conscience when the world saw the skull of fascism grinning over Berlin.

I believe Thomas Wolfe, the American novelist, defined the prevailing spirit in his letters of the time. He wrote a friend, then, "I also had a piece in the *New Masses*—my initiation." This was all the more significant, for at the outset of his meteoric career he had written scornfully of us, but the year before he died, so tragically young, he came in his shambling six-foot four hulk to our office to deliver a chapter of his forthcoming novel *You Can't Go Home Again.*

The advent of fascism had given the college instructor turned novelist a post-graduate course for which he never enrolled. He visited Hitler Germany on the invitation of his German publisher after his novel *Look Homeward Angel* enjoyed a remarkable triumph there. He was wined and dined and lionized in the Third Reich whose significance he had not originally understood. But his perceptive and honest eye finally saw past the flattering receptions of the herrs and the fraus when, one day, a small, shabby man furtively plucked his sleeve and begged help to escape the country. Then Wolfe began to look beyond the proud but past tradition of Goethe and Beethoven, past the gleaming streets and neat gabled towns, and he spied the present political horror beneath. How eloquently he asserted his philosophy in his agonized letters to Maxwell Perkins, his friend and editor at Harpers! Breaking with Perkins, he voiced what many believed in that time. "Your own ideas," he told his editor, "is that life is unchangeable, that the abuses I protest against—the greed, the waste, the poverty, the filth, the suffering—are inherent in humanity and that any other system than the one we have would be just as bad as this one." No, Wolfe cried, he would not accept that. "I think that almost every great poet and every great writer who ever wrote and whose works we all love has been on the side of the oppressed, the suffering, the confused and stricken of the earth. Do you know of a single exception to this?"

So, issue after issue of the *New Masses* carried the writings of men and women, Marxist and non-Marxist, who held with these ideas Wolfe expressed.

But saying this, I have not told the whole story: there is a sequel that requires consideration. The fateful months sped by, decades of history packed into weeks brought profound changes, sometimes overnight, like the signing of the Soviet-German non-aggression past.

I believed that the transcendent influence shaping that decade was the Soviet Union's persistent quest for a universal system of collective security against aggression: that, and the agreement of Marxists in all lands after the Seventh World Congress of the Communist International in 1935 to strive everywhere for an all-embracing coalition against fascism. *Le Front Populaire* in France preceded by months *El Frente Popular* of Spain. Everywhere, to one degree or another, Communists and non-Communists broke the ice of differences to reach working agreements against the marauding barbarians of the Wilhelmstrasse. The surge toward unity fired all thinking men with hope, for, as Tolstoy said, "The aim of life is the union of mankind."

But the enemies of mankind, the international appeasers of Hitler, blighted the time's green promise. A brief, but fateful, space of weeks separated the fall of Barcelona from the fall of Prague. Maxim Litvinov's pleas for a pact to halt aggressors failed to penetrate the glacial mentality of Chamberlain: the world faltered to the brink at Munich when Hitler, Mussolini, Daladier and the British prime minister signed the deadly pact designed to encourage the Nazis to turn their guns eastward, against the USSR.

And Moscow signed the non-aggression pact with the Third Reich.

The transatlantic cables hummed with the astonishing news, bringing consternation to many in our land. Our literary editor,

Granville Hicks, a university professor and author of a book on John Reed, resigned from the board, an unexpected blow indeed. He had seemed to me so solid, so certain of his Marxist convictions, this laconic professor who seemed to be the prototype of Emersonian New England, parsimonious in speech, firm in principle. And Sheean, among our occasional contributors, departed spectacularly. He wired me from Mexico City, hours after the news of the pact, to airmail him, if it was available, the text of Molotov's declaration. The next evening he spoke over a nationwide CBS hookup hailing the pact, but a few weeks later, in the *New Republic,* he reversed himself completely, comparing the Soviet action to Thermidor, Napoleon's betrayal of the French Revolution. Sheean wrote me a brief note, that I would probably be "irritated" by his articles, but he was certain that time would justify him.

True, the news of the pact surprised me as well as so many others: but after reflection and consideration of it with other Marxists, I concluded that this strategy differed little from that of Brest-Litovsk when Lenin desperately sought to buy time from the German invaders by ceding them a vast area; the greater stake, the primal imperative, was the life of the new-born republic. I had many turbulent controversies with disillusioned readers who contended that the Soviet Union betrayed international morality. One night I visited an old friend, that venerable Jewish scholar, Chaim Zhitlovsky, who lived near my home. He had devoted his lifetime to achieve the universal recognition of his mother tongue as an honorable language on a par with all others. He had braved the Czar's Okhrana as a Socialist-Revolutionary in his youth, and, he told me, had once debated Lenin. As a Jew and an advocate of social change, a passionate champion of the best of man's culture, he had seen the necessity of anti-fascist unity and welcomed the initiative of the Communists and of the USSR's foreign policy. I had a reverence for this aged warrior of the luminous eyes and saintly white beard.

"It is an astounding betrayal!" he greeted me as I came to visit him at his home, departing, the only time I ever knew, from his philosopher's calm.

I expressed my disagreement as gently as I could. Was it not obvious, I asked, that the Western capitalist democracies had finally decided against forming a grand anti-Axis coalition?

Didn't Munich foreshadow a new intervention against the first socialist state? And to survive, had that state any alternative, now, but to deflect, or to delay, the calculated blow?

"But how could Molotov take Ribbentrop's bloody hand? How can a socialist state ally itself with its precise opposite—the beast of Berlin! No, I cannot accept it; I will not accept it. It is the blackest betrayal in history! It equates fascism with Communism!"

"But Chaim, it is not an alliance, it is a non-aggression agreement. Haven't such pacts ample precedence in history?"

"How? Who? When?" he asked, shaking his magnificent head, bowed, the image of bewildered disillusion. "And you, Joe, who were in Spain, who saw the Junkers, you argue for it?"

I replied that our own country had acted similarly when old Franklin persuaded the French court to side with young America against King George. "Did that equate revolutionary America with one of the most tyrannical governments of its time?" The old man sat adamantly silent, resting both hands on his cane.

"Or consider an example in our own life, that is not *hoch-politik.*" Zhitlovsky then wrote a daily column for the New York *Jewish Day,* and I knew his pride of membership in the American Newspaper Guild, his respect for organized labor and his eager allegiance to it. "Suppose," I said, "the publishers contemplated breaking the Guild, the union against them, and considered a common front of publishers to do that. If the Guild were able to divide the publishers, to break their front, by signing good pacts with individual publishers, like say Hearst, would that equate the morality of the newspapermen with William Randolph's? Isn't that good tactics?"

"Morality," he said slowly, "is too sacred for tactics. That is Machiavelli, not Marx."

No, the grand old man would not give an iota, and though we remained friends his fine, wise eyes clouded when we greeted each other thereafter, until June 22, 1941, when he came to see me, coming up the path leaning on his sturdy cane, his noble face impassive in contemplation. "I came to say that I have changed my view. They were right and I was wrong. The pact was as necessary as it was horrifying." (Later even Winston Churchill said the pact was imperative for the Soviets to gain time to prepare their army and the people.)

Others, like Zhitlovsky originally, regarded any effort to vindicate the pact as the stone-blind rationalization of fanatical partisans. But there may well have been other considerations. "It was easy," a mutual friend of Sheean's and mine told me one day soon after the pact, "for Sheean to espouse Spain, and the Popular Front, when it was truly popular." Once that position became unfashionable, she said, and went counter to the views of Sheean's friends, Winston Churchill, and the State Department, he had to change. After all, the woman laughed, did I expect Sheean to end his career writing for the *New Masses* at a penny a word "if you can pay even that," when he is accustomed to twenty cents a word from the *Saturday Evening Post.* Had I illusions that he was made of martyr stuff?

I replied dolefully that her analysis of Sheean's motivations may well be oversimplified: that while his change of mind may work out the way she described, there was no proof that he changed solely to salvage his material interest. Fond of the man, I was loath to degrade him. She reminded me that Sheean had precedence for Sheean: in his *Personal History* he had deliberately turned from the Russian Revolution after a visit to the placid lovely campus of Cambridge where he asked himself by a silent pool why he should eschew an easy life, "sex and Stravinsky" and die for coal-miners in Pennsylvania or textile weavers in Gastonia whom he might never see. Yes, I reflected afterward, I remembered that he had written that.

I thought afterward of Wordsworth, a bright star of British liberalism, a flaming partisan in defense of the French Revolution: he too became disillusioned and was awarded a sinecure as poet laureate to the British Crown; of him Browning had written:

Just for a handful of silver he left us,
Just for a riband to stick in his coat.

But Browning later regretted his scathing poem as unduly severe, unjust, over-simple. Coleridge, too, repudiated his youthful loyalty to 1789, and thereafter lost that immortal fire which burned bright in the Rime of the Ancient Mariner and Kubla Khan. Like Wordsworth, he became an adherent of royalty and reaction, describing his earlier politics as

A wild and dream-like trade of bloody guile
Too foolish for a tear, too wicked for a smile.

And he resorted to opium and wandered in the mists of metaphysics for consolation, never again to write a line that faintly rivalled his early works. Would this, I reflected, be the fate of those like Sheean?

I have often brooded over this phenomenon which repeats itself dismally whenever history turns suddenly and unexpectedly. The image of the Revolution is lost to many in the blinding glare of the unforeseen new. But history moves deviously, it does not always travel the highroad in the noonday sun. Often it descends to the bleak lowlands, moving across fen and bog, obscured by mist and fog before it ascends once again into full view. It seemed to me that men like Hicks and Sheean understood the revolutionary ideas of socialism all too abstractly, more as spectators than as dedicated participants. Its ethical superiority drew them near, but they fell back, bruised, when the practical and imperative need arose to defend it. Hicks may have memorized chapter and verse of Marxist philosophy, accepted it cerebrally, but acquired no mastery of it in reality, perhaps like a medical student who absorbs his *materia medica* but is bewildered when a patient's symptoms are not as evident to the eye as ink on a white page. And finally, I thought, so many writers are the imprisoned captives of their past, their middle-class attitudes and modes of thought, and fail to comprehend realities that to workingmen schooled in a harsher classroom, are as plain as the blade of a shovel—or the muzzle of a Mauser. So much of the middle-class code derives from the upper class, to which they are reared to aspire. "Better *thyself,*" their elders exhort them, whereas the workingman has learned, or is learning, that he cannot better himself unless his fellows of the forge or on the belt go forward simultaneously. The stern circumstances of his life enables the workingman to understand and abide by the word "Solidarity," the most sacred of all words. The first person singular too often dominates the middle-class mind.

Needless to say, the magazine suffered, but it survived. Enough readers accepted our viewpoint to keep the *New Masses* afloat on the stormy sea. Well, I shrugged and swallowed my regrets: if politics makes strange bedfellows, it also makes unexpected estrangements. I respected the qualities I observed in Hicks, in Sheean, able men of good intention, but an old maxim describes the material Hell is paved with.

And yet, I believe that, I, we of *New Masses,* as well as they, committed error. Why, I have asked myself, could we not strive to maintain our personal friendships and find mutuality upon matters about which we still agreed. Sheean, for example, remained a partisan of the Abraham Lincoln Brigade, and of the Republic of Spain. He came to speak at gatherings of the Spanish veterans when they invited him. Yet when he stopped writing for us we made no overtures to him. Perhaps he would have rejected them, under the altered circumstances of the time, but we gave him no opportunity to say No. At least he would have understood that we did not consider him as an arch-enemy of humanity's progress which he decidedly is not.

A time will come when men of humanity can disagree and yet pull together, as of old, on their agreements.

14

Imperialismo Yanqui

THE POSTMAN BROUGHT us letters daily from our readers which I awaited as avidly as a swain anticipates word from his sweetheart. Some praised one or another article, always balm to an editor's uneasy heart, others differed with this or that viewpoint, still others proposed pieces on matters they felt we had overlooked. Most readers can be as plain-spoken as wives—and most editors worth their salt are, I believe, hen-pecked by their readers, or should be—within reasonable limits. There are moments when they should stand up and talk back; but seriously, unless they display sensitivity to their audience's will, and even its whim, divorce rapidly ensues. The magazine, in its best days, established a kind of family bond which is, I believe, the earmark of a periodical's success. Some editors on the staff answered every correspondent religiously; others, like negligent husbands, procrastinated or allowed over-long lapses of time before they took typewriter in hand. I resolved to allow no letter to lay in my basket longer than a work week and adhered fairly regularly to that schedule (thanks also to a wonderfully conscientious and able secretary). I suffered acute twinges of conscience if, on occasion, more than a week passed for I remembered my own youthful impatience when I sent off a letter to the monthly *New Masses* and virtually haunted the mail-box for the answer.

One day an impassioned letter came postmarked *Habana,* Cuba, which asked why "your eyes see only the lands across the Atlantic when history marches on the double-quick here, at your front door in the Caribbean." The writer had read the magazine for years he said, and with profit; but perhaps the *Marxistas Norteamericanos* unintentionally reflected an imperialist psychology when they ignored their neighboring people who, too, suffer oppression, and suffer it from your countrymen. "Like you," he wrote, "we hate Hitler; but come see what *imperialismo yanqui* does. Since your people is awakening to the Nazi fascism, now is a good time to come and write of us who yearn to air the grievous wrongs done us. And *camarada,* they are not few." He wrote that the Cuban people, tormented so long by General Gerardo Machado, familiarly known as The Butcher, knew the face of fascism before Germany did. And since the day they had overthrown the Caribbean Nero who fed trade-unionists and liberals to the sharks from a chute in the torture cellars of Morro Castle, almost in sight of Florida, they were in the midst of a resurgence. "Why do you not, you who travel so frequently (I missed no report you sent from Spain) come and write about us?" The letter was signed by Dr. Juan Marinello, poet and professor, who later became a Cuban senator.

No letter was this to answer hastily. I discussed it with my colleagues, and we concluded that our critic's grievance was just. They proposed that I go and I agreed instantly, like the European who wrote, "I learn by going where I have to go." That our till was chronically empty did not faze us. We fanned out among our more financially affluent readers who readily contributed the necessary sum.

The seaplane circled over Havana and I looked down on the gleaming streets, the spires that sparkled in the Caribbean sun, the broad avenues that ran down to the sea. My pulse quickens, to this day, when I come to a new city; magnetic always with human mystery and I hasten, impatient, to open the covers, to get among its people, speak with them, ferret out the secrets of their city's past, the shape of their present.

I arrived absurdly with a contingent of the ancient order of Lions, that American fraternity that roars its ritual. They went down the gangplank beating their chests, and danced a jig on the majestic Prado while Cuban longshoremen observed them with startled amusement. One alcoholic Lion, in a red fez, halted unsteadily at the marble statue of Cuba's hero, Jose Marti, *El Liberadore,* and exclaimed, frowning at the inscription, "Hell, it's in a foreign language."

I hurried away, across the gracious avenues lined with the royal palm and made my way to the Marxist newspaper *Hoy* that was housed in a neighborhood of six-story, white-faced tenements. The wrought-iron balconies above the tall windows brought painfully to mind the sacred streets of Cuatro Caminos, the working class neighborhood of Madrid. The staff of *Hoy* greeted me with true Latin cordiality and generously gave their time to consider an itinerary for the Yankee stranger who was a brother Marxist, a *camarada.*

Four towns had elected Communist mayors in the recent elections marked by "a progressive upsurge," they said jubilantly, and the Communists, leagued with the Liberals of Santiago de Cuba, in Oriente province at the eastern tip of the island, the second city of the nation, seated a Negro mayor for the first time in the country's history. A joyous buoyancy sparked from the surprisingly youthful staff who plied me, in turn, with questions about the States: our labor movement, the Negroes, the electoral prospects of Wendell Willkie, *El Presidente* Roosevelt; and the literary editor discoursed learnedly about Hollywood's art. The sports editor asked if Negroes would soon be admitted to the big leagues. Anibal Escalante, young, lean, intense, the scholarly editor, inquired in meticulous detail about the Marxist press in the States: its circulation, the size of the staffs, the proportion of readers who were workers, how many were Negroes, how many farmers?

I am forever moved by the warm kinship felt by men of different nationalities and races who are Marxists. Their common concern for humanity, their common ideology makes for a similarity in their approaches to questions, their modes of living, and even, I fancied, their mannerisms. Foes of Marxism are quick to call this regimentation: if that be so, then scientists who study the common laws of physics or chemistry must be indicted similarly. Not only did the Marxists abide by a science, they were the brotherhood of the good. "When now and then I have come across real goodness," Somerset Maugham has written, "I have found reverence rise naturally in my heart." I say—I believe without partisan bias—that I have found more "real goodness" among Marxists I have met in many lands than I have encountered among any other groups of men. Their passion, humor, zeal, are abundantly manifest if you will only look; it was Tolstoy who said: "Belief in the triumph of good vitalizes a race; enlightened optimism fosters in man a constructive purpose and frees him from fears that fetter his thoughts."

Four members of the *Hoy* staff escorted me to the train, after we had drunk some appropriate libations to the success of my journey, and they urged me to return on the way back. Escalante asked if I would write a piece for *Hoy* on my impressions of Cuba.

The narrow guage railway took me across the tawny, rolling pastureland of Camaguey that seemed so like the Castilian plain. The train puffed and halted at Caccoun, a straw-thatched sugar town where the conductor said we would halt a while for repairs. I encountered a fellow New Yorker on the train, a middle-aged, florid man sputtering his disgust at the delay, bemoaning the fate of any American "sent hell-and-gone to Cuba." Returning from vacation to his post as engineer in a large sugar *centrale* of the Atlantic Gulf Sugar Company, he had barricaded himself behind a copy of the *Saturday Evening Post,* a pile of *Time* magazines at his side. Learning that this was my first time in Cuba, he offered some amiable paternal advice: "Don't let them put ice in your highball, son, that's typhoid sure as hell. The island's full of it." Furthermore, he warned me, everybody down here has "black blood" in him, even Sergeant Fulgencio Batista, the president. "And you know they hate to work; it it wasn't for us, they'd starve to death." But one thing he had to admit, he said with honest admiration, "they're damn good ball-players, lightning on the diamond."

I arrived in Manzanillo, on the Caribbean, a town reminiscent of many along the Catalan coast; it stood lovely among the royal palm trees, gleaming white on the placid shores of the brilliantly blue sea. I was scarcely out of the railroad station when I encountered a procession of black-clad men and women moving in a funeral train, carrying aloft the small white coffin of a child. As I stood on the curb, several women in the procession noticed me, the obvious Yanqui, and averted their faces angrily: spectators near me edged away. Although I was not entirely surprised by the cold reception, its emphatic spontaneity disconcerted me, instilled in me a disturbing sense of guilt.

I checked in at a hostelry for businessmen, drummers, and encountered my traveling companion, the engineer. He had a day's business in town, he said wearily, and invited me to the bar. I excused myself, on the pretext that I wanted to look the town over. "The senoritas," he winked, "will roll you and dose you up for good measure. It's an old Cuban custom."

I made for the local quarters of the People's Socialist Party, as the Communists were known, and found them in a long, one-story whitewashed building the other end of town. Here, the *Hoy* friends told me, I would find a newly-elected Communist mayor.

El alcalde, the mayor, read my credentials from *Hoy,* glanced at me keenly, and took my hand, not warmly, I thought, possibly with a certain degree of reluctance. Or was it my fancy? He seemed in his mid-thirties, slim to the point of emaciation, dark, with sunken eyes in a bony, tan face. I mentioned the funeral procession and the hostility I sensed. He replied bluntly that his countrymen abhor *Norteamericanos.* As a Marxist he knew, of course, that the majority of my countrymen were not imperialists. "I know that *here,*" he tapped his forehead, "but my heart is slow to agree with my mind." I replied soberly, yes, I understood, but he shook his head. "Can a *Yanqui* truly understand the anguish of my people? That child in the white coffin died because of your countrymen," he said softly.

He would explain precisely how Wall Street killed that child, but at the moment he was occupied by some urgent business. He took my elbow and guided me through the narrow corridor to a long, bare room filled, to my surprise, with several hundred young Cubans, clad in the common white, whose voices fell as we entered. I felt many eyes upon me, a gaze more hostile than it was curious. The mayor quickly explained that these were party stalwarts he had summoned because he expected a raid shortly by the strong-arm men of the defeated party. "No few in the province regret that I, a tobacco worker, am now their *alcalde,*" he smiled. The Ramirez Leon clan that had ruled Manzanillo for forty years was challenging the election returns. Feudal lords, he said ironically, are unaccustomed to defeat, and they were raging. "Your countrymen have commanded them to challenge the election, and we have word to expect an armed raid today."

"The story I will tell you, when I have a moment," he said, "is a story of water. Surprising? Yet that is why you saw the funeral procession." Water in Manzanillo, he said evenly, does not quench your thirst. "Water is a war cry, water is death. Water, here, is Yankee imperialism." He turned to his lieutenants with some final instructions to meet the expected attack, speaking with that calm, ready certainty that I remembered as a quality of the people's generals in Loyalist Spain, Modesto,

Lister. Then, clapping his hand on the shoulder of a tall, sober-faced lad of twenty-two, he said, "Tomas, you have the air of an ambassador. Run and tell the Ramirez Leons that we are ready for them, and we can give two duros for one. Say that I am prepared to debate the election results on the plaza: that is in accord with the new constitution and it would save bloodshed. Say, too, that I have notified the newspapers, and that representatives of the foreign press are here," he said, with a glance toward me. He directed the youthful "ambassador" to persuade the foe that the nation and the world will know where to assign blame, will understand who attacked, and who defended. The opponents could propose a time for the debate. "But tell them if they choose war, to bring their father confessors with them. *Claro?*" The young man's stern face unlimbered in a smile, he clapped his hand to his forehead in a smart salute, and he was off in a long stride.

The mayor turned to me and proposed that I interview him now so that I would have the facts at hand for my story if and when the attack materialized. I agreed, and he faced his band of stalwarts. They have here, he said, a writer, a *Norteamericano,* who is not an imperialist. Two hundred pairs of eyes turned suspiciously upon the *yanqui* who was not an imperialist. The mayor described my publication as one similar to *Hoy,* and their manner eased. We would hold an interview publicly and aloud, now, while we awaited the Ramirez Leons. "It will be instructive," he smiled grimly, "a lecture on Cuba's economics is a good way to await the enemy."

Before the elections, he began, in a low, controlled voice, he had asked *Hoy* to dig up the truth about a Yankee corporation called Electric Bond and Share and publish it in a series of articles. "Why I chose this company? Because it is Cuba's curse. It control's Cuba's electric power; it controls Manzanillo's reservoir of water." He explained that it dominated Manzanillo by virtue of a lease granted it by a Ramirez Leon administration. Consequently, the company raised the water tax so steeply that none of the region's sixty thousand inhabitants could pay. "The *extranjero,* the foreigner, condemned us to death."

Manzanillo, he continued like a pedagogue, in a quiet, even tone, which concealed the gusts of passion underlying his words, "is the story of a single Cuban town," but it is typical of all Latin American cities which have been invaded by the Yankee dollar that is more powerful than the armies of the old Conquistadores. The Wall Street corporation has spread its might to Europe, China, India where it operates under the name of American and Foreign Power Company.

"We know that in every land flunkies can be bought for a price, and here Porro Orfilo, a traitor to our people, is the company's administrator." The corporation's hold on Cuba dates back to the first election in 1925 of Gerardo Machado, who sold out to this firm after American dollars enabled him to bribe a convention of the Liberal Party that nominated him for the presidency. After he won the election, he discharged his debt by allowing Wall Street to buy up the franchise of small, native power concerns throughout the island. The monopoly achieved, the corporation fixed prices at will. So now Wall Street controlled Manzanillo's water, which is life.

"But this is only the first charge in my bill of indictment," he said, his voice turning hard now, bitter. "Let none pass judgment until they have heard me out." Wall Street brought Manzanillo unemployment which struck the city like the black plague of old. "Three of every four breadwinners are jobless, and penniless, sentenced to degradation which every heart feels when the hand finds no work for its purpose. Condemned to search our own water without which we die, all Manzanillo can be seen, every morning at dawn, marching in processions, like aboriginals, to the wells and springs in the city's outskirts, carrying pails and pitchers. And death takes its toll, for the water is contaminated by typhoid. Hence we also see endless processions that march every day to the cemeteries where they carry those who have been condemned by the invader. Hundreds have died, thousands are struck by the fatal fever."

Therefore Manzanillans passionately debated a course of action. Some proposed to march on the water-works and take it by the force of their bare hands. Others replied, justly, the *alcalde* said, that the armored cars of Batista's National Guard would roar through the streets within hours. How, everybody asked, can you recapture the water that Almighty God meant for all of us to drink?

"We Communists, who are of the people, proposed a solution which our folk deemed wise. We searched out and discovered that the lease on the waterworks was about to end." Refuse to renew it, they cried, and they urged the municipal governors to regain the ownership so that Manzanillo can operate its own water supply, and to send the Wall Street usurpers packing. "Our brothers of the Liberal Party agreed with us and we formed a coalition on this issue and thus we won the elections." But the *Norteamericanos,* who are satisfied with nothing less than a total monopoly, bribed the Ramirez Leons to begin spurious proceedings in the courts to nullify the elections, and simultaneously to start a campaign of terror against the victors. "And so we are here this day of spring to defend our rights with our lives if need be."

"I have spoken of the plague of unemployment which has struck us. Unlike the black plague whose source science has not yet discovered, we know why Manzanillo is sick, Manzanillo that was once a rich and wonderful city." As a young boy, the mayor said, his voice rising now, his gestures becoming animated, he remembered his native town as the proudest in all of Cuba. "We shod our nation for we were the center of the shoe and leather industry." Then Washington manipulated the Treaty of Reciprocity, and Florsheim Shoes, Walkover, McAn "descended on us like locusts, devoured our trade from under our hands, and threw our men and women into the streets. We who shod a nation go barefoot today."

Once Manzanillo prospered as a center of the sugar industry. But Washington's imposts and tariffs usurped the sugar trade. Once Manzanillo was a leading seaport, it still enjoys the finest harbor on the Caribbean. "I remember when fleets of merchant ships lay anchored and once I counted the flags of seventeen nations. But the mills closed and our longshoremen joined the melancholy army of the unemployed." Once Manzanillo was the center of a flourishing lumber industry, not even a stick goes through the sawmills. Once Manzanillo's markets drew the farmers of a thriving countryside. "Now our farmers are as poor as the shoeless shoe workers." Seventy percent of them suffer from the disease caused by the parasites of the livestock which share the farmers' *bahias.* "This," he concluded simply, "is Manzanillo." He stood quiet now, a shade paler than when he began, his dark somber eyes fixed on me, and the gaze of his followers turned too, on the Yanqui.

I felt a tremulous compulsion to speak, to reply, my parched lips struggled for words. Before I could answer, the mayor raised his hand and said, in a suddenly contrite tone, that he feared he had wronged the *camarada* who could not be accused of guilt, for their guest was a Marxist and Marxists are brothers. My note of introduction from *Hoy* said I had been to Spain, he added respectfully as though that were an act of grace absolving me from sin. After all, hundreds of Cubans had fought for the Republic which was, for them as for us, sacred. Placing a hand on my shoulder, the mayor smiled warmly, and said: "He is our brother." The men who had listened silently, a great, brooding assembly of judges, applauded and cheered me, breaking the tension which had wrung me limp. I knew now the sensation that must have coursed through the nobles brought before tribunals of the people in the French Revolution, or the defeated bourgeois of the Russian Revolution.

I felt compelled to speak, however, and I replied in a strained voice, at first, thanking the mayor for exonerating and honoring me, but, I said, I feared that I must accept my share of guilt. As a Marxist, I am loyal to the precepts of international brotherhood, but truthfully, I must admit that I had made too little effort to rouse my countrymen on Cuba's behalf. I had not realized the scope of Cuba's tragedy, and I was grateful for my belated enlightenment. But I am a citizen of the United States, a Marxist, moreover, and I was culpable to a degree. A nation committing crimes implicates all its citizens. I pledged them that I would endeavor, with all the strength in me, to help right these terrible wrongs. I sat down feeling the sweat running through my shirt.

The Cubans pressed forward, many grasping for my hand, as though they, the injured, wished, too, to exonerate me, to evidence their regard for me as a friend, a comrade. I managed to restrain the tears I felt were welling up, and I was saved, in the nick of time, when Tomas, the ambassador, burst into the room, his face glowing. *"Camaradas,"* he laughed exultantly, "you should have seen them! I shall live ten years longer for it! What a buzzing and a gathering of heads when I delivered my message. They even neglected to order me to wait outside, as I had expected them to do. I watched them turn on one another, one shouting 'March!', the other shouting 'No'." The Ramirez Leons, hopelessly divided in counsel, told Tomas to return to his *jefe* and report that they had nothing to say to a Communist. But as Tomas departed, they fell upon each other in fierce argument and wrangling.

The mayor smiled, passing his hand over his forehead, and murmured *"cobardes"*—cowards. He addressed his assembly briefly, venturing his opinion that they would not now attack, but that the vigil must continue. It is true that the foe evidently recognized in time that discretion is the better part of valor, but their new-found wisdom may be temporary. The men, laughing, clapping each other on the back, returned to their places, some drawing copies of *Hoy* from their pockets to read, others shuffled cards for a game.

I waited an hour or so and the mayor finally suggested I return to my hotel and get a good night's sleep. He insisted on providing me with an escort. If I had the time and further questions I could return the next morning. *"Buenos noches,"* he said. "Please forgive my sorry hospitality."

Sleep lagged that night as I lay beneath the mosquito netting in the ancient, high-ceilinged room, but it was not the buzz of the formidable insects that kept me awake. At dawn, I slid out of bed and watched the magnificent sunrise that turned the serene waters to gold as a long dark ship neared the horizon. My head whirled with recollections of the mayor's indictment, his trusty band of defenders, the funeral procession. How indeed could they regard any *Norteamericano* without a measure of hatred or of distrust. What, truly, had I done to help ease their anguish, I, the editor of a respected Marxist journal who was disgracefully ignorant of tragedy at my door. How woefully unaware of the truth my compatriots were, even the most knowledgeable, how little they really knew of imperialism. Most of us believe that term implies the possession of colonies that were conquered by the force of arms, like the British captured India and Africa, and have yet to realize that finance capital has the might of many armies. I had learned from Lenin's work on imperialism that the export of capital reduces governments of states to a vassalage more effectively than marauding troops. Cuba was a case history that painfully confirmed my reading.

At breakfast in the beautiful dining room where the cutlery gleamed and the plates on the shelves shone bright in pink and turquoise I encountered my friend, the engineer. He sat alone, eating his eggs and ham, immersed in a copy of *Time.*

He glanced up as I entered and he gave me a hearty greeting. "So you had a look around?" he asked. I nodded. "God, man," he exclaimed, "it's duller than Philadelphia, isn't it?"

After Manzanillo I traveled to Santiago de Cuba, passing through the majestic arches formed by the giant palms that lined the roads. The country turned an overwhelming green as it rolled through impenetrable forests toward the hunched mass of mountains on the horizons. And suddenly Santiago gleamed white in the sunshine, a true city of old Spain, with its narrow winding streets and long vistas of low, two-story houses and frequent, fortress-like churches.

I interviewed the Negro mayor, a Catholic member of the Liberal Party who had cooperated with the Communists despite the clerical tirades against the *"rojos,"* the Reds, much as I remembered the hierarchy in Franco Spain had clamored. A small, handsome man with cameo-like features, the mayor spoke of much-needed municipal reforms and aid to the unemployed which the federal government in Havana must shoulder. In reply to my questions he said virtually half the population of Santiago was Negro, as he was, and that racism was not "indigenous" to Cuba and intermarriage had proceeded "for centuries."

I saw that he was loathe to discuss the Church and I consciously deferred to his reluctance realizing the difficulties he must have experienced as an electoral ally of the Communists.

I reflected afterward on the sagacious policy of the Communists which enabled them to campaign successfully with an electorate reared by the clergy. On the whole I found here what I observed elsewhere in my travels: in the final analysis the restraints of religion cannot deter cooperation with Marxists if their policies are demonstrably helpful to the devout masses. For Communists, notwithstanding the familiar propaganda, are not church-burners (like the anarchists of Spain), but proponents of religious freedom who hold that the right to disbelieve is as valid as the right to believe. And they realize that most believers in the rewards of the Hereafter live in the Here and Now and would not object to a Heaven on earth, or its nearest approximation.

At the Party's headquarters I met a trade-union leader, a powerfully-constructed longshoreman, coal-black of visage, who invited me to a fiesta of workers striking against Bacardi Rum, one of the region's principal industries. The fiesta, to raise strike funds, was held in the pavilion of a park skirting the city, a spot of serene tropical beauty, and the participants wore in ancient custom, gay-colored costumes that cowled their heads, peering at you through slits in the cloth. They danced old Cuban dances, the rhumba and the conga, to the intoxicating music of marimbas and the beat of long drums. They talked to me willingly, in fact eagerly, when they understood that I had come recommended, so to speak, by the Negro leader, and their talk was precisely that of trade unionists in Detroit or Pittsburgh—the need for more pay, shorter hours, the security of the job. As we proceeded in our conversations beyond the matter of the strike I discovered painfully again that our nation was understood solely in its worst light, its imperialist aspect. Imperialism cannot, by its nature, represent Jefferson or Lincoln or Emerson to peoples suffering from its rapacity.

Another factor saddened me when the orchestra shifted from its preponderance of native music and interspersed some numbers from Tin Pan Alley which were, by contrast, so painfully banal that I regretted hearing them. As a matter of fact everywhere I traveled through Cuba, particularly in its cities, I encountered the most tawdry tunes of our culture lapping into the strains of the lovely Caribbean music that seemed to be a blend of the heady rhythm of the African, the haunting melancholy of the Castilian and the added ingredient of the Cubans, a kind of gallant gaiety that was, I felt, essentially their quality. And everywhere I saw billboards that advertised the two-gun films of Hollywood. Economic imperialism, I noted, fosters a cultural imperialism to which the wealthier class rapidly accommodates itself. The plain folk, the common man of city and field, cling affectionately to their traditional song, dance and story, but the alien and aggressive new makes headway, especially among the young.

I noted, too, that the Communists, perennial target of the privileged as "foreign-minded," passionately defended their folk art and culture against the Hollywood invasion. The newspaper *Hoy* manifested an acute awareness to this invasion of the mind, and combatted it. Yet it propounded no national chauvinism or cultural claustrophobia: in fact, I found translations of Whitman, Sandburg, even some of Lincoln's speeches in its pages, and a long, thoughtful critique of Hollywood's better films. It was obvious to me that the Marxists of Cuba welcomed our nation's democratic heritage, while they mercilessly excoriated whatever they regarded as tawdry and socially harmful that came from our shores. In fact, as I read *Hoy* here (it was generally available everywhere throughout the island) I came to regard it as the finest Marxist newspaper of our hemisphere. So it did not surprise me when I came upon a middle-aged, weather-beaten worker seated outside his *bahia* on a sugar centrale near Santiago. He was reading, through a pair of ancient hexagonal spectacles his favorite newspaper, *Hoy*. He had never traveled abroad, nor had wandered more than twenty leagues from his birthplace, he said, when he learned I had been to Spain. "But with this newspaper, *camarada,* I roam the world." Within half an hour I recognized him as a man astonishingly aware of international developments who unhesitatingly expressed his canny judgment of them as he stood there, barefoot, in the sun. I speculated afterward what my traveling companion, the New York engineer, would have thought had he deigned to listen to the questions and comments of this penniless Cuban who lived in a one-room thatched hut. The Cuban had his views on the New Deal, on FDR, Chamberlain, Hitler, the Munich pact, all that concerned the most knowledgeable men of our metropolis. The haves measure a man's mind by the extent of his worldly possessions, which is a fatal miscalculation.

I thought, too, that many of my Marxist associates in the United States would have been amazed by this man, who was not untypical of many Cuban workingmen and farmers I met: most of us accept the image of the colonial as a total victim of colonialism steeped in an ignorance as dark as his oppression. It was, of course, natural to believe that the folk of the colonies or semi-colonies, deprived of schools, hag-ridden by a feudal-minded aristocracy and a medieval Church would know only their village. But that reckoning omits one transcendent fact, the existence of a Communist movement, a Marxist literature, a newspaper like *Hoy,* which enabled this barefoot villager "to roam the world." Men similar to him, like Blas Roca, shoemaker from Oriente, became Communist leaders, beloved and protected by their people who elected a sizeable number of Marxists to the Federal Congress.

15

Gone For a Soldier

I RETURNED FROM the Caribbean shortly before World War II exploded in full fury: the unleashed Wehrmacht sawed relentlessly through France, a giant oak rotted by the termites of a treasonous policy. Daladier, Chamberlain, the men of Munich had done their work, and history exacted a dreadful price. Paris, proud and beautiful Paris, soon heard the gutteral Prussian command on the Champs Elysees and under the Arc de Triomphe. It was little profit for Marxists to admonish those who scorned their counsel during the war in Spain and after Munich: the capacity for self-delusion is infinite in those who are blinded by their superior-class bias. For on June 22, 1941, when the Wehrmacht finally turned East, storming across the frontiers of the Soviet Union, these self-same prophets confidently predicted, with the certitude of omniscience (despite their colossal miscalculations of the recent past) that the Blitzkriegers would reduce Russia within six weeks.

That awful morning of December, 1941, I heard the radio flash the news from Pearl Harbor, and I experienced that maddening recognition of tragedy which one foresees in a nightmare but which one is helpless to forestall. So this was it—all that we had sought to prevent through the Thirties, through Spain, through the Munich pact days. Little man, what now? Yet I knew this was not Armageddon: yes, blood and sweat and tears, as Churchill said, but the pale horseman would not finally ride over a globe denuded of mankind. My confidence in Marxism excluded a cataclysmic view of life. Humanity was not born to commit suicide even though that bellicose and strange two-legged creature Man periodically beat his plowshores into swords to bloody them on his neighbors. For so long as man lived by the compulsions of capitalism so long would he shed his brother's blood. But, I speculated hopefully, perhaps this was the last universal war to afflict mankind, perhaps out of this carnage a universal peace would emerge, not the peace of the graveyard but that of a lasting fraternity among nations. I had confidence that a war against fascism would unlock the mighty potential of our own democratic heritage: furthermore I had certainty that the socialism of the Soviet Union could never be crushed. The union of these two forces in war could conquer the enemy. I did not believe this would happen automatically, without enormous labor and heartbreak. History never hands Man his victories generously and willingly like a loving mother.

Listening to the news from Hawaii, hearing of the shattered dreadnoughts, I thought: and now, my nation, my people, were under the bombs in a war that need never have been. To work, little man, to work: your country is in danger.

The editors assembled within an hour, sober and taciturn, and we mapped an immediate editorial policy for the magazine. None of the editors disagreed with the Communist Party's call for an all-embracing national unity to create a war economy that would manufacture the material that meant disaster to the enemy: we could be the workshop of victory. But that required the submersion of domestic differences for the common goal. Every resource, human and natural, must be unfettered. To win as quickly as possible and with a minimum of loss demanded the farthest extension of democracy in our history, which in turn required the prompt grant of all constitutional rights to that tenth of our people denied them, the Negroes; it meant the sincere compliance with Labor's needs and respect for its hard-won rights, as well as Labor's total exertion to turn out the tanks, airplanes and cannon that would devastate the enemy in the field.

Like Marxists everywhere, in all countries, and most patriots generally, we deemed it our obligation to strive to enhance the coalition of anti-fascist allies, to create the understanding imperative to full cooperation between the western powers and the socialist Soviet Union. This, Marxists argued, was the keystone in victory's arch.

Many men in high office, like a senator from Missouri named Harry S. Truman, had proposed that we stand, like the Pharisees, to a side and allow the Germans and Russians destroy each other. That idea did not die after Pearl Harbor. Herbert Hoover, Charles S. Lindbergh, Captain Patterson of the *Daily News,* and a powerful circle of similar-minded men preached a corollary to the Truman view: that we, the U.S.A., concentrate our fire upon the Japanese enemy and let our European allies and the Soviets grapple with the Hitlerites. If this strategy prevailed, we felt, the anti-fascist coalition was doomed and victory would become more than problematic.

"Greater love hath no man for his country," I wrote that week amending an old maxim, "than to lay down his prejudices for his country." And unlike the preacher in the familiar story who advised his flock, "Don't do as I do, but do as I say do," we practiced what we preached. For shortly afterward a well-known New York attorney, Sol Rosenblatt, served us papers on behalf of James H. R. Cromwell, the United States Minister to Canada, who charged us with slander for reporting, in an expose several months before, that the diplomat belonged to Mrs. Evelyn McLean's "Cliveden Set" in Washington, which we had described as "a nest of appeasers." The article named the names of familiar guests at the lady's sumptuous, pro-fascist functions. Cromwell sued *New Masses* for the round sum of one million dollars.

My first impulse was to let Cromwell sue and be damned, for our author, a man careful of fact, convinced the editors that his information was unimpeachable. We could prove that we were right. But the next day I met Alexander Trachtenberg, the Marxist publisher, a man of sagacity whose opinions I valued. One of the early editors of the old *Masses,* he retained a lively interest in the magazine, aiding us often with his counsel born of a wealth of experience as editor and publisher. His canny, dark eyes twinkled as he took my lapel. "One million dollars," he said. "I am sure you will be able to raise it, for Cromwell is right." Despite the irony in his voice the man wasn't joking. Startled, I replied that we could prove our case, certainly in the court of public opinion, if not before judges who would certainly be judiciously neutral—on the side of a Cromwell.

Trachtenberg shook his head impatiently. The proof was not to the point today, for Cromwell's statement accompanying the announcement of his suit declared his opposition to Hitler, his willingness to cooperate for victory by using all possible means. It could well have been that Cromwell was a member of good standing in Mrs. McLean's entourage, but it was also possible, the publisher said, that he experienced a change of heart once his country was attacked. Men changed. He did not question our facts, they could well have been right, but we would be wrong if we did not make the best of this opportunity to submerge past differences for present mutuality. Decisive was the matter of national unity: that transcended journalistic pride. The Marxist *New Masses* had an opportunity to illustrate our sincerity as advocates for that nation-wide unity. It was decidedly his counsel that we should take Cromwell at his word, apologize, and welcome his declaration that he would fight Hitlerism to the end.

I weighed Trachtenberg's words carefully and discussed them with the editors. Many writers and readers had already indicated their support for us against Cromwell. The editorial board debated the matter earnestly and finally agreed that Trachtenberg's advice was sound.

We published an apology. Cromwell publicly accepted it, dropped his suit for a million dollars and agreed to settle for one-thousandth of that sum. We had difficulty raising that thousand dollars—over and above our operating income—but we managed it, that plus another thousand to compensate his lawyer for his labors. As it happened, Cromwell's original intention "to sue *New Masses* to death," as he had announced to the paper, actually turned to the magazine's benefit for it did help to establish the reality that we, the Marxists, sincerely sought national unity in the common interest.

So, not long afterward when we ran an editorial agreeing to a proposal to put a ceiling on prices, but demurred on wages, we received a letter from Bernard Baruch, the famous financier —"adviser to Presidents"—which argued that the nation's well-being and the success of its war effort required a ceiling on both. Certainly we could not agree with that: the profits of the corporations were skyrocketing and although labor was earning more, primarily through over-time, prices of necessities kept advancing unconscionably. Besides, in principle, we would not support any proposition to keep wages down since capital inevitably got the lion's share by the sheer workings of the law of surplus value.

I decided to attempt an interview with the financier and say that; I believed you could gauge the changing temper of the times when his secretary phoned to say yes, he would see me.

At his office on Madison Avenue, I met a tall, erect, powerfully-built man, a mane of silvery hair above his keen, aquiline face. Surprisingly youthful and alert for all his seventy-odd years, his air was that of the Southern gentleman as he rose from his chair behind the gleaming, glass-topped desk which had nothing on it but a telephone and a photograph of Woodrow Wilson inscribed to Baruch. No, the financier said regretfully, he could not grant an interview for publication, but it was his practice to listen to men of all viewpoints no matter how unpopular they were. Though we were at opposite poles, he, the capitalist, and I, the Marxist, must after all, reconcile our differences "to win this thing."

The amenities over, the multi-millionaire, now a respected elder statesman, a national sage, cocksure of his power and his sagacity, philosophized serenely as we talked. He had been described as the ablest speculator in Wall Street, a Statesman of the Ticker Tape. It was charged that his cultivation of government leaders enabled him to multiply his fortunes. He leaned back and stared at the ceiling saying he had lived long enough to know a few things and one of them was the face of an honest man. "You look honest to me," he smiled. He also knew that no lie ever succeeded for long, and that honesty inevitably triumphs. It was a cynic who said honesty is its own reward: actually it had paid him more dividends than any lie he had ever told, and, humorously, "a man is a liar who denies that he has never lied." I sat back, expecting to hear a catalogue of homilies, but I was agreeably surprised when his words took a different twist. "You people," he said directly, "have recently called me a capitalist, but a progressive capitalist." That, he laughed, was fairly accurate. But it might be of interest to realize that as a capitalist he had "never exploited a single workingman." He had merely played the stock market more shrewdly than most speculators, for he was born with enough sense to duck when a punch was thrown his way. And so he prospered. "I guess you can call me a lucky gambler with a share of God-given common-sense, a quality that has a wrong label on it, for it is the most uncommon thing in this world." For, were it truly "common," could the world be in the mess it is in?

Why, he asked, his voice suddenly sober, is man so cruel to man? Need life be so ordered? As for himself, "I never hit a man hard enough to kill him": that was common sense for he had observed that today's foe is often tomorrow's friend. "Your

Marxist philosophy," he continued, "proposes to end the cruelty of man to man, yet consider how cruel folk in Russia are to each other." He was sailing on at a fine clip and it seemed out of place for me to suggest that I had come to see him on the matter of prices and wages. Besides, he was interesting and I was more than curious to discern the shape of his mind, this first top-flight capitalist I had ever met in the flesh. True, I had met no few of lesser dimensions, most of them cast in the mold of the Rotarians I had known in my home town. So he continued his soliloquy interrupting it occasionally to suddenly ask "Right?" And when I attempted to reply, he would push on, possibly because I was largely inaudible, for he wore a long-stringed hearing aid, but, more likely I thought, because he was accustommed to walk a one-way street in conversation in the way of elder statesmen.

After his comment on man's cruelty to man in the socialist country, he surprised me by saying, in almost the same breath, that he had no illusion about building a new country. "Birth presupposes pain. We had plenty of it here when we built the railroads and dug the mines. As the Prophet said there is a time for everything, a time to live and a time to die—and a time for violence, I suppose. But you people seem to go around hunting for it." Yet, he mused, there would inevitably be a lot of it in a land whose traditions stemmed from the tsars who were the cruelest of all rulers.

"I've observed another thing," he raised a finger, oracularly. "There is, oddly enough, a similarity between Marxist Russia and democratic America. The two systems revolve around a similar idea. The Soviets promise every man equality in the goods of life, the Americans guarantee every man equality of opportunity to get the goods of life." The American system obliges a man to work hard, at his level best, but doesn't the socialist system drain the God-given gift of drive, initiative, out of men? Socialism, as he understands it, promises a man all he needs if he will work; capitalism requires him to work well to get his needs. Still, time has the answer, and it will be generations before the Russians get to where they want to go, but you've got to admit they've made progress. "You'd have to be bat-blind not see it in the scrap they've put up against Hitler." He was happy he had survived this long, he said, and although he had gotten as much out of life as any man, he wanted to endure beyond his allotted three-score and ten so he could see how it all works out. "Though I am," he assured me, "a thousand percent adherent of capitalism, I always have an interest in the ways of other men, in other philosophies." As a matter of fact that was so clear that Lenin (he pronounced it Len-een) "a great man he was," knew this, and invited him over in the Twenties. Lenin said he would pay him a million dollars, any price, but he answered he had all the money he needed; "What good is one more million to a millionaire?" He merely wanted to help these people, in fact he would help any people, and Lenin figured he knew more about coal, its digging and its financing, than anybody alive. "He was probably right," he smiled. "I was ready to help clothe, feed, house, or transport the people of this new country, and gratis." But Krassin, headman of the negotiations up and died and the deal died with him.

Suddenly Baruch asked if I were Jewish, and when I nodded, he said he thought so, "we Jews develop a sort of sixth sense about each other," and shrugging his wide shoulders, he said the Nazis called him a Judeo-capitalist or whatever the damned word was, and Gerald L. K. Smith said he was Public Enemy No. 1, a Jew millionaire who influences presidents to betray their country. Looking hard at me suddenly, he said, "If Hitler wins, you know that I, the Jew capitalist, and you, the Jew Communist, will walk down the same long road together with our ass sticking out." It makes no difference to a fascist that he opposed Communism as a philosophy all his life and the record shows it. "But I am a Jew, a rich Jew, so off with my head." True, other heads would roll afterward, Gentile heads as well, but his was scheduled to roll first, a dubious honor. "Yes, son, there is more anti-semitism in this world than you are aware of, even in high places in Washington."

Now, smiling his oddly winning smile again, "a man requires a lot of criticism." No one man has all the brains, and the wise man heeds others who think he is wrong. That makes a man wise." Woodrow Wilson, the champ of them all, once told him a story: Wilson came upon two senators wrangling on a staircase. One struck the other, knocked him tumbling down the steps. "My God," Wilson said to the senator who remained standing. "What's going on, what'd you do that for?" "Well," the senator replied, "We got into an argument when he was criticizing me." "Why," the president said, "you told me you liked criticism." "I do," the senator replied, "but this sonofabitch was telling the truth." Baruch sat back, roaring at his own story, then, bouncing forward, asserted that he really did like criticism, from any source, welcomed it from the Communists who could truly pour it on, but he could not brook it from this Gerald L. K. Smith fellow. "My differences with Communists are real, over real things, but this Hitler-man has the thinking of bygone ages when men cut each other's throats because they didn't like the way the other worshipped God."

As he was speaking, a vagrant thought wandered through my head; why was this mighty captain of finance unburdening himself of these reflections to me, "a man at the opposite pole," as he said? Did it serve some purpose, or was it merely the provocative novelty of talking to a Marxist? Did some egotistic compulsion move him to avow his humanity to a man who professed a credo based on humanity's good? As I wondered, he interjected casually, "Know what's wrong with you fellows? People think you're in this war only because the Russians are in it." He said it diffidently, as though he were commenting on the weather, but a keen glance from his appraising eyes hit me like an arrow. Had he unburdened himself in that man-to-man manner to gain my confidence, and now, man-to-man, tell me the truth: are you really concerned in the defense of our native land or do you have a prior loyalty to another country? Was that his game?

"Well," I replied, in my first opportunity at speech, "It is a tradition that dates back to old Tom Jefferson. The Hamilton crowd raised their cups to drink toasts to the death of that cursed Jacobin, that 'agent of Paris.'" I said it happens everywhere whenever a man of one land admires an idea that derives from another country. "But," I added, "Philosophy has no geography. Marx himself said he drew from the Germans, the British, the French and I suppose God knows who else."

"But to get back to Jefferson," Baruch intervened, adjusting his hearing aid and bending toward me, "did he ever set the interests of France above ours?"

No, I replied, but he saw that the interests of both countries coincided. The Federalists charged him with a greater loyalty to France because he refused to back Hamilton's war-hawks who wanted war against France in 1793. "And why?" the old man asked, setting his elbows on the desk and cupping his head in his hands, his eyes frankly surveying me. "Well," I replied, vaguely uneasy at being catechised, but I was wound up by now, "Jefferson regarded the French, who helped us in our war with Britain, as an ally: furthermore, since 1789, it was two young Republics in a world of monarchies; the assembly of kings allied and marched against revolutionary France. If the kings crushed France, maybe Jefferson feared we would be next. Moreover, didn't we have a treaty with France which Hamilton refused to honor? His heart beat for monarchical England, Jefferson's with republican France."

The old man rose to his full height of six foot three, and adjusted his hearing aid, laughing delightedly, seeming to enjoy himself vastly. "Well, I know something about history too," he said. "Would you have had our young Republic, just getting on its feet, thrown into a new war against mighty England?" Obviously, the man relished disputation, but I feared that our argument would get us nowhere. We were certainly remote from ceilings on prices and wages; I endeavored to steer away from history with a remark that I believed *he* would have been a Jeffersonian in 1793, like Madison and Adams, though he would have me believe that he favored the Federalists, with Hamilton, who urged Washington to be a king, not a president.

"You are right," he chuckled, thumping the desk top, "I would have been on Jefferson's side, but I would have been with him all the way! Don't forget wily old Jefferson finally had France's man, this crazy Citizen Genet, kicked out of the country, got Genet's own government to recall him, but he did it in a way that kept France a friend while he steered clear of war with England. *That* was statesmanship. What I want to know," he added, "is why you people opposed the war until the Russians got hit."

Just then the old man's secretary popped her head into the door and whispered that his next appointment was waiting impatiently. "Have him wait a few minutes more," he dismissed her, and turning a sternly humorous scrutiny on me, he admonished me not to hate all capitalists. "Young man, you've got a head, use it. Don't let your ideas freeze into dogmas. That's how I've stayed young. Now, *you* know all workingmen aren't heroes: and all capitalists aren't villains."

"No, Mr. Baruch,"I replied hesitantly. I was really taken with the old man's engaging buoyancy, his youthful vigor, whatever his possible design. "I would wish you were on the workingman's side. But I remember what old Mark Twain said, 'You gets your ideas where you gets your corn pone.' When it's over I have a suspicion where you will be."

"When it's over, young man," he replied firmly, "I will be what I am. Believe me, I am not labor's enemy. I wish the workingman well. For myself, I have merely abided by the old rabbi's injunction: 'If I am not for myself, who shall be for me? If I am for myself alone, what good am I? And if not now, when?' So I became a capitalist. But don't forget you people called me a forward-looking one. I am not for myself alone. I made my fortune, that was for myself, but I wanted more than money. It gave me standing in the community which is not always easy for a Jew to achieve, as you probably know. I am not for myself alone. I want mankind to prosper, to live together, like brothers, put down the sword after this war is won, or else we will succeed in just about wiping each other off the face of the earth." He spoke so earnestly that it was difficult to suspect his sincerity.

His secretary, worried and frustrated, looked in again and again; he waved her off, "Another minute." Finally he rose, extended his hand and in parting vouchsafed his authority to speak about labor: many do not know that as a youth he had worked in the Colorado mines. True, he went there not merely for the wages, but he sought experience, wanted to learn all about mining. Then, he laughed, he was "a strong stallion," and had enough bounce after a day's work with the pick, to go to the local gym and box. "I was pretty good with my mitts. You know old John L. Sullivan once came into a gym where I was working out. He took me aside afterward and offered to make me the heavyweight champion of the world." Baruch said he always seriously considered every proposition any man made him, but he rejected this one and went into finance. "Maybe that was a wrong decision," he laughed. "Many a man would swap life in heaven for the heavyweight championship on earth. But at that I've had my fun and even did a little good."

The old man bid me phone him again sometime. "We never did get around to wages and prices," he said surprisingly, for I was certain he had utterly forgotten my purpose in coming. "But you know where I stand. I enjoyed talking with you. I like to talk to saint and devil." He was chuckling as the door closed.

Going down on the elevator I thought, well, I really got scarce opportunity to explain my motives in supporting the war. But could my explanation convince him? I would match my patriotism against his, or any man's for that matter. I regretted, however, that I didn't make the point that the acceptance of *any* war a Government favored was no prima facie proof of patriotism. Opposition to certain wars was better evidence. Abe Lincoln condemned the war of 1847 against Mexico as unjust and didn't Henry Thoreau go to jail rather than pay taxes to support that war?

And Baruch. Didn't he help Wilson in World War I which I regarded as an imperialist war we entered to safeguard J. P. Morgan's billions invested in an Allied victory. Surely that was a rich man's war and a poor man's fight, as folk back home said. Wilson later in effect admitted that. Baruch had reference, of course, to the Marxist opposition to World War II during its phony period—when the French and the German troops gazed at each other across the front-line; well, I regarded the war, *then,* as a duplication of the first holocaust, a contest of the rival imperialists for world markets. And all that time the powers behind the scenes desperately tried to switch the "wrong war" to the "right war" via the piney wastes of Finland. But I believed that the fundamental character of the war changed when its flames enveloped the first land of socialism which was the bright banner of man's hope. And after the Panzer-division men roared across the frontiers of socialism, it was in the sacred interest of humanity's advocates to muster help for that nation's survival—for the sovereignty of all lands was at stake —ours included. If der Feuhrer were to win, like-minded gaul-eiters would spring up in our land to crush our democracy underfoot. However, I concluded as I walked down 57th Street past the art galleries, it would have been a fruitless disputation. Intriguing doubtless, but Baruch, who revered Wilson and was one of his marshals, was doubtless related to the Morgan crowd: how could he, with all his avowed declarations of tolerance, understand the validity of my view. But he was a fascinating enigma—to me.

I recalled Jack London's image of the capitalist, Wickson, in the *Iron Heel* who listened to the socialist Ernest Everhard indict the inhumanity of Wickson's class, and he agreed, yes, the indictment was valid.

And how coldly London has Wickson respond: "The world is ours, we are its lords, and ours it shall remain." He, his class, had Power—"that king of words," and he bade the socialist "to pour it on your tongue til it tingles with it." The world had rolled on since Jack London, the workingman, wrote his book: a workingman's state existed and the Wicksons—canny and crafty as always—mastered a new vocabulary, borrowing, without credit, of course that singing word from socialism—Brotherhood.

This hard-headed financier, a captain among capitalists, possessed a set of brains he handled as dexterously as he did his "mitts" that old John L. Sullivan admired. No, this was no latter-day St. Francis of Assissi walking barefoot in the Stock Exchange. He may perhaps have trusted his own words, believed them—the capacity for self-delusion is infinite, even in the hard-headed men of finance. But doubtless he reflected, in his own uniquely magnetic way, the mind of the decisive segment of America's capitalism: the realization that the survival of the House of Morgan required the suppression of the Haus of Krupp. And anybody, to survive, will take assistance from any source, even from an erstwhile foe. Baruch had said just that: "I never hit a man hard enough to kill him," for today's enemy might be tomorrow's friend. Nor could you deny that a capitalist can be a patriot. After all, FDR was no sharecropper. True, most of France's 200 Families preferred the swastika to the tri-color, but Winston Churchill in Britain—cigar, Scotch and all—was no Chamberlain.

Yet realizing this, one had to be bat-blind to ignore capitalism's basic compulsion to reap profit wherever profit could be reaped: a compulsion that moved even the patriotic capitalists.

Certainly the business-as-usual morality was embodied in General Motors man, William Knudsen who headed the government's effort to lift the level of war production. Knudsen came before the nation as a genius of American industry—hard-headed, hard-fisted, driving, resourceful, imaginative and peerless as organizer. He revealed those qualities for GM: but as superintendent of the war effort, he displayed all the piratical qualities of a Robber Baron out to corner the market. How arrogantly he rejected all proposals of labor as inimical to "management's prerogatives" while he steered fabulous contracts to a cluster of giant corporations, cold-shouldering the smaller. His policies induced perilous shortages in many crucial war materials—aluminum for our planes, steel for the tanks, the cannon, the warships, copper and God knows what else. Whatever his words, his patriotism had the dimensions of a silver dollar. Obviously what labor termed Knudsenism would not prevail over the Axis.

But, inexorably, I reflected, wouldn't a just war generate manifestations—the assertion of our patriotic and democratic heritage? Was that not the genuine soul of our people? True, we were woefully ignorant politically, in the broadest sense, knew virtually nothing of what I had seen in Cuba, but wouldn't most of us have recoiled in shamed consternation, as I had, if they too saw the white coffins of Manzanillo? Certainly the cause of Republican Spain broke through to most of us despite the hostility of most publishers? The tradition of '76 and '61—wasn't that truly sacred? Of course, Henry Ford, who published the anti-semitic "Dearborn Independent", and who took an Iron Cross from Der Feuhrer, said "History is bunk."

Could he be right? No, the wizard of Dearborn played his magic on cogs and carburetors but man's heart is no sparkplug. No, I was certain that war to destroy fascism had to evoke its opposite—the democratic spirit. And our role as Marxists necessarily demanded that we strive to stimulate that spirit, nurse it, bring it emergent, to the fore. Communists by the thousands were going to war: leaders like Robert Thompson, of Oregon, John Gates, of New York, Gus Hall, of Ohio, Henry Winston, of Mississippi, were in the ranks; the veterans of the Lincoln Brigade, by the hundreds, were at the fronts. Some 15,000 Communists were soon enrolled in the various fighting contingents, no few becoming national heroes, like Thompson who won the Distinguished Service Cross, and that "one-man army," Rudy Boettcher, who was awarded it posthumously.

Hence, as the months rolled on, the president amnestied the jailed Earl Browder, the secretary of the Communist Party then—"in the interests of national unity"; later Wendell Wilkie, the Republican presidential candidate of 1940, appeared in

Supreme Court to argue—successfully—on behalf of William Schneiderman, the Party's California leader, whose citizenship was challenged by the Department of Justice. Signs of the time? There were other signs. Our democracy is so far from monolithic that no day passed without its tragic budget of news from the South describing atrocities against Negroes; and we had our troubadours of defeat, like the New York *Daily News,* the Hearst syndicate, McCormick's *Chicago Tribune.* Daily in every edition they assailed every forward move of the Administration and purveyed pessimism like a drug peddler pushes narcotics. Certainly the Civil War suffered grievously from the machinations of the Copperheads; their descendants swarmed over America today. The business-as-usual psychosis of Wall Street braked progress on the industrial front; newspapers impaired morale; and, in addition, the canebrakes and the city streets heard the croak of outright fascists, aping Hitler: Gerald L. K. Smith, the Rev. Charles Coughlin, James Colescott, the Imperial Wizard of the Ku Klux Klan, Rep. Martin Dies, first chairman of the House Committee on Unamerican Activites—these and many others sniped from their lairs, financed and encouraged by shadowy men of wealth.

Our magazine assumed a two-fold obligation: the publication of anything that would sustain and strengthen a fighting morale, and simultaneously to expose to the public those who undermine confidence in victory. The series "What I Am Doing to Fight Fascism" illustrated the former: series like John L. Spivak's scorching expose of Coughlin and the Ku Klux leader and Smith helped to ruin their authority.

And when Dies, the Texan Himmler, took the Congress floor to defame prominent men and women of the arts and letters whom the President appointed to a committee that would bring the truths and goals of the war to the public, we carried a symposium in our pages that brought response from nationally-known figures like Senator Sheridan Downey, of California, Senator James M. Mead, of New York, Budd Schulberg, the Hollywood writer, Arthur Upham Pope, the educator who said in our pages: "There is nobody so intellectually pure and lofty that he doesn't carry inside some kind of bias that he ought to uproot. These various prejudices interfere with our elementary understanding of the great issues. They make trouble from one end of the country to the other, and they are the fertile soil for rumor, with all the poison and demoralization that rumor breeds."

The magazine could attest to that: I, for one, did, pounding my testimony out on a typewriter perched across my knees, as I traversed the continent describing America at war. The first leg of my journey took me South again, and traveling across the green rolling lands of Virginia during apple-blossom time, I sat in the packed club-car contemplating a dozen young aviators and their lady-friends jitter-bugging to the tune of a radio. Their gaiety had that desperation which is so common in war time: eat, drink and be merry, for tomorrow. . . . Tomorrow these rosy-cheeked boys in uniform would be goggled and helmeted in planes dodging and dancing through the lethal flak. As I watched moodily a tall, fleshy, well-dressed man, waved a bottle of whiskey over his head and called, through the din, for everybody to join him in a toast: "Here's to Washington," he shouted, "where the Catholics are in church, the Protestants are in bed and the Jews are running the war."

A trim, solid army major of forty or so, seated beside me drinking beer, carefully set his bottle of Schlitz to a side, rose deliberately, pushed his way through the startled crowd to the drunk, tapped him on the shoulder and demanded an apology. The man, a head taller than the major, looked down on him and asked snickering, if his name was Cohen. "No," the officer said, "and it isn't Hitler." He measured the drunk with a careful glance, then let loose with a haymaker that seemed to come up from the knees and the big drunk went down, collapsing like a smokestack sprawled on the floor, stretched out flat and was dead to the world. Everyone, having frozen in their places like an absurd still-life, came to and rushed the major, thumping his back with congratulations. He glanced down at the body, and returned to his bottle of beer. A couple of the apple-cheeked aviators enthusiastically hauled the drunk out of the smoker by his heels and deposited him in the next car, brushing their hands ostentatiously as they grinned, returning to their dance.

The train rattled on into the sun setting behind the purple slopes of the Smokies as I reflected on the significance of this episode. It grew on me as a symbol of our war. The jubilation that exploded when the major uncorked his lethal haymaker revealed more than satisfaction that an obnoxious boor got his come-uppance. The drunk personified Nuerenberg, the Hitler idea: the major's deliberate initiative bespoke our code. I recalled the spontaneous national celebrations which Joe Louis set off when he knocked Max Schmeling unconscious: the Alabama Negro represented the democracy of the USA and the Black Uhlan, as they called his antagonist, the nazism of Hitler.

I congratulated the major and jokingly referred to the Louis fight. He seemed pleased by the comparison: the ring, it happened, was his passion, and in a trice his talk veered to his old favorites, Ad Wolgast, Benny Leonard, Leach Cross, Lew Tendler, Jack Johnson. I was somewhat crestfallen for I had expected the conversation to take a different turn. Intending to plumb his mind concerning the intruder's expression of the fascist idea, I hoped to inspire some philosophic discourse on the war's meaning: instead, we were suddenly transported to Madison Square Garden. Having introduced myself as a newspaper writer, I mentioned that I once covered sports, personally knew the Baron of Leiperville who trained Big Sam Langford, a celebrated Negro heavyweight of championship calibre. "Yes, yes, I remember," he replied excitedly, "*there* was a fighter. As a matter of fact I've noticed that niggers are as sweet a bunch of fighters we've got," and he added, lightly, pouring some beer into his glass, "I suppose there must be something to what they say, that they've got thicker skulls than we got, and they can take a shellacking that would kill a white man." His words cooled me off; but he went serenely on, describing the battle-royals, as they called them in his day, when half a dozen brawlers were let loose in a ring to slug anyone within reach, each the other man's enemy, and the fellow who remained standing won the purse. "Generally they were niggers, and the punishment they could absorb!" Some other admirers of the major crowded around convivially and terminated our conversation.

I reflected on the episode, its original glow dimming for me, but later I thought its disappointing postlude had its logic too. Actually, the person of this single man, this doughty major of the United States Army embodied the complex of qualities characteristic of our nation. Our heritage embraced contradictory elements: we cherish the concept that all men are created equal—that it is uniquely ours since 1776—and yet so many of us are prey to the ideas that ignited this war. Yes, Arthur Upham Pope spoke perhaps more truly than he knew when he wrote in my magazine. "There is nobody so intellectually pure and lofty that he doesn't carry some kind of bias that he ought to uproot." Do we suffer from a sort of national schizophrenia, a split personality: part Jefferson, part Goebbels? The afternoon's experience crystallized my determination to search this thing out, to assess, if at all possible, the dimensions of our split mental—and political—malady.

I started with another go at last night's hero, our major, to explore, if at all possible, the dark corners of his mind where the concepts of racism still lived. It could well be that he was, like so many of us, serenely unconscious of his own bias. I cornered him at breakfast and led as delicately as I could into the matter, finding an opportunity when the Negro waiter—an erect, graying man of forty with that remote dignity characteristic of many Pullman employes—took the order. Noticing that the waiter's erect bearing had caught the major's eye, I recalled aloud that I had written of Pullman car porters and discovered an extraordinary number of B.A's and Ph.D's among them, sociologists and scientists who waited on tables because convention on the campus regarded the color of the skin more seriously than the quality of their mind. The major glanced at me quizzically as he poured the coffee, and he remained silent. I pursued the point, perhaps recklessly, despite his obvious reluctance to respond, and I remarked that our nation required the full mobilization of every man's talent and energy, and that the exclusion of any group from the war effort aided the enemy. "Well, yes," he replied slowly, but his canny blue eyes did not meet mine and I risked a blunt, direct question. "You demonstrated your feelings beautifuly on that score yesterday: what is *your* opinion on the integration of Negroes into the war effort?"

He was staring out the window at a wild, sun-struck slope of the Appalachians outside, and finally, laying down his fork, and leaning across the table his eyes finally turning to meet mine, he said: "I was reared in Tennessee, mister. I say the nigger deserves his rights, but let him stay in his corner and I'll stay in mine. He's got ways I don't like and I know he feels the same about me. I told you I like him in the ring. I like him on the stage. He's a natural-born musician and performer. I can watch Cab Calloway clown all night long: he's tops. Nobody is as good with a band as Duke Ellington. But I don't want nigger doctors treating my family. They just aren't up to us, not yet. Maybe in a few generations . . ." his voice trailed off tentatively. I sensed no defiance in his tone, but rather, an uncertainty. I thanked him for his frank reply, surmising the man's honesty, which perhaps suspected the irrationality of his prejudice. He was still able to examine it, like one inspected one's face before washing in the morning, but he could no more shed his bias than he could his nose. Not then, at least.

There was, too, something peculiarly civilian about him despite his rank. He did not respond like a Brahmin of the military caste, but rather, as an ordinary citizen in uniform. I asked if he were a professional army man. "No," he smiled, "I haven't got the martial temperament: I'm an architect in private life." He was "ordained" a captain upon his entry into barracks life a year before and he won his spurs as a major for professional services rendered, building officers' quarters. I felt that I could speak more freely to him than I could if he were weaned at West Point trained to regard civilians as his wards; much as a priest considers the parishioners his flock. Unquestionably, I said, bias against the black man is deep in the fibre of the South. But isn't this precisely the time—now, at war—to try seriously to eliminate it? Perhaps I was crowding the issue upon a man who confessed an ancient prejudice, for furrows were appearing ominously in his brow: this explosive question, I knew too well, rarely lent itself to calm argument. "How," he asked, a troubled note in his voice, "would you tangle with this question without stirring up general hell? Truth is I don't trust you Northerners on this question. You're bulls in a china shop. Before you know it you'd bring everything down in a crash."

I reiterated my point that the nation desperately needed the Negro in war industry. It was a patriotic necessity, and, in fact FDR's presidential order 8802 exhorted industry to honor that need. I would also, I continued, institute a governmental campaign to educate all Americans on the question of race: explain that prejudice on this score is the precise equivalent to Hitler's fatal dogma. And finally, we should insist that the Department of Justice move against the breakers of laws guaranteeing Negro rights. Silence answered my words, as he toyed with a spoon. "You know, mister," he finally said, shaking his head dubiously,

"I think that would be the quickest way to stir up a race-war that could put the Hitler war in the shade." No, let sleeping dogs lie, it will work itself out in due time, he concluded, glancing at his wrist-watch. I rose, thanking him for his courtesy and attention. I comprehend his viewpoint, I said, shaking hands, but I believed his bias was operating against his better judgment. "Maybe," he smiled, "time will tell." As I was about to leave he raised a finger, "By the way," he said, hesitantly, "That was all off the record, you understand. No quotes. The Army, you know." I understood, I replied, I understood very well.

That afternoon I wrote in my notebook: "Herndon once said to me that the South is chock-full of decent white folks who've been taken for a ride on this race question. I met one today: a Southern patriot—ready to die for his country, much readier to die than to lay down his bias. True, he came from a border state, and the hydrophobia of racism is not so virulent in him as it is farther south. He can discuss the matter rationally; does not regard race differences as fixed and immutable, a law of nature. He foresees a time 'several generations hence' when the differences will vanish. 'Go slow,' is his advice: willing to hear proposals to improve matters immediately, he is skeptical of their chances to succeed."

16

Marching Through Dixie 

Birmingham, which I had visited almost a decade before, remembering it as a rundown, depression town, raged and roared with war in its blood. A center of industry, counting nearby Bessemer, part of the empire of Tennessee Coal and Iron, its streets pulsed with crowds of workingmen—and workingwomen—tramping from their daily work-shifts, or heading to them—black faces and white. I telephoned a Negro I had met in New York who invited me to visit him when and if I came South. He'd show me around, he had said, after I interviewed him for a story I wrote on a Communist convention which he attended as a delegate. I remembered I had described him as a "black son of Alabama." Born and reared in Chambers County, in the heart of the Black Belt, a hundred miles south of Birmingham, he had left his hoe and plow and gone into industry a couple decades back, to become a steel worker, and a Marxist. He maintained close ties with his rural kin.

I met him at an appointed spot, recognizing his warm smile as he waved to me from his rattle-trap Ford. A man in his middle years, he stood a tall and spare six feet, his lean and wrinkled dark face had the mien of a man ten years older. "It's high time you came," he clapped me on the shoulder, "there's enough to write a book about." And promptly—in the quiet of his small, neat room where several homemade bookcases held well-worn volumes of Marxist classics—he began a story of today's South, telling it in the soft, melodious drawl I remembered when I spoke to him in New York. I wrote then that he was a prototype of Negro Communists I had known: men and women who are 'doubly Communists," as he had said; "doubly dedicated," I had written: once, as members of the working class and twice, as spokesmen for an oppressed nationality, and hence, one who bore a two-fold burden.

Most Negro Communists I had known had chosen Marxism as their philosophy primarily because they were Negroes, and collaterally, because they were proletarians. I never questioned the justice of this motivation: simply to acquire the status of the average white workingman was a climb out of the latter-day bondage, somewhat like a slave who yearned first to become a freedman, just that. Later he would strive for the advantages that come with freedom. Merely to live in the house you preferred; to educate your children in the schools you chose; to exercise the franchise without risking your life—all these were incalculable boons the white workingman enjoys without second thought. And my friend, I shall call him Henry Tompkin, was typically one of those who chose Communism because it realized, he had said to me, quoting Marx, that "Labor in the white skin cannot be free while labor in the black skin was branded."

Folk up North needed considerable light on matters down here, he murmurred. "Thing are moving slow. A lot good is happening, but bad dogs the good." Yes, Negroes were going into war industry, true, but solely as unskilled labor. Those who had the experience for up-graded jobs, were denied the opportunity. Furthermore, the most rabid of Dixie's racists were on the rampage again, determined to stop progress dead and restore the status quo ante. For example, Tompkins said: two days ago a Negro army nurse, Nora Green, stationed at the Tuskegee Army Flying School was beaten by a white bus driver for protesting when he denied her the right to a seat she had reserved. The nurse had received orders to go overseas and she was traveling to Montgomery for the proper clothes to make the journey. Now she lay battered, in the hospital, brought down, not by a Nazi, but by an American, Tompkins said. More: three Negroes were lynched the previous month in Mississippi, two of them boys of fourteen. In Georgia Governor Talmadge inspired the formation of a new, streamlined Klan, the Vigilantes Incorporated.

Here in Alabama, Governor Dixon publicly rejected President Roosevelt's injunction that Negroes be hired in all factories working on government contracts. And the *Dothan Eagle,* my friend said, tossing me a clipping he drew from an old wallet, wrote: "Governor Dixon has set a splendid example for other southern governors."

Another clipping from the *Greensboro Watchman* spoke

more plainly: if the President's injunction were observed, "The night-riders will be out again. There will be hangings, burnings."

"Naturally," my friend said, "the rumor-factory is working overtime: tales of Negro soldiers throwing kisses at white women; of Negroes jeering, 'When you white men go to war, we'll take care of your womenfolk.' "

Last week one of Birmingham's foremost attorneys, "Judge" Horace Wilkinson harangued the Bessemer Kiwanis Club to form a League of White Supremacy and he had roared that "Negro troops threw kisses at white college girls." Another leading figure, Borden Burr, attorney for the powerful Tennessee Coal and Iron Company, an affiliate of U.S. Steel, served as intermediary for the governor and Wilkinson, the moving spirit among the racists. E. Le May, public relations counsel for the steel corporation urged the Alabama Press Association to endorse Dixon's defiance of President Roosevelt. "He didn't get it," my friend said, "It ain't running all one way. There's a big tug of war going on." He suggested I interview the racists.

He had more clippings, from the *Montgomery Advertiser* and the *Birmingham Age-Herald,* two of the foremost dailies of the state. Both journals supported the President's plea to enforce federal war policies and opposed the behavior of Governor Dixon. "The greatest duty of us all at this critical moment," the *Age-Herald* wrote, "is to increase understanding, to keep down misunderstanding, incitement of internal animosities of any kind. The government in our conviction is trying to advance unity by combating fundamental injustice."

Yes, the tug of war was indeed evident; I agreed with my friend that I would try to interview some of the racists. But first I wished to go into the Black Belt. After a pause, Tompkins replied that was possible, but it was easier said than done. "It wouldn't do for a Communist to try to get around there on his own," he said. "The landlords got their eyes peeled these days for any white stranger, any stranger for that matter, colored or white. And you might get yourself in a parcel of trouble."

First he would want to notify his friends in Chambers County that he would "come by" with a friend from New York. "We got folk there think the way we do," he said. They would be happy to meet me. But this is a matter that might imperil them, as well as myself, and caution was in order. "We need to organize the trip," he smiled. "Got to organize everything down here. Can't do nothing haphazard like maybe you folks do up North."

Two days later, after word went down and came back, we travelled south, in the cautious dark, along a lonely road, off the main highway. Some sixty miles south of Birmingham he stopped the Ford on a deserted byway, hidden among clumps of scrub pine; I saw a dim light, as of a candle, in a cabin some 100 yards off the road, gleaming faintly, the sole evidence of life in the vast dark. Tompkins quickly stepped to a large oak amid the pine, and with a rapid motion, inserted something in a hollow of the tree. He was back in the car in a trice and off: and then, casually, referred to the hollow as a "mailbox" where he delivered five copies of the *Daily Worker* every week. "Postmaster," he shrugged, "reads everything they get."

With some reluctance, he answered my query about the "organization" of our trip to the Black Belt. It required notification of a particular sharecropper we were to visit, and his agreement; this sharecropper, a man he would trust with his life, would, after my arrival, bring me to half a dozen of his most certain friends. So far only the single sharecropper knew I was coming. "This requires more doing than going to a foreign country," I observed, and he chuckled. "Ain't no foreign country in the world foreign as Alabama to a New Yorker. They know all about England, maybe, and France, never met one who knew 'Bama." The sharecropper whom we would first visit, where I would stay the night, he informed me, had a family of six children and a wife: he was accustomed to occasional nocturnal guests. "They knows who's friend, who's foe." The cropper himself had read the *Worker* for years; solid and reliable, he was respected by his folk here, who regarded his as "a man with answers." The sharecropper was an elder in the Zion M. E. Church, who "trusts God but keeps his powder dry"; reads his Bible every night, can quote from the Book of Daniel and the Book of Job, name any, and he's been studying the Stalin book on the nation question, read everything he could lay hands on. "Can quote them as well as Genesis."

After midnight we arrived at the tumble-down cottage of our sharecropper who had awaited us, reading by lamplight while his wife and brood of six slept in the two big, brass beds of the bedroom, the sole room in addition to the kitchen. In the moonlight I saw a square-built man of thirty or so, sober of manner, and soft of speech, in overalls. He came out on the porch in his bare feet. "Glad to meet a comrade from the North," he said earnestly. "I read your articles a long time now." He had set up a cot for me in the kitchen.

I watched the sun rise over the cotton fields that gleamed as they had for centuries, the white fluff bursting through the bolls. Overhead a squadron of great-winged bombers streaked across the sky, probably from the field at Tuskegee; the planes were obviously so familiar a sight here by now that a solitary hawk wheeling over the fields continued unperturbed to circle gracefully, unafraid: the scene might have been that of rural Alabama in Jefferson Davis' time—were it not for the bombers overhead.

The next evening my host guided me cautiously across the rolling hills, under a small crescent of moon, to the cabin of a neighbor, two miles off. About nine o'clock six men drifted in, singly and silently. They came every night, to hear the nine o'clock broadcast from the world capitals.

Each man, I learned had carefully counted out an equal share of his scarce cash to get the radio which they kept here, in the cabin that was equidistant from their homes. They settled on the floor, in shadows cast by a candle flickering on the mantelpiece near the radio dial. Worn by the day's labor in the field, they seemed to be resting their body's weariness, but I soon saw, their minds were resiliently fresh. For when the broadcasts ended, from Washington and London, announcing the news from the fronts, they sat up to debate, in deliberately low tones, the broadcasters' conclusions. From a dark corner where I could barely discern the bulk of the man's body I heard a disembodied voice drawl a question about the Western Front. Another shadowy form from the opposite end of the room murmurred that Russia alone seemed to be in a hurry. "The Allies got the stuff to do it," the voice commented, "but there's generals want to see Russia tore up some more."

The symposium conducted in darkness continued on, with intervals of thoughtful silence as a whip-poor-will outside called insistently and occasionally a hoot-owl moaned low. I noticed that one of the Negroes lay on the porch outside the open door, listening to the men inside but keeping vigil on the approaches to the cabin. The irony, in the midst of a war against a Gestapo civilization Americans required sentries to discuss that war! And yet we demanded these Americans to offer their sons up to the altar of democracy, their lives and their energies. The questions with which they grappled reflected a resentful concern, revealing simultaneously a steady interest and preoccupation with the dominant issues and developments since the bombs fell on Pearl Harbor. Each man in the room read the *Daily Worker* occasionally if not regularly, I guessed from their words.

When they learned my identity, they edged nearer and deluged me with questions. Now, in the pale gleam of light I saw their faces, the vivid and searching eyes, and, as happened to me frequently in such circumstances, I experienced a mingled emotion of pride and humility: pride, because these harassed men regarded me as friend, a white man they could trust in this world of white hostility; humility, because of my uncertainty that I could measure up to the dimensions of their courage, the scope of their eagerness for truth. I knew something of the penalties they could incur for their rebellious independence of mind. Their faces in the candlelight etched into my memory, dark and unknown Galileos pursuing knowledge, aware of the faggots ready for the Inquisitor's torch. Should the landlord or anyone beholden to him whisper "smart nigger" as a charge against them, disaster could descend within the hour: prompt exile from their home and family, or a visitation accompanied by flogging, or worse. How much then had really changed since the slaves of Frederick Douglass' time were flogged to death for daring to learn to read—and yet he had dared as men will, and as these did.

And so their questions came fast: what did I think of Roosevelt? Doubtless a good man, one ventured, but was he not surrounded by bad advisers? Another asking, did he truly favor collaboration with the Soviet Union? If so, why was the Western Front delayed? And others; what manner of man was Churchill? How long could the Russians bear the brunt alone? Were war supplies reaching the Soviet ports? Was it true that the convoys were going down, torpedoed by submarines or by the bombs of Goering's aviators? I replied as best I could, advising first that no civilian knew the answers to all their questions, but I offered my opinions for what they were worth.

Another sequence of questions followed that struck nearer

home: how could a war for democracy allow Negro blood donated to the Red Cross stand in bottles unopened on the shelves? They had read or heard of that and it rankled like a whiplash across the face. And these lynchings that went unpunished by federal authority! Hadn't Roosevelt a greater power to act than he exercised? Was I aware that many a Negro was saying it was safer for black Americans to fight as soldiers in the Pacific than to train to be soldiers in the southern camps? And a whisper rose bitterly from the shadows: "We got two wars on *our* hands, one against Hitler over yonder and the other against the one in the Big House here." And another added, "Maybe the Hitler nearer me is the one to handle first."

My host, the church elder, who knew Daniel and John and Genesis rose, a sturdy block of a man, his head obscured in the dark, the dim cast of light falling upon his bare feet. "Hitler," he said, "was a Pharaoh reaching out beyond Egypt, beyond Jerusalem, to make the whole world his slaves." If *he* won this war, the landlord in the Big House would work for Berlin. Here, at least we have a Constitution; here at least our homeland's law promised equality. Should Hitler win we Negroes would be back in Jefferson Davis' time. And that he sure did not favor. His soft, controlled voice did not conceal the stern certainty of his convictions: he spoke evenly, almost in a monotone, without rancor or anger, like a scientist demonstrating a truth in an amphitheater of listeners.

So the conversation swirled up like a surging river whose might is visible but almost soundless. Suddenly I heard the repeated cry of the hoot-owl and there was a stirring at the door where the Negro lay sentry. A hand snuffed out the candlelight as the men in the room rose in the darkness: my host took my arm firmly, leading me through a back door into a dense thicket a few feet away and I stumbled among the trees, at his side, noting that everyone had vanished soundlessly and invisibly. We retreated for more than a mile before he even whispered a word. We had come to the end of the woods, to the clearing beyond, and he stood alert in the black shadows, by a tree, scrutinizing the landscape. We remained silent for several moments that seemed to stretch endlessly, broken only by my heavy breathing and the night-sounds of a bird or a cricket. I felt that the thump of my heart was audible as I strained my eyes to survey the long slope of the meadow, a distant tree trunk, the bright stars overhead and the crescent of the moon in a cloudless sky. We heard the sudden far-off bay of a dog to the south, from the opposite side of the woods, and my host, giving my elbow an almost imperceptible shove, strode into the meadow. We hastened toward the crest of the slope and suddenly were in his cabin which lay just beyond it. The sentry had signalled that a suspicious stir neared, and they had decided to take no chances. I lay on my cot, wide-eyed, pondering the evening's meaningfulness.

The children were stirring at dawn and we sat down to a breakfast which my host's wife cooked over a wood fire in the stove: of biscuits, greens and clabber, a kind of fermented milk. The children eyed me curiously, stealing glances as they ate, and after the meal they went off, bare-foot, to the school a mile away. My hostess, a slim, light-brown woman of thirty-five, with lustrous eyes, asked shyly if I came from New York. She had never been far from Chambers County, once to Birmingham, but she read of buildings one hundred stories high, and she dreamed that she would go North some day and stand on the top of a skyscraper and look down. She inquired of my family, the number of my children, their ages, their schooling. Was it true that all children owned two pairs of shoes in New York, one for every day and one for church? I discovered that hers had no shoes at all, that she had a pair "for Sundays," and none for daily wear; her husband owned shoes for work in the fields and another pair for the Sabbath when they attended church services.

Occasionally they got a Birmingham paper and she studied the advertisements, and knew precisely the kind of footwear she would get her children, speaking of the possibility as something remote, but attainable, and with a timid smile she asked if I knew the style of shoe my wife wore, for she studied the advertisements of ladies' footwear and had a fashion in mind that she would buy for herself when the day came. She brought me, bashfully, a clipping from the *Birmingham Age-Herald* and placed her finger on an ad displaying a pair of shoes with slender, high heels and a small oval buckle. They were "truly beautiful" but she feared she would stumble in them, "big and country as her feet were."

The poignancy of her questions moved me, and, I suspected, her husband, who interjected that were it not for a stroke of bad luck, an unexpected drought, she would have had shoes this year, "even them with stilts," he added with a gruff tenderness. But his luck would change, and she would have her shoes and the children theirs, "God be willing."

Oh, of that she was certain, she replied, impatience might be sinful and she was not impatient, but it did feel good talking about it. At the last "sing" they held on the church grounds—the sharecroppers came by the hundreds from miles around, I learned, occasionally, to lift their voices in spirituals and hymns—she had seen some croppers' wives wearing high-heeled shoes and she couldn't help feeling a little bit of envy. She, too, some day would come in fashionable footwear to sing hymns to the Lord. "I'd probably feel a little nearer Him on them stilts," she added with a humorous, side-glance at her husband. Then, as though she suspected that her sally—and her confidences—might be misunderstood, she said with a lovely simplicity that she trusted I would not consider her words as complaint; I would understand, being a "comrade from New York," which is such a rarity. Would I convey her respects to my wife and to my family and would I come again? By then their luck would have changed and they could offer the hospitality they felt "but showed so po'ly."

Back in Birmingham I turned my attention to the whites, in the course of which I interviewed the editors of the *Birmingham Age-Herald,* and John Temple Graves, III—a spokesman of liberal views. Graves, a man of grace, worldly, impressive in his bearing, who described himself as a Roosevelt adherent, listened politely. I indicated what I had just learned in a Black Belt county not far thence, and he replied cautiously, that a Communist might possibly exaggerate the Negro's awareness of the world beyond. As a Southerner, "by profession as well as by birth," he smiled, he may know the colored folk better. True, their lot was miserable, he would not deny that: it was a tragic condition history imposed upon the South but that too would change in time. There was advance, unspectacular but steady; slow, possibly too slow. But a leisurely tempo was decisive, for the impoverished white mass of the South held so profound a prejudice that speed might provoke the horrors of a race war. History, tradition, held both white as well as black in thrall; the past came down "by word of mouth" to the illiterates of his region, and they know too well the terrors of the Reconstruction. "You should have heard my gentle grandmother on the question." Then I would have realized the white southerner's problem. I must know that the colored folk were one step removed from savagery when Lee surrendered. "With the help of your carpetbaggers and scalawags the blacks set up a reign of terror exceeding the French Revolution."

The tone of his cultured voice hardened perceptibly as he related the tale his grandmother told of a time when no white woman walked alone because rape and rapine were the order of the day. The slaves, freed of bondage but not of ignorance, egged on by disreputable Northern adventurers, were elected to the state legislature where they behaved like tribal medicine men in frock coats, passing fantastic legislation, squandering fabulous sums of public moneys on such civilized equipment "as golden spittoons." Naturally the whites adopted desperate measures, became night-riders, formed the Ku Klux Klan, to curb the fearful license. This man of culture who had spoken rationally a few moments before was transformed on this matter, into a yokel of primitive bias. I felt his reason shrink and I assumed it would be profitless to recall the Reconstruction other historians had described, scholars possibly more objective than his grandmother, who had doubtless viewed the new time through the spectacles of a disinherited slave owner. The curtain of his mind had slammed down, and he would have dismissed the established facts I could have cited from Dr. W. E. B. Du Bois' *Black Reconstruction* or James S. Allen's *Reconstruction,* which described the noble endeavors of the black freedmen to institute free, compulsory education for white children as well as their own, to climb into the Nineteenth Century. I bade Graves adieu and returned to my room, wondering if any educated whites (barring those of Marxist orientation) were free of the virus. I decided to interview some learned men of the South, the professors of Birmingham-Southern, to discover their frame of mind.

The campus lay serene under the hot Alabama sky, hushed in that gracious quiet befitting the halls of learning. The receptionist appeared puzzled when I asked to see the head of the anthropology department. She was uncertain whether the college taught the subject, and she connected me with the dean of science. Tall, portly, bespectacled, a man of dignified carriage and aplomb, he listened gravely to my question and promptly summoned two assistant professors to his side. The trio stood in an empty classroom surveying me with a worried air as I stated my purpose: to write a survey on the South at war. It seemed to me, as a Northerner, I repeated, that maximum efficiency for the war effort depended upon the maximum acceptance of the Negro as a first-class citizen. But the majority of whites I've spoken to seem to regard him as an inferior race, at least in our time. What, frankly, did *they* feel?

Apprehension seemed to become positive alarm and the two younger educators turned automatically to their senior. "Well, sir," he replied very carefully, "this is a subject we rarely discuss for publication." I should understand the dangers that were involved. If, and he hesitated a moment, if I understood that and agreed to, ah, omit names from my account they would gladly oblige. Both younger men nodded vigorously and I assured them the safeguard of anonymity, "a common practice," I said heartily. The professor, relaxing, said he could then speak truths most Northerners found unpalatable. "The fact, sir, is that the Negro has not yet attained the mental stature of the white. His race is a stage below ours in evolution." The others agreed instantly, reeling off a routine of argument all too familiar. How, I responded, could they explain, let us say, George Washington Carver, or Paul Robeson, or Langston Hughes. The professor smiled easily: "No question but that nature produces biological sports and all races have their geniuses. We are discussing the norm of both races."

How then, I pressed him, would they assess the findings of Professor Franz Boas, of Columbia, the world-esteemed anthropologist, who proved, after thousands of experiments, that all races are equal in mental capacity? "Boaz?" the professor repeated, turning perplexed to his junior colleagues. Both duplicated his air of bewilderment: no, they had never heard the name. I stared from one to the other, and thanking them, I departed quickly for the college's library building. In a fever of haste I thumbed through the index cards and, my heart leaping, I found the name of Boaz, where it belonged, under the B's. Taking his volumes down from the shelves, I opened to the back-cover where the names of borrowers are tabulated.

I confess to a curious shock when I discovered the names of the three educators. I sat down hard, reflecting on the infinitude of dissimulation, and I had believed I encountered enough to recognize all varieties. Obviously these educators feared to admit, to a stranger and a Northern stranger, that they read Boaz' works and knew his findings. I realized that the intellectual pall that settled over Germany had a considerable measure of its counterpart here, in my southern states—less spectacular, perhaps, than Hitler's, but equally as perfidious.

I could scarcely leave the South until I sought out the men of organized labor. Experience had already taught me that the new, "the nascent" would more likely be found among workingmen. At Bessemer, the coal and steel town outside Birmingham, dingy with smoke and smokestacks, I attended a union meeting in a great, barn-like structure, hard by the Southern Railway tracks where a green locomotive backed and filled a few yards from the entrance. Black and white workingmen met, self-consciously, in the same hall, members of the Mine, Mill and Smelter Workers Union. A tall, gaunt, white man of middle age presided; a solid, coal-black Negro sat by him as vice chairman: at the next meeting, I was told, the roles would be reversed. The members did not sit side by side, however; the colored men massed on one side of the aisle, the whites opposite, a preliminary arrangement that met the requirements of local law, as well as the lingering bias of new members.

After the meeting the chairman told me they had, the week before, won a contract—verbal—after nine hard years of campaigning, but the company inserted a treacherous joker in the written contract which cancelled out the concessions. Consequently, Negroes and white, womenfolk as well as men, picketed the Birmingham offices of the company demanding the restoration of the advances promised in the verbal agreement. White and black pickets paired off to stand sentry on each floor of the company's skyscraper office building, bearing placards that said: "Nobody leaves the building until the contract is signed." But this was no strike, the chairman assured me, they had no intention of striking in wartime: this was a device, he smiled, to achieve their objectives without a strike, for all pickets came for their round of duty after the workday shifts. I was in Birmingham when the astonished white residents saw the two races march shoulder to shoulder, and observed that the police turned their backs on the sight and continued to direct traffic.

The Negro vice president told me similar stories: how at an important manganese smelter—"important war stuff"—white members overhead a foreman refer to Negroes in the plant as "niggers." They notified the grievance committee, whereupon a delegation of five whites and two Negroes brought a complaint to the superintendent—no paragon in the past—but who listened gravely today, summoned the foreman and forbade him to use that word again on pain of dismissal. As my face lit up, the unionists added quickly that I should not regard these episodes as the rule: they are still exceptions, but they show the way the Southern winds are blowing. Most AFL locals still clung to the old exclusion policy, yet even there you could discover the promise of progress. The AFL state convention in North Carolina had elected a Negro to the executive board, for the first time in their memory, and an AFL journal approvingly quoted a CIO Negro leader who said: "The labor movement in the South will never amount to a hill of beans until the unions are prepared squarely to face and solve the Negro problem."

Afterward I spoke to the white president and the Negro vice-president separately. The white said he had been reared in the traditional bias against Negroes. "But it came to my attention that Tennessee Coal and Iron used us—us against them, and them against us. That way they kept wages down for both." He had realized then, he said, that no Southern union could be successful unless it contained members of both races equally. "I figgered then that the War Between the States was dead and gone; it was a war between the bosses and us workers, whether we were white or black." This, the organizers of the union taught, "and I came to see they were right." Logic vanquished prejudice—or rather, and prior, his individual desire—selfish, if you will—to secure a higher standard of living for himself and his family, required the submersion of prejudice, and a resolve crystallized to set aside his prejudices. He discovered that the Negroes revealed understanding as clear as his, in fact, they proved to be solid, reliable union men, and gradually, in fact, rapidly, he accepted them as his equals. "That's the way it will come in the South," he said earnestly. "The poor white will learn that he stays poor as long as the colored fellow stays poorer." Yes, I replied, "It was Booker T. Washington, I think, who said 'to keep the other man down in the gutter you got to get down there yourself.'" He nodded assent. "Took me a long time, forty years in fact, but I got to see that."

The Negro vice-president told me a similar story, with one divergence. Negroes working in industry realized, very quickly, that their fate embraced the lives of their white co-workers. Life taught them long back that the boss-man holds the races apart for his particular advantage. "Leave the ordinary man alone, white and black, and we would be friends. But the law's against that. And we know who passes the laws." When the Mine, Mill and Smelter men came along and preached what the Negroes already believed, they heeded their counsel as union organizers. "The problem is to get to the white man, the white workingman, catch his ear, and that ain't easy." But it *is* possible; given will and leadership success was inevitable. There would be setbacks but time worked for the union. "It might take a year, might take ten, maybe more, but come it must." True, he said, "it takes patience, but that's what the black man has a lot of, maybe too much. They realize that many in the government expect to win the war with one hand; one hand against Hitler, the other to keep the Negro down." But that would change; it was already changing for the unions, the new thousands of Negroes in the unions would help speed the change along.

So I saw again another verification of the Marxist philosophy, if affirmation I needed. As a matter of fact I was not unprepared to find this, and find it I did. The emergent new first thrusts its shoots up in the soil of the working class, the class destined to shape the future. What I saw in Bessemer was a tender shoot that augured that future. So I mingled with many Negroes in the Southern cities and I believed I detected, in their concealed impatience, a confidence in tomorrow. Advance had been slow but it was steady this past New Deal decade. A conscious unity was emerging, and many had a pre-vision of their mighty potential, politically, economically, as industry wooed the sons of sharecroppers from the fields, these new recruits of labor. And many, though suspicious of all that was not Negro, yet realized the advantages that came from concerted action with their paler brothers of the factories.

In considerable measure the crusades of the Communists in the Thirties stimulated this realization. So many, I discovered here, knew that a Negro, James W. Ford, was the vice-presidential candidate of the Communists; that some of their finest sons, like Benjamin J. Davis, Jr., member of an old Georgia Negro family, was a leading Communist. And it was personally most gratifying to me that I encountered Negroes who remembered my writings on Herndon, the work of the International Labor Defense in the successful campaign to deliver the Scottsboro boys from the executioner. I could knock on virtually any door, of any Negro newspaper office, or parish house, introduce myself as a representative of my magazine or from *The Worker,* and be a welcome guest.

In fact, my last week in Birmingham, a Negro editor invited me to his home one evening to meet some of his friends. Unlike the sharecroppers of Chambers County, they were unacquainted with the periodicals I represented. The window shades were carefully drawn: the apartment was on the ground floor and they invited no prying eye; the metropolis was not unlike the countryside. "Well," the Negro editor said at one point in the evening, "I am no Marxist. If I studied your philosophy I might well disagree with it. But concerning the Negro I know this: Your people put the white Christian church to shame and I say that as an elder of the Baptist church." An aged minister who sat quietly through the evening, who had listened carefully throughout, added quietly: "I follow the works of the Communists from afar. I remember the case at Scottsboro; somebody gave me a copy of the Herndon book which I read. I have come to this conclusion: Communists and Christians, true Christians, are headed the same way on different roads. Bound for Paradise. But when they get there it will be the Communists who will sit at God's right hand. Why? We Christians walk in righteousness because we expect a reward in Heaven. You Communists recognize no Heaven and no God. But the Lord said ye shall know them by their deeds which is the true expression of faith. Will not their reward be the greater?"

Before I departed for the Far West, I determined to talk with some of the movers and shakers of the State: the men behind the scenes. Congressman-elect John P. Newsome, a handsome, tall man in a well-tailored, double-breasted business suit who had campaigned on the slogan "Victory is my only purpose," said of the Negroes, "Nobody's stopping them from serving." Donald L. Park, director of the Birmingham Chamber of Commerce, smiled at my misgivings. "Negroes are one hundred percent behind the war; they're satisfied with conditions unless outsiders stir them up." I reminded him of "Judge" Wilkinson's speech at the Kiwanis Club urging the formation of a League of White Supremacy. "That," he scoffed, "had no practical significance. It merely served as a warning to some Negroes to, er, retain the status quo." State Senator James Simpson, urbane, suave, articulate to the point of eloquence, "the ablest Tory of them all," I had heard, spoke with the solid confidence of power. Attorney for the biggest interests of the state, his office in the city's biggest skyscraper, overlooked the industrial terrain like a high outpost of a defending army. From his windows I sad Red Mountain smoking, turning out the steel which brought Birmingham to the fore. A political opponent of "Judge" Wilkinson, he berated the proposition to form a newfangled Klan. But he supported Governor Dixon's defiance of Roosevelt's Executive Order 8802, which declared the Negroes' right to equal employment in war industry. "No," he responded with finality, the Negro was not the issue. At stake, he said coldly, "are the sovereign rights of the State of Alabama." I outlined my views drawn from my first-hand observations; he listened carefully, his shrewd eyes veiled, measuring me. When I concluded he said with deliberation, "I believe you must realize this, sir. We cannot allow Washington to cram legislation down the throat of Alabama, on the pretext of winning the war."

The pretext of winning the war . . . ! A chilling phrase, demonstrating the man's scale of values counterposing victory to the grant of rights to Negroes. Truly, as my friend Tompkins, said, "bad dogs the good," and these men of power stood guard over the old South, watchdogs ready to leap at the new. Indeed, as he put it, there was a "tug-of-war," the pull of titanic forces.

* an unusually good piece of writing and observations – This alone should have prevented the Browder revisionism –

17

To a Beloved Ragamuffin

AND FINALLY, AFTER winding north again through the grain states, across Nebraska's seas of wheat billowing endlessly like golden waves, over the peaks of the Rockies, down through the wild, tawny Southwest, I came to Los Angeles—vast, garish, aquiver with energy. The City of Angels at war. I walked the neon streets of the endless metropolis that churned and eddied with crowds of newcomers from the forty-eight states. At the bus depot I saw the Greyhounds disgorging men, women, children, of every race and national origin: Negroes from the deep South, dark-skinned immigrants in stiff, yellow, brand-new shoes, the frightened women bearing nursing babies at the breast, the older children trailing behind, grasping one another's hand, too timid to look about them; Okies and Arkies, sandy-haired, tall and gaunt so often, loose of limb and of speech, in from the Ozarks, Steinbeck's Joads of a later migration; round-faced, swarthy Mexicans in wide-brimmed sombreros whose fathers, I mused, may have ridden with Pancho Villa; long-striding farmhands whose blue eyes and fair skins spoke of Scandinavian heritage—all flocking to the industries creating the stuff for war.

The girded might of our nation was, somehow, most palpable in this city of blue skies and palm fronds, which seemed to forego sleep. Every hour, daytime or night, men and women in those shapeless, industrial overalls and tin helmets were walking, driving or jamming the busses on their way to work, their hours merging in a production schedule that displaced the sidereal day. I spoke with hundreds, in the coffee-pots, at the factory gates, in the taverns, on the streets, savored the flavor of their lives and found it good. Men who handled the hoe and plow yesterday on the western and southern slopes of the continent today clambered over the tilted wings of giant bombers, mastering the instruments of the time, the pneumatic drill, the rivet gun, the fierce acetylene torch. My fingers could almost touch the social process of the proletarianization Marx and Engels forecast a century before; my eyes beheld the majestic metamorphosis of society. The tiller of the land, solitary since Hesiod, becoming the *masse-mensch* Ernst Toller apostrophised—the man of the masses, shedding the baggage of centuries, his fear of the new. Everywhere on the streets I heard whites of all origins and Negroes, exchanging amenities, friendly sallies, observations, ideas, in the rough camaraderie city life imposes—the flat, mid-continent drawl replying to the soft, slurred southern accent.

And yet, everywhere on my journey, the new contained within it the old—like a bright day of early spring when the sun suddenly surrenders to clouds bearing snow. In the midst of this surge of commonality, the ancient racism jealously lifted its dagger, for the day after I arrived mobs of "Anglos" assaulted Americans of Mexican origin in the notorious "zoot-suit riots," as the headlines called them, pursuing their prey through the streets and beating them without mercy, singling out those dubbed *"pachucos,"* youngsters who wore clothes of an unorthodox cut. News of the racist outbreaks sounded on Tokyo's short-wave within hours, sounded across all Asia, damaging our cause inestimably. How many times, I reflected bitterly, was I to witness the horror I had first seen in 1919 when the barbarous Kluxers pursued Negro children through the streets of my home town?

I sought out the *"pachucos,"* Mexican boys in their teens who wore the tight-cuffed trousers and broad-shouldered jackets that ostensibly enraged their tormentors. Their raiment was no more bizarre to my eye than the loose, high-cuffed trousers the boys at Yale affected, but these were the sons of immigrants at the bottom rung of society, hence their indulgence of youth's flamboyant taste was something peculiarly sinister. The Hearst newspapers described them as "packs of thrill-killers" in the sickeningly familiar jargon of the front-page headlines. How ardently such a press perpetuates the worst of our nation's prejudices, sows the dissentient seed to reap its immoral growth in circulation and dividends.

That night I spoke to Alvah Bessie, my old friend of Spain, whose letters I had meticulously mailed to his sons. He was here now writing movie scripts for Hollywood, and I discovered the same, curmudgeony Alvah, whose tart, acrimonious manner was belied by the kindly pair of luminous blue eyes that sparked under the high bald forehead. As I could have suspected, he knew the picture, and was, as a matter of fact, an ardent member of a committee of film writers aiding victims in the Sleepy Lagoon case. It was a *cause celêbre* of the region, wherein some seventeen *"pachucos"* faced possible death penalties on murder charges manufactured by a hostile District Attorney's office. Alvah had carefully compiled a reference file of newspaper clippings on the case from which he read to me, his voice rasping that articulate indignation so characteristic of him. He seemed always to be in a state of combustion, incapable, as he was, of encountering injustice coolly. So I remembered him on Hill 666 in Spain, and as drama critic and now as film writer. And I loved him all the more for it.

The first clipping he read reported that Karl Holton, of the Los Angeles Probation Department, insisted that "no wave of lawlessness" existed "among Mexican children." Less, in fact, than among other of the city's categories. "But," Alvah sputtered, "the bastards who do the dirty work are the Hearst papers and characters in the prosecution's office, like this cannibal Edward Duran Ayres." Alvah read from a speech that official had delivered before a jury trying the Mexican boys; it began with the proposition that "The biological basis is the main basis to work from." The police-anthropologist mesmerized the twelve good men and true by his description of ancient Aztecs "given to human sacrifice. As many as 30,000 Indians would be offered up to the heathen gods in one day, their bodies opened by stone knives and their hearts torn out while still beating." This "total disregard for human life," Ayres, the cop, concluded, "has always been universal throughout the Americas among the Indian population, a fact well known to everyone."

That, Alvah snorted, his bald forehead wrinkling in despair, "passes for science in this war against the *Uebermensch.*" Naturally the jury of Anglo-Saxon origin was affected as it turned its gaze upon the strong Indian features of the youngsters in the dock. "Where," Alvah demanded oratorically, "is the outcry of civilized men?" The next evening he took me to a protest meeting in Hollywood where many civilized men of the film colony opposed these shibboleths smacking of Nuerenberg and Goebbels. At the meeting, which was jammed to the windows,

I heard the outcry Alvah demanded. Men and women long maligned by the press as profligates squandering fabulous salaries in orgies of licentious brawls, revealed a zealous decency and patriotic elan. Emerson and Thoreau of old Concord would have welcomed them as kin, I reflected, yet to avow that in public the newspapers would have laughed you out of court.

I could not have come across the continent to Hollywood without a journey through the movie-lots, I told Alvah, and he replied dourly that I was like every other smiling, slap-happy yokel who could scarcely await the grand moment when he could go gaping through the never-never land of Metro-Goldwyn-Mayer and the rest. And since none are more profoundly bumpkin than the New Yorkers, naturally I too must do the sights like every breathless tourist. Yes, I said, that was true. All right, he replied wearily, he'd arrange it. He telephoned a director I once met back East and made the appointment for my filmic hegira.

The director was a slim, immaculately-clothed man with a thin, angular sensitive face. He guided me through the wooden streets of a wild and woolly Western town of Billy the Kid's day, replete with an assortment of bars which looked as though each should be called "The Last Chance Saloon." Suddenly we slid back to Lincoln's time to walk the Civil War streets of old Atlanta, promenading along Peachtree Avenue past the statues of black stable-boys in jockey's caps who held out their hands for the reins of the dappled gray; then, incongruously, we stood on a platform overlooking the Athens of Socrates' time, the ersatz Acropolis of wood high on a height; past many imposing cameras and all the mysterious apparatus for sound, the accoutrements of the billion dollar industry which registers the art of the actor. I mused over the fantastically intricate machinery required to register the art of the film: to capture a smile, a tear, the laugh of a man.

Viewing it all, I marveled aloud, wondering how something so fragile and tender as a work of art can grow in this confected megalopolis. The director reminded me of films like "Grapes of Wrath," and "Juarez," and "The Informer," of "Mr. Deeds Goes to Town," and now the latest masterpiece, he said, "Action in the North Atlantic," which John Howard Lawson had written. At least a score more he cited were touched by genius and humanity.

The director who was, I knew, an adherent of Marx, argued thus: true, the cinema art was Big Business, more so than the legitimate stage or the publishing of books. Certainly the Chase National Bank which captured the industry would tolerate no heretical art portraying the reality of wealth and of poverty; its principal motif was to make money. But if the public would clamor for a better film, the bankers and their willing (or unwilling) satraps, the producers and the directors, would respond, and many of them would do so gladly. During a requisite political climate such as the New Deal, and, as today, the circumstances of a just and necessary war, we could win an improved cinema. As an instance he cited "Action in the North Atlantic," portraying the simple and timeless heroism of our seamen, members of the CIO's National Maritime Union, who carried on through the hells of bombers and submarines. If the public demanded such films, the bankers would yield, reluctantly, but inevitably, for the box-office was the arbiter. But the public manifested a sorry sloth. Why has labor failed to throw its mighty mass against the moguls?

Perhaps, I replied tentatively, Hollywood's bad art—far outweighing its achievements—had already corrupted the public's standards. "You," he cried indignantly, "a Marxist to say that?" Had I forgotten the WPA days when the public responded enthusiastically to the classics in art and the theater? The common man readily adopted Bach, Beethoven, Debussy which the unemployed musicians "on the dole" offered them. Did I forget the acclaim greeting the murals of Benton and Gropper and Refregier? I dare not return East, he said passionately, without visiting San Francisco and see Refregier's murals of California's history. Had I forgotten the response to the honest realism of "The Living Newspaper," or to Orson Welles' version of Shakespeare's "Julius Caesar"? Give people an art that illumines their lives and you will see how phony this "degraded taste" theory is.

I found his views so congenial, his passionate convictions so infectious, that I gladly accepted an invitation to dine at his home. Home was a sumptuous (to me, at least) establishment, beautifully appointed, overlooking the grand expanse of San Fernando Valley. Paintings of the masters hung on the walls, and he mixed a cocktail from a well-stocked bar tucked into the living room—the accoutrements, I thought, of $100,000 a year. This man, I mused, enjoyed a wealth few could imagine, certainly very few from among those he favored, like, say, the seamen of Lawson's film. How could he retain his undeniable integrity?

I knew enough of men who lost their ideals in the fleshpots, a story as old as Esau. Through the evening I learned, too, that he came from no world like mine. His father, a prosperous garment manufacturer, had sent him to Princeton; he had gone on to the Sorbonne, studying literature, mainly the French classics—Voltaire, Balzac, Stendhal, Baudelaire, Anatole France—his favorites. Fired by the honesty of the young, he recoiled at the insanity of the depression and in the course of those years he encountered men whose intelligence and humanity he respected, and discovered to his confusion that they were Marxists—a phenomenon Princeton had scarcely prepared him for. He opened the books they lauded, Marx, Engels, all the classics, consuming long nights in their pages, absenting himself from the company of his fraternity brothers. "And so I chose Marxism." He could not join the Communist Party, pleading an aversion to the discipline of organization. But he regarded himself as "a confirmed adherent of the Marxist philosophy" which gave him, as he said, "the key to history." I studied his thin, angular face, the glow of his eyes, noted the heady fervor with which he spoke: no, this man was not deluding himself, nor me, as he professed his allegiance to this heresy, while he sat in a luxurious arm-chair.

Wealth, of itself, is not necessarily the thief of integrity among men of certain conviction. Zola, established in fame and social position, persisted, defending the Jew Dreyfuss, chose voluntary exile to injustice. Before him Karl Marx, son of a prosperous father, himself the graduate of a foremost univer·ity, willingly forsook comfort and status for social truth and justice. And before him, Robert Owen, one of the wealthy industrialists of his day, abandoned his privileged world to champion a humane way of life embodied in the ideas of Utopian Socialism. But sympathy for the oppressed, even a passion for their advancement, is not ultimately decisive. It needs coupling with program, with philosophy, with a solution—before a man would act and clothe his naked emotion. Sympathy is of the heart: program, philosophy, of the mind: marry the two and men like this is the issue.

How could I leave Hollywood without a visit of homage to Charlie Chaplin, whose comic genius I admired beyond that of any living artist—the poor man's Aristophanes? His vagabond of the outsized feet, patched trousers, his pretentious but battered derby and ridiculous cane was as much my boyhood companion as Huckleberry Finn. I remembered a generation of children, puarticularly those of the poor, who joyously aped his walk, shuffling along, with occasional little hops, twirling imaginary canes. I had seen the gamins of Cuatro Caminos in Madrid imitate their idol a few moments before the Junkers and Capronis came. They dubbed him Carlitos, in the affectionate diminutive, as they would a beloved member of the family. His "City Lights" drew long queues to the Madrid theater at the moment Generalissimo Franco's Moroccan cavalrymen waited across the Manzanares for the signal to enter triumphantly.

This genius enabled men to transcend their woes, gave them the gift of the gods, laughter, without which homo sapiens could never have made it. I had religiously attended every picture he filmed to see his satire which revealed a tender affection for all earthlings enchained by poverty: the minstrel of the Twentieth Century.

Few contemporaries enjoyed so much praise—and fewer still were subjected to as much scorn. Journalistic wiseacres were repelled by his effrontery when he dared to argue politics and economics with Winston Churchill. The nerve of the clown! —and they raked over his private affairs mercilessly. But fame he had and wealth. Most men can withstand adversity better than they can endure adulation: our world is so arranged that hardship, the common lot of mankind, renders a man close kin to his fellows whereas success isolates him. Peasants long ago observed that a full belly cannot understand the empty one, as an old Slavic adage has it, but *Carlitos* kicked up his heels at misfortune as he eluded the club-wielding cops, chasing him not because he was a felon but because he was a pauper—the most heinous of crimes. Rich as Croesus according to the newspaper gendarmerie which dogged him remorselessly, he never lost the common touch—at least in his films. Something indestructibly good must persist in the graceful frame of this little Cockney who said perversely, according to our scorning press, that he was a citizen of the world. Like all stage-struck *aficionados,* I hoped to get a close-up glimpse of him and learn, possibly, something of his nature.

My telephone call resulted in an invitation to dinner that evening. I had, of course, expected to find him in lush surroundings, yet I was disconcerted by his imposing home, a Georgian mansion I associated with English nobility whose green lawns required four hundred years of cultivation. As the august butler let me in I reflected on the changed fortune of this erstwhile indigent vaudevillian of Britain's provincial stage. Charlie, handsome, urbane, of middle height, met me with his familiar radiant smile, the white teeth agleam in the sensitive face whose astonishing eyes could register fright, sorrow, wonder, joy—the gamut of universal emotion.

At his side stood a young woman of a dark, somber beauty, his wife, Oona O'Neill, the daughter of Eugene O'Neill. Chairley's hair was gray, his age twice and more hers, yet his boyish, gay and light-hearted air matched her youth so that they seemed happily companionate. He had looked forward to meeting the editor of the *New Masses,* he said in welcome, for he had known its predecessors, the *Liberator* and the old *Masses* which he had read "with relish and profit." Although he regretted the absence of "that carefree, go-to-hell air the earlier magazine had," he still awaited it expectantly, for it published "facts from a Marxist viewpoint" which men concerned with truth should know.

Over a decanter of wine in the huge living room he inquired about my journeys across the country and I offered my observations. On the whole, then, he responded with satisfaction, "You would say the democratic spirit is definitely ascendant?" Yes, that was my opinion, despite the brutality of racism I encountered so frequently, and the stubborn persistence of "business-as-usual" among the wealthiest class. "You see, Oona," he said gleefully slipping an arm about her shoulder, "That's what I told you. Oona," he turned to me, "worried about that Sleepy Lagoon case, these zoot-suit riots, how much there was of that in the country." He had assured her that though such outbreaks were inherent in the scene, "as of today," inevitable "in a competitive society," history was on a forward march. Barbarism will live at our side a long time, but, thank God, we would live to bury it.

Throughout the evening he impressed me with his buoyant optimism, speaking, as he put it, as "an old timer," revealing facts of his past I had not known. "I am no politician," he shrugged, "only a clown," but it was evident that he had astutely kept abreast of politics through his personal associations and his readings. He knew intimately Jim Larkin, the Irish labor leader, and Big Bill Haywood, the giant, one-eyed miners' leader who became a founder of the IWW, the Wobblies, and later, a Communist, dying, a political refugee, in Moscow. Charley recalled that he had helped to provide bail money for Haywood who needed bail so damned often. Tom Mooney, too, corresponded with Chaplin for years and had his admiration and his help.

The actor described himself as a disciple of Lincoln Steffens, and like his master, an old friend, he had welcomed the advent of the first nation of socialism, the USSR whose course since October he had studied, and respected. "It is, as old Stef said, 'the future' and it is proving that socialism 'works'." If he, Chaplin, needed further proof, the Soviet cinema afforded it.

The surest guage to the culture of a modern nation is the film, and "we have never even approached Eisenstein and Pudovkin in daring and depth"—whose works were an earnest, he said, that there would be Shakespeares and Tolstoys of the celluloid. He had informed the Soviet artists of his admiration and now "we have a kind of mutual admiration society." In fact, each Soviet freighter docking at San Pedro sent a delegation offering greetings and gifts.

He became so imbued with his story that he began unconsciously to act it out, describing the hesitance and shyness of the customary trio of seamen who came to his house. There was an odd tenderness as he depicted their astonishment at the magnificence of his abode, their stolen glances at the furnishings and their bewildered skepticism as they looked back at him for assurance that they had the right man now that he was stripped of his ragged shoes, mustache, and cane. The last delegation that came a fortnight before struggled up the steps with an enormous decanter of *Zubrovka,* a seventy-year-old brand of vodka, the container standing five feet high and three feet across and he took me into an adjoining room to point it out. "Bless them," he said, and he pantomimed the little speech the spokesman had made, a young, squat sailor with the slanted eyes of Asia, who said that they represented the working class of the socialist Soviet Union, and "in this gift we wish to express our love for an artist whose works we love for they are on the side of the world's toilers and the downtrodden." A previous delegation led a baby panda into the house. Chaplin had an enclosure built for it on his estate; several months later he had gone out to inspect it and discovered it had grown alarmingly, and his gift chased him over the fence. The master of pantomime emerged as, telling his tale, he stooped to stroke a baby panda, like a kitten, his eyes full of tenderness that widened suddenly into astonishment as he beheld what might have been a giant grizzly: his eyes wide now, reflecting horror as he fled comically across the room.

After the laughter he turned serious again, disclaiming any pretensions to the status of philosopher or scholar, but he had read history and this he knew: mankind had stumbled up the stair of time into the age of the ordinary man, and somehow, all his life he had known it would. He who had come from poverty, and had for decades mingled with the rich, realized the "plutocrat" had no "God-given gift of superior intelligence," for he had known many a penniless, obscure man who "could match brains with any of them." As a youth he concluded that society, not unalterable fate, brought the misery he observed everywhere.

As he carved the roast beef in the handsome wainscoated dining room, he told a story of his past, when he first encountered the ideas of socialism. One day, crossing Hyde Park, he stopped to listen to an orator on a soapbox. The man's gestures, not his words, had caught his attention, for the speaker's arms flailed violently "like the sails of a windmill in a storm." Interest in the man's gymnastics departed as the words penetrated. The young Chaplin, fascinated, remained to the end of the speech. "Are we men or are we mice?" the orator concluded after denouncing the passivity or fear of men and Charley departed for his lodging house pondering that question. His initiation at Hyde Park induced him to heed the conversation of workingmen he met in the lonely provincial travels and he found himself purchasing and reading socialistic literature. Soon afterward he knew that a giant of the theater, George Bernard Shaw, advocated the ideas of Karl Marx, and later he noted that the writers he most admired, Anatole France and Romain Rolland, regarded socialism as the key to mankind's salvation. Hollywood, he regretted, is not noted for its hospitality to such ideas and ignores the fact that the "greatest artists favored social changes—Moliere, Voltaire, Schiller, Tolstoy were enemies of the status quo." His unorthodox ideas were confirmed by the testimony of the wisest of men and so, although he had acquired his share of wealth, he had never abandoned his point of view.

"And now," he said, "we've got a war on our hands." He asked my opinion of the chances for a Western Front, which, he was certain, victory demanded. He had not only read *New Masses* on that crucial matter, but many other publications, and he had listened to men whose opinions he respected. The new front was already feasible, as well as imperative. And though the newspapers believed that a comedian somehow abdicated his rights to a viewpoint, to politics, he had no hesitance to speak his mind. So convinced was he that, it turned out, he flew to New York not long afterward to speak on the matter at a Carnegie Hall meeting which called for the opening of the Western Front. And, of course, he received a hostile response in the press which ridiculed "the clown who presumed to tell generals how to run the war." I met him briefly after the meeting and he said lightly, "They're giving me hell and I tell them what Clemenceau said about wars being too serious to be left to the generals."

I think of Chaplin often, and the place of satirists in our culture. Our nation, and an Emancipator loved a sharp-eyed funny man named Artemus Ward whose works Abe read to a Cabinet that recoiled at this literary exercise as the nadir of frivolous caprice. Later we revered Mark Twain and chuckled over Peter Finley Dunne's loquacious but sage bartender Mr. Dooley. All peoples, since the days of Aristophanes, display a tender reverence for their satirists, those artists who dare to prick the hides of the lordly and to demonstrate that kings can be naked. The art, here, has declined disastrously in recent times, for ours is a thin-skinned regency even though it has relinquished ermine and velvet. Where, since the business royalists and their newspapers have driven Chaplin from our shores is there another? I am certain such talents walk the land, I have heard their private observations and witnessed their parlor performances—but they are denied the public platforms, of press, radio, television, movies or stage. The art of lampooning avoids that target which is the greatest of all themes—the inhumanity of privileged might. Oh, General Motors can evidence enormous forbearance when one of its own amateur satirists compares workingmen to hunting dogs but it is spectacularly ungrateful to satirists who have the temerity to direct a shaft toward its sensitive skin. Consider the consternation in the skyscraper offices if say, Jackie Gleason or Sid Caesar insisted on producing a M. Verdoux or a Mr. Dooley on the General Motors hour. The comedians would be considered bereft of their senses and deprived of an audience even in Keokuk or Tallahassee.

Several years after my evening with Chaplin I happened to discuss his art with Louis Aragon, the French poet and novelist whom I met in London and who was, also, a fervent admirer of the comedian. I told Aragon the story of a Filipino writer who came to *New Masses'* office in 1945 eager to "shake hands with the editors" of his "favorite" magazine whose pages he had read since his early youth. When Manila, his home town, was declared an open city as the Japanese advanced, he frantically gathered together all the books in his library that revealed any concern for social welfare and burned them in the dark of night. Marx made an alarmingly bright blaze. Tolstoy, Shaw, Zola, France, Dreiser, went into the bonfire as he controlled his tears. He came to two books that he found impossible to burn. "It would have been like burning my children." Naturally I speculated on their titles, but I confess I could never have guessed right. One was *Redder Than the Rose,* a collection of satiric essays by Robert Forsythe, a *New Masses* writer in the Thirties, and the other, a book of drawings by William Gropper, who is, in my estimate, the Daumier of our time. The Filipino dug a deep hole and buried the two books for disinterment if he survived. "Why?" I asked curiously, taken by the story, "didn't you do the same say, for Marx, or Tolstoy?" He shook his head, "I have wondered about that myself. Like Shaw I could say Marx made a man of me. But these two books made me laugh. Maybe laughter helps a man live."

I also told this story to Forsythe whom I accidentally encountered at a cocktail party some time later: he had resigned from our magazine after the publisher of the big periodical on which he earned his livelihood lay down the law. It was "either the *New Masses* or the job." As I told the story, tears began to form in Forsythe's eyes, this vast man who stood well over six feet with proportionate bulk. "My satire in *New Masses*," he said, "was respected and I respected myself. I got letters from all over the country and the world. I left it for a big slick magazine with a thousand times your circulation and so I became a well-paid, unknown hack. On the little magazine I wrote what I pleased: on the big magazine I wrote to please the advertisers."

18

It Happened in London

I FLEW EAST after this instructive journey that revealed to me an America transforming itself into the arsenal for victory: like men who reveal themselves in crisis, the defects of our democracy emerged more clearly to view. How stubbornly the medieval shibboleths persist, poking their cowled heads through our Twentieth Century life, confirming the observation of the antiquarian, James Henry Breasted, who said, after studying the Egyptian dynasties, that civilization is one hour old.

The advance of science beguiles us as we fly our riveted version of the Magic Carpet through the skies and fondly assume that we are qualitatively different from our remote ancestors who dreamed, like Daedalus, of soaring sun-high on wax wings. We check our luggage at the airport, carrying an antique baggage in our heads. The smart, young woman in gold ear-rings and a silvery stole who sat across the aisle made the sign of the cross, tapping her forehead, shoulders and chest as the plane took off. A few moments afterward she spoke familiarly of headwinds and tailwinds, of Douglasses and DC-7's and their relative merits, speaking with all the authoritative aplomb of a pilot. Soaring above the tawny plains and craggy deserts of Arizona I mentioned the Indian tribes in their adobe dwellings below and humorously she related an experience when, on a summer vacation, she had accidentally driven upon them while they danced their barbaric dance begging the Great Spirit for rain. She was fingering a small medallion that hung about her neck, of St. Christopher who heeds the prayers of travelers seeking safe journey.

Like this lady our civilization is prone to every variety of superstition that lurks beneath the turbines and skyscrapers, the veneer of technology. True, the industrial revolution had brought concomitant revolutions in our social and economic mores, is creating the circumstances that will inevitably bring a socialist transformation. Meanwhile superstitions of race supremacy, of national chauvinism, of religious intolerance, of an infinity of ancient misconceptions and witch-doctor ways of life, die astonishingly hard. Perhaps the most ingrained of all American superstitions is the assumption that the capitalist order constitutes the best of all possible worlds. It was shaken for a time during the early thirties when it failed spectacularly to supply the life needs of our nation, but it was restored by the restoration of our economy which began to improve with the prospects of a universal war that would destroy millions of mankind. The fraternity of varied nations, the international brotherhood of man, was a prerequisite for a sane world of the future.

So I was elated when I picked up a copy of the *New York Times* one morning of December in 1944 to learn that the British trade union movement had invited the world's labor unions to London the following February to consider the creation of a world labor federation. Abe Magil, my associate editor, asked drily if my suitcase was packed; this was one of the war's great moments, perhaps the greatest, and the magazine should be there. He was right: I must be there, to write that story, and if I could, reach the battlefronts to cover the Gotterdammerung of the Nazi pantheon.

All the world's workers banded into one brotherhood! How had Tennyson put it?

Far along the world wide whisper of the south wind
rushing warm,
With the standards of the peoples plunging through
the thunder-storm;
Till the war-drum throbb'd no longer, and the battle
flags were furl'd
In the Parliament of man, the Federation of the world.

The parliament of man . . . if this gathering in London was not yet it, it certainly was the prelude. By God, I had to get there. The magazine, of course, as ever, lacked means, but our readers had their way of responding. Again we scurried about, sounded them out, and again we could make it. The finances assured, I filled out endless forms for travel in wartime, in duplicate, triplicate, quadruplicate; name, place of birth, age, why, when, for whom, how long, what intention. And moreover, the Government said, I must have the endorsement of a dozen responsible citizens for my trip. I ran here, there, wrote letters to eminent citizens I knew and who knew me to vouch for my existence, my intention, my honor. Charlie Chaplin wrote, A. F. Whitney, head of the Trainmen, wrote, Theodore Dreiser wrote, a round dozen of "notables," and finally I had my passport.

I was to appear at a certain dock at a certain hour, carrying my precious copy of the quadruplicates—and the receipt for my passage money, of course. So, on a bright, frosty January dawn, suitcase in hand, I walked down the road from my little home, took a long lingering backward look at the cottage amid the black bare oaks, the snow on the hills, thinking of the family within. . . .

The low-lying Liberty ship I boarded lay in dock near the Battery on Manhattan. I slept fitfully the first night out, and when I awoke I went on deck and saw a sight no eyes had seen until our time. Ships stretched from horizon to horizon, east, west, north, south, dark pawns on a green checkerboard, spaced in the center of equal squares about a mile apart. They rolled gently on, slowly, deliberately, under the bright winter sky: a convoy of ninety-six ships were visible to my awed eyes.

Several days later the spokesman for the ship's local of the National Maritime Union, a gnarled, middle-aged man with a mop of gray hair approached me as I stood on deck and invited me to speak to the crew about the forthcoming conference. The ship's purser had noticed my name on the passenger list of seven, and knowing the *New Masses,* passed the word on. A member of the crew who read the magazine had seen the announcement of my trip to the labor congress. Of course, I would be glad to speak.

The crew, off-duty, sat in the jammed mess-room in their dungarees, a score of young men, a few grizzled old-timers among them. They listened intently through the throbbing of the engines. When I finished, the gnarled man read the resolution of the CIO that had accepted the invitation of the British unionists to attend. There were questions, answers, and the chairman proposed a cable to London: "We, the crew of the S.S. ———, wish you all the success in the world. A peaceful world after victory requires world labor unity." A swift show of hands accepted it unanimously.

A trim engineer, cap aslant on a handsome young head, sought me out when he was off-duty. The London conference was on his mind, and it was an energetic mind, probing, zestful, alert. He also talked about Communists he had met on the Brooklyn waterside where he was reared: they seemed "wacky" to him, he said, baiting me. They came down to Red Hook, set up a stand to harangue the gangster-ridden waterfront; he had seen the gangsters rip them from the stand, "beat the living hell out of them," and they returned, the next time and the next. They had guts, he grinned, but he was damned if he could understand them half the time. He was not given to martyrdom, he laughed. "What's in it for *them?*" Nobody does anything for nothing; some material consideration was in the picture, "what's the payoff?"

He could understand getting your head knocked off trying to build a trade union; that made sense because out of the effort came higher wages and the sole defense a workingman had. But Communists were impossible to satisfy: "They want the earth and the moon thrown in, with this socialism of theirs." It would never work, he said with all the certitude of twenty-five and a gamin-like cockiness.

We had many talks in the twenty-four long days and nights at sea in the slow-moving convoy proceeding through dangerous waters, the destroyers racing like shepherd's watchdogs about the ships, plumbing the waters for the schnorkels which were somewhere nearby. The young engineer shook his gay, boyish head scornfully as I answered, puzzling me by his instant rejections. He manifested a quick comprehension of all matters but those pertaining to Marxist philosophic objectives about which he grilled me. I had no original intention to discuss them with him, but he returned to them again and again with questions such as, "You call yourself materialists: how can you explain the creation of matter?" Or, "You deny that sin is inherent in Man, how do you explain the war we're in, or the fact that we've always had wars, have them, and always will have them." He talked, elbows on the rail, gazing into the sea which fascinated him endlessly, as he indicated: the deeps contained mysteries no man could fathom, and hence, proof, for him, that the God Marxists denied, existed. I had delineated my understanding of dialectical materialism and he had stared at me, his clear, alert eyes widening with mock astonishment.

I asked, at one point if he had studied for the priesthood and somewhat startled, he admitted that he had been an altar boy at the Roman Catholic church in the parish that included Red Hook, which, I remembered, received its religious and political instructions from Father Curran, editor of the *Brooklyn Tablet,* a vigorous disciple of Father Coughlin. This priest, who described himself as an inveterate foe of Communism, had encouraged him to adopt the priesthood and my friend responded zealously. But he abandoned his resolve after two years at Fordham when he discovered, he said, that he lacked the stuff for the holy life. Born into a sea-going family, he preferred to follow the mast. But he retained his interest in matters ecclesiastical and hence, long felt a curiosity about Marxists who denied, he understood, everything that he regarded as sacred. I tried to disabuse him of the notion that Marxism is the diametric opposite of the Church: we advocated the right to religious freedom, but he smiled superciliously. "Not that I would call a man a liar," he retorted, "but some men take as gospel everything the Commissars tell them. And it seems to me you're one." As a matter of fact he felt, I sensed, that I was an honest fellow, but he said, I was too gullible, begging my pardon. "I talked to some of those fellows who came down to Red Hook to get beat up hunting martyrdom to advertise their Party"; these, he insisted, boasted their hatred for the Mother Church, its clergy and its faithful whom they would "liquidate" once they achieved power. Nor could I dissuade him. I cited various clergymen like the Rev. Hewlett Johnson, the Dean of Canterbury, who attest to the right of worship in the Soviet Union and he dismissed such testimony indicating, without specifically saying so, that no Catholic priest had written similarly and hence the avowals were worthless. He was indeed a dogmatic young fellow (I have found that the alleged dogmatism of Communists is certainly no monopoly of theirs), but he was engaging in his manner, quick of retort, which he expressed in the inimitable vernacular of Brooklyn. He revealed the admiration I encountered everywhere on my travels for "the Russkies" as fighting men, "as good as any the way they've stood up to Hitler," and he regretted that they had been deluded by the Bolshies, "Satan's priests on earth." Nationalism, not

Communism, explained their heroism. He had all the pat answers of the anti-Communist dogmatists.

One night as we stood on deck watching the silver of the moon shimmering on the sea, the inexpressible beauty of the earth's solitude, he swept his hands wide, and laughing, said: "All right, your dialectical materialism argues that matter is indestructible, that it always was and always will be. Look out there now and tell me how that happened without a Supreme Intelligence. Some things are beyond reason, and if you can look at that and still deny Faith, I surrender you to the flames you will deserve." There was indisputable poetry in that young head which was, at once, devout and irreverent. Irreverent, I insisted, because he lacked faith in Man, demanded to know "the payoff" for example, that induced Communists to come back again after they had "had their blocks knocked off by the waterfront gangsters." But Man, he retorted, was a compound of unfathomable contradictions: Adam, created by God, was perpetually wooed by Satan. Several times I repeated my determination to avoid theological debate, but he drew me on, provocatively, insisting that the explanation of my philosophy compelled him to counter with his, the Teachings. "Let's keep it clean," I insisted finally, "and talk about mundane things —trade unions, for example. Is there room in the unions for all faiths including those of no faith?" "Okay," he agreed, "Let's call it a draw. I can't get you to see the Light and you can't convince me that Marx and Stalin are latter-day saints." We concluded on that note but a moment afterward as a dolphin leaped across the waves catcing our eye with its serene grace he waved a grateful hand across the railing, commenting, "Let your dialectical materialism explain that."

Yet we remained friends, for he seemed to cotton to me, drawn perhaps by the intriguing mystery of my disbelief, and he invited me to give the intricate vitals of the ship "the once-over." "You say I don't have faith in Man," he taunted, "Come see what Man made." The world of machinery moving with such magical precision, the vast boilers and turbines throbbing like the organs of a vast sea animal seemed to fascinate him as well as it did me. He stood on the iron platform, hands on his hips, surveying the maze of steel and gleaming brass like a young mother appraising her child. I sensed the workingman's pride in the machinery he had mastered, that he alone can work, not those who have the juridical deed to the property. Yet, withal, that bright, cocky head of his could not imagine a time when those who work the machinery could own it, so ingrained is the superstitious sanctity of private ownership.

The ninth night out the Atlantic unfolded a magnificent spectacle: the wailing wind churned the sea into great, angry waves that rocked the ship violently. I gave up lying on my bunk trying to read Clausewitz's *On War* that Robert Minor gave me as a gift on my departure, inscribing it to "A Fellow War Correspondent." In the messroom I found my six fellow-passengers had preceded me, sitting around the long table, their heads bent toward the young engineer in argument. They had avoided me, had not gone beyond the amenities, and I assumed they too read the purser's list of passengers and knew I was from the *New Masses,* and they were either government officials or some sort of businessmen. Okay, I thought, like the miller of Dee, who sang, "I care for nobody, no, not I—if nobody cares for me," and kept my dignified distance.

As I stepped inside I heard the young Brooklynite say angrily, "Labor has a right to join with whoever the hell it pleases; Communists, too, if they play the game." The voices died down as I appeared, and one of the passengers glanced, embarrassed, in my direction. "What do you mean they'll dominate us?" the young engineer's voice continued, his back to me, unaware of my presence. "What do you think we are, school kids?" I was in so far I could not retreat, and though the conversation did not include me, I felt involved, of course. As I considered my course, a tremendous wave, the first of many giants, crashed onto the upper deck and sent a cascade of water tumbling into the messroom, scattering the passengers, rolling them around the room. I rose drenched, as an alarm bell sounded imperiously and the young engineer leaped to his feet and bounded away, a queer expression on his face. The ship began to quiver in a strange, unaccustomed trembling and the passengers glanced toward each other with apprehensive surmise. The wind howled outside, a rejected giant demanding entry. Another wave cascaded into the messroom and again we went down. This time matters were really getting serious. Outside I heard loud cries and a seaman in his oily poncho ran through the room. The man who had led the argument with the young engineer clutched at the seaman's shoulder. "What's happening?" he cried, but he was shaken off without a reply.

I groped my way to the deck, gripping the rail tightly, managing a precarious footing. About me was an impenetrable icy, rainswept black in which a wild wind strummed the taut cables maniacally. When my eyes became accustomed to the dark I made out a looming shadow a hundred feet or so off the leeward side. My heart leaped, these ships carried cargoes for war, explosive-laden doubtless, and a seaman had said jocularly, "If we ever sideswipe one of them bastards," pointing to the ship a mile off, "it's sweet Jesus, brother, for us all." Was it to be sweet Jesus? All about me I felt the shadowy shapes of the men clambering about the deck, the black void filled by the gale's roar and now and then a man shouted, his words drowned by the crashing volume of sound. No ship dared flash a light for the storm was not their sole enemy, if anything, it was their least, for we were approaching Cemetery Lane where Doenitz's torpedoes were well within distance. It was a distinctly unpleasant prospect. Yet I was not really afraid: if anything, I was awe-struck by the fury of nature that I had read of so often but as I saw now, never comprehended, so feeble are the best of words. I could not envisage the Liberty going down, nor even, though the danger was at our elbow, almost literally, could I believe the two ships would smash together. It had happened, of course, often enough, but I had a greater confidence in the gleaming machinery down below and in the quiet, confident men to whom I had spoken. I had survived too many bombings in Spain to believe that my number was up.

After about an hour the ship stopped trembling, and the young engineer re-appeared, his face streaked with grease, his nattiness gone, but a triumphant smile lit his face. "Okay," he laughed and ran on. Though the storm continued in its crescendo, the ship proceeded with its customary roll. The air of tension abated and the passengers breathed easier, like reprieved men. The young engineer turned up, natty again, his boyish grin taunting us, for he refused to enlighten the passengers on the reasons for the past hour's trial. I learned later that collision was averted by a hair's breadth, miraculously, and that the deft work of the crew was responsible.

At mess, the young engineer mischievously addressed the passengers: "Now, as we were saying when we were so rudely interrupted "—and he lashed into them on the score that they regarded workingmen as gullible simpletons who could be led around by the nose. The others sat silent, shamefaced; the implication seemed clear to me: that he and the crew had mastered the crisis that threatened us all and no landlubbers had warrant to advise them on any score. The ship, I reflected, was society—that mastered storms and calamities because laboring men sweated in its hold while their superiors rolled helplessly on the floors. The youngster would not let matters rest. "Yes, American labor should join the federation of trade unions. It is the smartest thing they could do." There was no dissenting voice.

After a stormy voyage of twenty-three days, we came safely through Dead Man's Alley, off the west coast of England and docked in blacked-out Bristol. My young friend shook hands warmly in departure: "I haven't abandoned you to the devil," he laughed. "Don't forget St. Augustine was a worse sinner than you'll ever be." He gave me his address in Brooklyn with an invitation to look him up "when this damn thing is over." I had relished our conversations, realizing that our philosophical differences did not forbid our friendship. He sensed my regard and I hope he concluded that Communists and Catholics can walk as brother-earthlings ignoring our disagreements on the Hereafter. After all, in the clutch, as we say, he and I agreed on the Here—the need for a world fraternity of labor.

London, vast, a city of endless brick and stone, drab beneath the gray fog and "austerity," had an air of incalculable grandeur. I had scarcely arrived at the cavernous Paddington station in a chilly dawn hour when I heard a distant rumble and crash and Londoners murmured, "V-2's," proceeding calmly on their way. Their ears were attuned to the distinctions between the two current varieties of bombs, the V-1's and the V-2's, rhythms of death, easy enough to discern I discovered. An hour later I saw a V-1 putter through the skies, like a winged motorboat chug-chugging overhead, the chaser planes of the Royal Air Force scurrying after the pilotless intruder. The V-1 chugged over the rooftops and with crazy abandon the motor cut out and the flying bomb crashed down. There was no way to judge its course or its objective: it had none except to float somewhere, anywhere over the great metropolis and dive to destroy as many women, children and men as its explosives could reach. The V-2 had even less logic, save that it multiplied havoc, traveled with a speed beyond sound, a rocket longer than a telephone pole that arched across the Channel to be heard only after it brought its desolation.

I passed a dozen children on their way to school and watched them press against a wall carrying the poster of a movie I had recently seen in New York—"A Tree Grows in Brooklyn"—which drew me as though they were my own dear brood. Multiply this bomb a thousand times, make it a way of life for four years, and you began to understand how London lived since the first big Blitz. But this was the final thrashing spasm of the monster: daily the Beaverbrook papers and the others described the shrinking fronts that hemmed Hitler in, the surge eastward of the western allies as the Red Army galloped westward to Berlin. But you felt a people panting for the war to end, and, I wondered, would this be the end of war for all time.

The answer, I believed, lay in London's City Hall where the conference of the world's trade unions was to be held. A great, gray granite structure on the Thames, with that obdurate solidity common to many London public buildings, it reflected I felt, the might of the British. For Great Britain was not solely, nor was it primarily, the imperialism that held so many lands in thrall for centuries. This was the nation, too, of the warrior queen who died in battle against the Roman invader, the land of Piers Plowman and of Cromwell, of the Chartists, of a working class and a people that had amply justified their eminence among the world's nations. Britain which I learned to abhor as a child, when I fought the Redcoats under my kitchen lamp, became, through the years, my cultural homeland, where Chaucer moved, and Shakespeare, the giant spirits of the Elizabethan age, and later Bunyan and Byron, Shelley, Keats and Burns, Thackeray, Dickens, Hardy, Conrad, Shaw and O'Casey. In Spain I remembered two races of men in the British contingents to the International Brigades—the wiry, slight incredibly hardy proletarians, and the massive red-faced, big-boned recruits from the upper classes, the students from Oxford and Cambridge, built in the image of old Dr. J. B. S. Haldane, that mortal behemoth. I attributed the physical difference to the rigid stratification of the classes. Due to many historic factors, the opportunity to move from lower to higher classes was denied the descendants of the Chartists; the workingman born, died a workingman.

I had a few days to spare before the conference convened and I spent my time well. I sought out my old friend, the late William Rust, then editing the London *Daily Worker,* remembering the many nights I had come upon him in his Barcelona room, the window-shades drawn, writing until dawn, checked only by brief spells for a spot of his unbelievable brackish tea. Here, at the *Daily Worker* offices I saw him labor with the same zestful intensity I remembered from Spain. A gay, witty man who loved music, literature, good conversation and his mug of ale, at his editor's desk he was brisk, efficient, single-minded and aggressive as the cinema imagined an executive of Wall Street to be. He had mastered in incredibly short time the sweep and the minutiae of editing and publishing, and the *Worker,* emerging from under the government ban, set on it early in the war, soon won the admiration of the British journalists I met on Fleet Street. After the day's work I accompanied Bill to several pubs he regularly visited on the way home and noted how the workers, in for a glass before supper, crowded around "Ould Bill" affectionately, asking for the latest news.

And on Fleet Street I met various journalists and editors of London's newspapers, including the famous cartoonist David Low, a stocky, broad-shouldered, whiskered man who knew the *New Masses,* he said, and admired its art work though he could not accept its politics. At dinner he asked many questions of America, and after a while, beetling his great, black eyebrows, he remarked: "Why do you damn Yanks insist on calling yours a young country! Man, you're middle-aged over there. We can't always be treating the States like some bloody adolescent." We, he said, signed our Declaration of Independence over a century and a half ago, by God, and we should be held to account as a mature land. He scorned our Army's attitude toward its Negro soldiers and recounted his favorite story of the day: two old codgers outside a pub watched a detachment of GI's swing by and one old Briton asked the other, 'I say, Jock, how do you like the Yanks?' The other, puffing reflectively on his pipe, replied, 'Fine, but why did they bring the white ones with them?' "

I heard similar comments from many men, on the streets, in the pubs, on the trams, realizing again the depth of skepticism about our democracy we had engendered by our benighted Jim Crow policies. They regarded us as arch-hypocrites, we who vociferously boasted that ours was the land of the free. One day, on a tram, I overheard a white Southerner remonstrate against a Negro GI seated nearby, and the conductor, a young, buxom woman clapped a stern hand on the southerner's shoulder: "I'm sorry, mister," she said coldly, "This is London, not Alabama."

Harry Pollitt, secretary of the British Communist Party, a jolly, round-faced, keen-eyed man I met on the fronts in Spain suggested I visit the Rhondda Valley, in Wales, a great coal center, while I awaited the conference opening. I accompanied a comrade who drove out the next morning, and came to the country of low, rolling hills and steep valleys dotted with the ancient stone villages of the miners. I stayed overnight at the home of the regional leader of the Communist Party, a young, jolly, wiry miner who was also the head of the union local, as his father had been before him. Dinner, their best, for the American guest, consisted of a sparse ration of French fried potatoes, two narrow strips of cheese, two pieces of unbuttered toast and a hot cup of tea.

I accompanied the miner to his lodge, as they called their union hall, the center of their recreation as well as their trade union life. Some forty miners sat playing checkers or chess, drinking their thin beer, their custom after each day's work deep underground, and I was welcomed as "the comrade from the States, from *New Masses*," pleased to learn that far off here in the fastnesses of Wales they knew the magazine. A tall, middle-aged miner clapped his hand on my shoulder saying this was the scene of "How Green Is My Valley," an American film they had all seen. The men were bony, great-eyed, hollow of cheek, subsisting evidently on the fare I had noted at dinner, yet they evidenced a remarkable elan and intellectual eagerness. I overheard two men in a quaintly humorous argument debating a point of Hegelian philosophy—when do the quantitative changes in a chicken's egg become qualitative?

My host explained that most of the miners adhered to the Marxist philosophy, although not all were Communists, in fact about half of their number voted Labor. But they lived on friendliest terms, earnestly respecting the other man's right to political difference. That was certainly evident throughout the evening. They mounted an impromptu show in my honor: each was obliged to sing a song, recite a poem or make a brief speech. I heard the magnificent Welsh chorals and songs, and was flabbergasted when the master of ceremonies—my host—called on me. I was hard put to it, but I remembered two old Negro work songs of our South, one of them saying:

I went to Atlanta
Never been there befo'
White man eat the apple
Black man get the core.
Catch that Southern
Grab that train
Never come back no mo'.

Despite my wretched voice the song made a hit with these gifted singers, and after the applause they set upon me to explain America's racism, demanding tough explanations. One asked, in an injured voice if John L. Lewis (whom they universally admired as a union leader) went along with this damn nonsense. After all, the Welshman said, it was a war against Hitler and his gibberish about Aryan democracy and how can Americans condone it at home. "Come now," another asked, "how democratic is your country?"

And so, in the plain union hall nestled in the ancient valleys of the Welsh I talked well into the morning about America—its merits and its demerits—with workingmen three thousand miles from Alabama who wanted to know all I could tell them of Alabama. I recounted my recent experiences with the sharecroppers of Chambers County and their eyes glistened at the story of the common radio. Here, visibly, was that "international brotherhood" which Abe Lincoln described as the "strongest bond" of the working class.

They responded frankly to my questions concerning their lives, their union and they seemed to agree that the American miners worked more safely "underground" than they, but that theirs was a richer life "above ground." Silicosis ravaged their lungs and my host quietly indicated a slim, emaciated youth in his mid-twenties who "had six months to live." I was horrified when, on my return to London, relating my impressions of Rhonnda to Harry Pollitt he replied soberly, "And yes, that splendid lad, your host, is himself a doomed man." His cough, a year ago, was diagnosed in London as a fatal case of silicosis.

The Nazis gave London a greater dose of bombs as the day for the world conference approached. The air seemed to be thick with the pilotless monsters that virtually criss-crossed their lethal way across the London skies, slashing into the homes, falling most heavily in London's East End, near the great dome of St. Paul's Cathedral, transforming the ancient slum into a wilderness of brick. Yet that courage of man, accommodating himself to death, struck me everywhere I went, recalling the heroism of the Spaniards a brief few years before who pleaded this would curse the nations rejecting their plea for arms.

The newspaper headlines were big with news of the impending conference of labor whose portents few misunderstood. They day it opened I sat in the balcony, looking down on the delegates, my heart pounding. The sight ravished the eye and the mind—this Assembly of Mankind that old Briton Tennyson had foreseen. Below, on the conference floor, stood a tall African from Gambia, a man greater-sized than life, possibly seven foot tall, his face a chiseled ebony: he was clad in blue and golden robes that fell to his feet. Nearby stood a group of Arabs in maroon fezzes, and a few feet farther I saw the delicate faces of Chinese and Indians, the colored delegates from many colonial countries. The British contingent clustered about the urbane figure of Walter Citrine, a lord of the Empire, Sir Walter, as the papers called him. An imposing delegation of Russians, some thirty-five, seemed invested with the grandeur of their resistance, some of them limping to their seats on canes, veterans of Stalingrad. The French contingent was led by Benoit Franchon, veteran, too, of the underground resistance; Spaniards, lean, taciturn, who managed to survive the Franco holocaust, were here. My eyes hunted out the Americans, led by Sidney Hillman and I recognized the various CIO leaders, James Carey, slight, curly of hair and dark of eye, of the electrical workers; Joe Curran, brawny, red-faced, of maritime—all the familiar faces. At another corner Latin Americans caucused with Lombardo Toledano, listening earnestly, his handsome, dark-eyed face somber. There was a perceptible stir when a V-2 crashed somewhere in the city, sending its tremor here, rattling the windows like the hostile warning of a jealous enemy who realized that here, on the banks of the Thames, spokesmen for sixty million workingmen had gathered.

After the first session and lunch, I returned to the conference hall with George Sinfield, of the London *Daily Worker* who responded to my enthusiasm with an ironic smile: "Hold it," he said grimly, "until you've heard His Majesty's Knight Sir Walter. And you've heard of Schevenels, of course."

I knew that Citrine, the British labor leader headed the International Federation of Trade Unions which obdurately excluded the Soviet trade unions from membership since 1919, and consistently persecuted unionists suspected of Communist leanings. But I believed that the inexorable logic of wartime would impose unity upon the IFTU: fascism which murdered trade unions, required this conclusion. I should have been sobered by Sinfield's warning, for I was not unaware of an old infirmity: so sure a conviction have I that the spiral of history moves upward inexorably that I tend to ignore the possible presence of history's concealed road-blocks. Impatient to move on from the Kingdom of Necessity, out of the dark pre-history that Engels described, I assess matters wishfully all too often. I panted for Utopia, so much so, that Malcolm Cowley once described the *New Masses* as the magazine of "the Happiness Boys." I accepted the ironic appellation as a green laurel in this world where so many confidently predict doom: but experience should have warned me to judge matters more soberly, to remember that mankind traveling toward the sun often twists back, makes its unpredictable zig-zags, and that this conference would scarcely proceed in a straight, brave line to that unity which seems so simple, so irrefutable to minds like mine.

What I yearned to hear came from the spokesmen of those unions whose homelands suffered most grievously in the war. They argued ardently and cogently for the immediate creation of a world federation, and so, I exulted to hear, did the American delegation. Hillman, wearing his thick spectacles, bobbing his head of curly hair, his shoulders bent slightly, warned the delegates in the familiar accent of the East Sider that the voice of labor must be heard, and it must be heard unmistakably, in the negotiations for peace terms now that the war was nearing its victorious close. Though labor here had agreed on "excellent" fundamentals, it lacked the instrument to register its enormous totality. Time moved fast and there was none to waste. Labor was not represented at the current international aviation conference: nor was it promised a place at more vital conferences coming up. We must, he reiterated, construct "at once," a "unified, monolithic trade-union federation, submerging our differences to achieve it." Had we done that before 1939 "we could have prevented this holocaust." The coalition forged in the fires of war must continue in the quiet of peace. Labor, the first victim of fascism, heroically bore the brunt of war, therefore "it must be the prime guardian of the peace, of the unity of nations that want freedom"; to achieve that labor must unite. "Old factional quarrels can be fatal." Such differences proved the tragic error of the Thirties: if they were repeated, we would betray the trust reposed in us, "and all will pay an awful penalty." He exhorted all delegates to create a democratic federation that would admit all trade unions, large and small, of all free countries "on the basis of equality."

Vladimir Kuznetzov, spokesman for the Soviet unions, whose youthful face and boyish dip of hair suggested Wendell Willkie to the correspondents, said the war had brought all workingmen together to confront Hitler, and together, they stood on victory's threshold. Now, despite all past differences, they came to London to achieve a lasting and indestructible world unity. So spoke the French trade unionists who had bled beneath the boot of the Occupation: so, too, the Republican Spaniards still bleeding under the Franco despotism.

Their arguments seemed unassailable, but by now I should have learned, logic is not impregnable against the adroit tongues of those who would spread confusion. Walter Schevenels, a king pin of the moribund IFTU rose, a tall, heavy-set man of middle age, responded forcefully, shrewdly, peering at his sheaf of notes through thick glasses. "The IFTU leaders had long recognized the all-around desire for world unity." But, to his mind, *his* organization was the place for that unity, and blandly, he ignored the fact which shot through the mind like a tracer bullet, that the IFTU had contested the idea of trade-union unity wilfully, stubbornly, desperately, for a generation. It was clear, too, though Schevenels did not put it into specific words, that he chafed at Hillman's sharp observation that the IFTU had consumed years talking of reorganizing its ranks into an effective instrumentality of world labor and still its executive body deferred consideration of such a proposal—made by its own committee—until the next September. "For three years," Hillman said, "they have been unable to agree among themselves." Hence the obvious, the imperative, need for a new and fresh organization.

But, Schevenels argued maliciously, Hillman merely expressed "a mystical desire" for unity, and offered "no concrete way" to achieve it. Hillman and his friends merely demonstrated their prejudiced conviction that "the IFTU must go." Pointing an oracular finger toward the ceiling, he said his organization had learned hard lessons "which Hillman and his friends have yet to learn." World labor unity will not be achieved by mere "enthusiasm." If the IFTU had tried hard through the years after World War I, and if it had failed, the cause was not due to a paralysis of the will. "Let us not overlook the history of the last forty years. There was a great enthusiasm for unity in 1919, but we did not succeed." Then, after he dashed an abundant shower of chilly water over the baneful quality of "enthusiasm," he concluded: "Nevertheless we must conciliate our differences." Sir Walter Citrine rose, a handsome, silvery-headed figure who comported himself like a courtier, a rare "son of horny-handed toil" indeed. Of course, he purred, toying with his cuff, Hillman's report was "constructive." But let us all remember that this conference is merely "advisory and consultative." We must build "solidly and carefully." Then he lay the groundwork to defer the immediate formation of a new labor center. "You cannot discard the IFTU unless you are certain of the new organization. Will it work? Who knows? Who can tell? What, for example, will we do for finances?" He spoke with polished eloquence, concise in expression, respectable and as suave as a King's Advocate could possibly be. He concluded with a plea for "realism not romanticism."

His words jarred me, for I certainly could see no hostility between the concepts of "realism and romanticism." *Realistic* it was indeed to found a new world labor organization here; to achieve that required what Sir Walter contemptuously called *romanticism,* which, to my mind, is daring, courage, ardor, imagination, the considered abandonment of the old.

Well, the story is long and the time is late. Unity, in this world of contrary forces, remains a goal, elusive as a will o' the wisp. I may say that I did not quite see the birth of Tennyson's "Parliament of Man, the Federation of the World." I did see a brave beginning. The preamble to the final statement of the conference pledged the creation of "a powerful democratic world union federation at the earliest practicable date." A Continuations Committee of fifty delegates, "fully representative of the composition of the conference" was empowered to act as agent of this conference to ensure trade union representation at the coming peace conference and at all preparatory commissions. A Federation later did come into existence that included the CIO. The Federation exists today, even though the unions of the CIO departed in the cold war that began not long after the hot war ended, but that is running ahead of my story. Suffice it to say that most of the world's unions took a giant step forward despite the Labor Canutes who bid history's tides to stand still. Events have demonstrated, since these days in the City Hall on the Thames which shook under the V-2's despite its massive solidity, that the workingmen of the world will soon stand as one for peace despite all other differences. Bridges will be thrown across the gulf of opposing ideologies as Mankind realizes even more urgently that it is one world—or no world. There was a prevision of that on the Thames under Hitler's rocketing explosives the late winter and early spring of 1945.

19

Red Roses for Paris

DETERMINED TO REACH the Continent and the fronts despite the obvious reluctance of the officials, I haunted the appropriate offices as the war raced, thundering, to its finale. The Allied troops overran the installations in Holland whence the Nazis discharged their awful missiles, and the newspapers displayed Churchill in his familiar and absurd overalls, cigar between his lips, triumphantly examining the lethal machinery. The fronts dwindled hourly as the Red Armies charged westward, sweeping the wretched remnants of the Panzers before them. I was in London making my interminable rounds when the last bombs fell on the city. "No bombs today," a notice in the *News Chronicle* said laconically as though it were a weather note, a matter of small moment. Six days passed, seven, eight, and the Londoner seemed to scan the skies more distrustfully, apprehensive of the eery quiet. Rumor spread through the byways that the enemy had perfected a super-deadly weapon that would soon come crashing into the capital, and the sudden silence after four and a half years of bombs brought a strange tension instead of jubilance. "Hope deferred maketh the heart sick," and few men could trust their fortune. The populace was jumpier in the quiet than it was under the crash of the familiar bombs.

I finally broke the blockade about me, and, hallelluiah, I could proceed to France. I crossed the gray choppy channel on a cold April morning in a fussy little steamer carrying contingents of returning French soldiers—escaped from Nazi prison camps to England. They were half-crazy to catch the first glimpse of the shoreline, stood hours at the bow with their own thoughts, staring silently at the horizon. When the first penciled strip of land rose from the sea the young veteran at my elbow turned to a side and wept.

Chattering gamins in torn blouses clambered over the channel train at Le Havre, begging for chocolate or a cigarette *"pour mon pere,"* and the veterans swept them up in their arms, kissing their thin cheeks, thrusting coins into their hands, chocolate bars and little brown loaves of bread.

Paris was indescribable: the pride of the city struck you first, like a brilliant sunburst at dawn, for, the novelty of liberation still fresh, the tri-color flew from every flagpole and, it seemed, from every chestnut on the Boulevards. The city glowed and the city wept. Wherever I set foot I found bright fresh wreathes of roses laid at the spot where some loved one had fallen in the Liberation. On the corner of the Place de la Concorde, above a garland of fresh flowers hung a placard, the inscription written in a woman's careful script: "Marcel Dornier, twenty, student of pharmacy, died gloriously on this sacred spot for France." The buildings were still pocked and scarred with bullet pits that told the story.

Though I encountered everywhere the hollow eye of hunger, the capital glowed with pride. Paris was Paris once again, the buds faintly green on the great horse-chestnut trees that lined the boulevards, the bookstalls on the Left Bank crowded with bibliophiles, the streets jammed with young and old who fairly swallowed the clean air of freedom. True, the massive job of reconstruction engaged their energies, and materials were scarce, food meagre, and the politicians were at work, no few of them at dirty work, striving to re-establish the men of wealth who had collaborated with the Nazi occupation. But overriding all was the news, printed in the tiny newspapers they called "postage stamps," the headlines breathless, mere bulletins, but they sang a triumphant hymn of victory: Extra: "Our Troops Nearing Berlin!" Special extra: "Hitler Reported Dead!" Special, special extra: "Herriot Alive: Freed by Red Army!!!" The newspapers carried the photographs of GI's meeting the Red Army at the Elbe, drinking beer from the same mugs: it was a moment frightening with immensity even as it intoxicated you.

Phillipe Reval (a pseudonym), *New Masses* correspondent since liberation, a young somber-eyed Frenchman about twenty-five years old, an honored veteran of the Resistance, took me in tow. Despite his crowded day engaged in the furious hustle of reconstruction, he carted me around the capital in his tiny car appropriated from the Nazis. He brought me to *L'Humanite,* the principal organ of the Communists, to the headquarters of the Communist Party, a great, stone building with barred, guarded doors against possible assassins left by the underground collaborationists; to the home of Louis Aragon, the Communist poet who had for four years led a hunted life in Petain's France where he managed to organize some forty thousand professionals, doctors, teachers, clerks into the Resistance, writing three books of poetry in the choking days when the Gestapo hunted him, smashing through the front door one day while he escaped through the kitchen window.

Eager to cable the story of Paris under the Occupation, I found my man in Phillipe. I wanted this told, for civilian America had been spared the agony of quartering a conqueror in our homes, our schools, our public buildings. This was one of the truths our people must know to understand our allies' trials, and achieve a clearer understanding of postwar needs.

Phillipe fought the war as a partisan, I knew, and urging him on, over innumerable cups of thick coffee, through the spare hours of a week of nights, he reluctantly related his experiences, that were "typical," he insisted, of thousands more.

At seventeen, a student in the Sorbonne, he attended an underground university conference at Heidelberg, was betrayed and arrested by the Gestapo at the border. That was 1939, just prior to the outbreak of war. The students of Europe saved him by raising a furore across the continent that Himmler could not ignore. Scarcely home, this lean, eager-eyed student of botany, the son of a science professor in the old university at Caen, was one of thousands arrested when Petain's government of quislings rounded up all Communists and known anti-fascists when Paris fell. It was prison again, escape again, in the chaos of the moment. Like hundreds of thousands of Communists (70,000 of whom perished in resisting the invader) he remained at his post.

Agents of the Resistance found him work as an insurance salesman which provided an acceptable reason to travel through the land: expert hands supplied the forged identification papers which the Gestapo conned when they swaggered in pairs through a subway car, a cafe or a train, suddenly demanding the domestic passports. "That," he smiled ruefully, "was the worst." You watched their faces as they looked over your papers, your heart pumping so loud that you were certain the Gestapo must hear it. "I could master everything," he added, dolefully, "but my heart-beat." Assigned to ascertain the moment a Nazi troop train would pass a given point, he conveyed that information to French railwaymen who dynamited the rails at the appropriate moment—a job, I understood, of extraordinary complexity and hair-trigger precision, and apprehension meant torture in a Gestapo cell. He sat there, in the clattering cafe off the Boulevard Hausseman, his black hair parted neatly in the center, his manner modest, almost diffident, talking in a massive understatement as though he described work in a library sorting out books.

We became friends fast, and Phillipe invited me to accompany him on his first visit to his father and mother since Paris was liberated. His folk lived in a small coastal town by the channel, where the university had been totally destroyed by bombs.

His father, the professor of botany, small, wizened, with a white goatee, impeccably clad in the threadbare garb of a provincial pedagogue, a pair of pince-nez glasses perched on his nose, greeted his son stiffly, almost coldly. The professor, Phillipe told me enroute, had stamped apoplectically through the house when he learned his son had enlisted in the Resistance. Why should his boy be the one to risk his life? He had a university career cut out for him, and politics belonged to others, not to the elite dedicated to science. A bitter scene concluded when he ordered Phillipe from the ancestral home.

During the Occupation his mother sent Phillipe word that she understood, and gave him her blessing. Mama Reval, a tall, matronly woman, clad in an ancient black gown, stiff with starch, the picture of a respectable village bourgeois, fell to weeping when her son entered the door. The old professor tried gallantly to conceal his emotion and play the host, brought out a decanter of Normandy brandy, but he could not conquer his aloof embarrassment. Father and son carried on their reconciliation with averted faces. "You are well, Phillipe?" the old man asked. "Reasonably," the son replied. "And when will you return to the university?" A moment of silence before the reply: "When the job, father, is done."

The old man turned away, his pince-nez uncertain on his quivering nose. The long, painful evening passed as the mother, with a determined show of joyousness, tried fruitlessly to restore an old, bygone harmony. As each desperately gay effort failed, a shadow of grief crossed her face. When the evening ended in frustration and we were to go upstairs to our beds the old man, with a strong effort, turned to his son: "You must go see Professor Willenbroek," he mumbled, "He has just returned from Buchenwald." And the mother, wringing her hands cried, "Oh, see what the beasts did to the dear old man!"

The next day we visited the old professor who sat silently in the flagstone courtyard of his small, whitewashed cottage, a cloth cap on his head, his feet in great, loose slippers, the wreck of a magnificent man, all skin and bones, an angry red rash running across his cheek and when he doffed his cap his white hair hung in patches, falling across a high domed forehead; but a pair of deep-set, burning eyes greeted Phillipe when we entered. He kissed his young friend on both cheeks, gripping his wrists, a tremor shaking his shoulders. "My son, my son," he murmured, "I rejoice that they did not lay hands on you." Later, Phillipe gently asked of Buchenwald and the old man replied sadly, "I am only a professor of terrestrial geography, Phillipe; you must find another Dante to describe Inferno." Before we departed, he gripped the young man's hands in his again. "Your father," he said slowly, "is a man of profound sorrow and regret." Phillipe stood before him, silent. "Remember that, my son," he added deliberately. "If he erred it was from excess of paternal love, not from a deficiency of patriotism."

That evening as we lay in the high, wooden beds of Phillipe's boyhood room, I glanced across the room to find him staring up at the ceiling and finally he spoke. His father, he reflected, and the old geography professor were life-long companions, born and reared in the same Normandy town, and doubtless the professor of botany had persuaded the professor of geography to intervene and heal the family rift. "My father, who was untouched by this war, pleads with that hero of Buchenwald to help him, to help him salve his conscience." He lay silent a long time and I found no word to offer. Two generations, I thought, an ancient conflict, remembering Turgeniev's *Fathers and Sons* when the drama was played in an earlier time. I imagined the turmoil in the old man who, too, doubtless lay staring at the ceiling in the next room, and my heart went out to him. I finally indicated my thoughts to my friend, who replied softly, "And what of the fathers of those who will not return, fathers who stood by their sons? Has he no heart for them?"

But at breakfast, the table glistening with the best of the family ware, the silver polished, the cut-glass gleaming, Phillipe walked slowly across the room to his father, gripped his shoulders and kissed his cheeks. The old man's dignity departed abruptly, his eyes filled, his pince-nez fell, and he rose hastily, awkwardly embracing his son and stumbled from the room. The mother lay down the copper coffee pot, bent her head and wept.

On our return to Paris through a sun-swept countryside like a Breughel painting Phillipe talked of many things, the political scene, the municipal elections being held that day, the effort of the Communists to maintain the unity of the various Resistance parties, the conspiracy of the collaborators to retain their wealth. He talked of America and of Russia, but as we reached the outskirts of Paris, he said suddenly, "If Professor Willenbroek could forgive him, I can too." And frowning, "His weakness is that he is only the father of a son, not a father of France."

I repeat this story because it seemed to me to illustrate the spirit of France as I saw it in the spring of 1945. It must suffice for the many epics I heard during my stay.

Being the editor of a magazine read primarily by intellectuals I asked Phillipe of their role in the Resistance. Phillipe hesitated, at a loss to begin. Naturally, he responded slowly, the principal actors in the Resistance were the proletarians, the trade unionists, like the railwaymen with whom he worked. And, it must be said, the most trustworthy and able among them were the Communists. Evidence of that was the political might of the party now, since Liberation. No power on earth could dissuade the hard-headed, suffering masses of France from some unalterable conclusions—*they* knew. They had seen the collaboration in action through the long, bitter years; they had few illusions. The ablest, the most self-sacrificing were the Communists, "for the historic reasons we understand," he added in a matter-of-fact tone. That held for the Communist intellectuals as well as the major resistance force, the workingmen.

But one erred if he believed the Communists alone played an honorable part. He had been spirited from one home to another through the years, was often harbored by professionals, middle-class folk of various parties who asked no questions though they doubtless suspected his political affiliations. He smiled faintly as he described his life in the handsome home of an upper-class family for a month, appearing at breakfast every morning with his host, a portly, dignified pedagogue who inquired politely how he had slept, handed him a morning newspaper, opened another himself, consumed his coffee and croisson silently, and, finishing his meal, shook hands and went off, with nary a question. And yet the penalty for such hospitality was death in some torture chamber. He had even stayed in the homes of some Roman Catholic priests. Yes, many intellectuals surmounted their political differences to confront an enemy that made few distinctions. That was inherent in a war of national liberation.

Whether the unity could hold for the future? He spread his hands. The differences of class would re-emerge since capitalism still reigned. Money divides: oppression unites. The men of the trusts are stubborn fighters and Lenin had said they contrive to find many ways to rule. The political battle will be to win the middle classes whose loyalties waver under duress. True, many intellectuals opposed to the Communists had displayed heroism in the Resistance, "cooperated with us against the Nazi," but now they will feel the centrifugal pull of class loyalties. Some will remember who stood most staunchly when the Gestapo ruled, and will not forget whose counsel proved steadiest and sagest; but "memory is not enough, even the fondest memories," he observed with a small smile. A livelihood must be made, a career pursued. "And no few will accommodate their memory to their present." The Party is not unaware of these truisms, he added grimly, as our policies amply show. "Much depends," Phillipe continued, turning his somber eyes on me, "on what your Wall Street does." The impenetrable future held the answers. Meanwhile, he predicted, the Communists would make considerable gains in the municipal elections; the returns verified his prediction. To this day despite all the blandishments of the franc and the dollar one of every three Frenchmen casts his ballot for Communists, knowing that they are the most trustworthy guarantors of 1789—and of a future that will bring, as a Frenchman predicted, "the singing tomorrows."

At the Rue Scribe I learned that SHAEF—Supreme Headquarters of the Allied Expeditionary Force—planned to send several planeloads of editors and correspondents to visit the concentration camps that had been liberated a few days before. The first photographs of Belsen, Ravensbrook, Buchenwald, Dachau had appeared, and I realized that few in America would find them believable. I chased about Paris to the proper offices, determined to reach the camps. Authorities shunted me from one office to another, and I was out again, back again, in again, out again, arguing that my magazine be accorded rights equal to all publications who opposed the enemy. My persistence finally triumphed.

The Paris sun shone bright that early morning, May 6, 1945, when I stood with some twenty-seven correspondents, editors and publishers at the airfield awaiting the plane to carry us to Dachau. My companions were English, Dutch, Swiss, a Spaniard, and two very young newspapermen from Palestine. I was assigned a seat beside a middle-aged man impeccably dressed in a pin-stripe suit, a Homberg hat, a silk handkerchief peeping correctly from his breast pocket and his shoes gleamed mirror-like. His long ivory face sported a small waxed mustache and behind his gold-rimmed spectacles peered a pair of small, sharp, jet-black eyes. I detected the aroma of a perfume. The man lifted his trousers carefully as he took the seat by the window, and smiling carefully, he handed me a small, gold-engraved card. The foreign editor of *Ahora,* a daily newspaper of Madrid, was introducing himself. Senor Manuel Jaime Diaz ingratiatingly asked me the name of the newspaper I represented. I replied that I wrote for the New York daily press which he seemed to interpret as the *New York Daily News.* I did not, at the moment, correct his impression, suspecting that he would doubtless recoil from the presence of a *Rojo* at his side and I would lose my unexpected opportunity to probe a Falangist mind. "Ah yes," he exclaimed with delight, "I know your paper very well. In fact I have read your articles." I took his extended hand with less than enthusiasm but with a sufficient grip to observe the amenity.

As one journalist to another, I asked how matters stood in his beautiful Spain. Ah, he replied, quickly, the ravages of war were being repaired, the past glories of his land were restored. It was a terrible war, all wars in Spain are terrible, he smiled, and there was still much to do. "But," he said flashing a set of brilliant white teeth, "The Generalissimo has things well in hand." The editor had just toured the country, from San Sebastian to Port Bou, the peasants were happily tilling the fields, the workingmen were in the factories, the churches the Reds destroyed were rebuilt, miracles of reconstruction were achieved in the half dozen years since peace was re-established. "There were a few recalcitrants," of course, but they were behind bars. "We are re-educating them," he explained, smiling brilliantly again.

I had no present intention to challenge the man, and I ventured to ask if the methods of rehabilitation were successful. "Oh, senor," he replied enthusiastically, "we have new prisons, model prisons, with educational classes. We free those who signify their intention to cooperate with our new order." And many had already been freed. Yes, many, many. I replied that I was happy that Spain had no concentration camps like this one at Dachau we were approaching: no gas chambers, no crematoria. He listened carefully and replied with a shrug: Spain had nothing like that. "The Spanish soul is violent, true, but only in battle: it is compassionate in peace." For of all nations Spain is "the most Christian, the most devout." I nodded. (So far, the man talked according to rote.) Then with a surprising fall in his voice he volunteered his familiarity with the diplomatic reports on the Nazi camps, which reveal that the excesses "were exaggerated." As journalists we would understand that all wartime reports of the enemy are exaggerated; "that is a concomitant of war." Europe remembered the atrocity stories of the first world war, the non-existent Belgian nurses whose arms were cut off at the wrists. We must allow a normal amount of propaganda about our enemies, he said, accenting the word "our." But the Germans, after all, were a Christian nation, too, cultured beyond most, the homeland of Kant and Hegel and Goethe, after all, senor. Therefore we must take such tales with a fair amount of salt.

We were high over the Rhine and I looked down to see a broken steel bridge, twisted and gnarled, one half pointing toward the sky like an accusing finger. *"C'est la guerre,"* the editor observed dolefully. A scene for Goya, I commented, and he responded enthusiastically. Oh, I knew the work of the master "who next to Velazquez is our greatest." Goya, he went on, was peerless in his depiction of war and was doubtless the supreme patriot among Spain's artists for none better than he recreated the heroism of its people whose valiant resistance to Napoleon lived eternally in his art. True, I agreed, but hadn't the master run afoul of the authorities somehow, dying in exile in Bordeaux? Ah, he replied cheerfully, "the soul of the artist is frequently recalcitrant, retaining as it must, a certain child-like naivete that enables him to preceive beauty beyond the prosaic reason of mature men." This man has all the answers, I mused sourly, and added maliciously, "And he had trouble with the Inquisition, didn't he?" Ah, my planemate exclaimed, "You are a student of Goya, I see."

He was happy America evinced such interest in Spain's art, but he must say that Goya had no trouble with the Inquisition; personally, Goya was an exceedingly devout man at heart but one who tried the patience of the Church with his immoral escapades in which, like artists, he displayed "a lamentable lack of discretion." I asked how art and literature was flourishing now "under the new order," to which he replied, "Splendidly; peace has brought a renaissance."

Well, I concluded, I won't get far with this fellow, and our talk dwindled to silence the rest of the journey.

An hour later the plane banked over a great brown cathedral whose spire had evidently been hit by a bomb, and hung to the side like a man with a broken neck. We were on the outskirts of Munich. The plane landed with a bounce on the golden soil of Bavaria, the sun brilliant overhead. Three GI's came running out of the airdrome and when the propellors slowed to silence one asked the pilot was it true, "Is it all over?" The pilot, a six foot stalwart with tousled yellow hair smiled. "Yep, Jackson, all over. Got the news over Strasbourg." So the war in Europe came to an end while we were above German soil. A chunky, grinning soldier from Jersey City mumbled, "Well, that's that."

Enroute to the Munich City Hall where we were to lunch with the American command, the bus took us through the narrow, gabled residential streets where all windows displayed white sheets or towels, tokens of surrender, as though each family individually turned itself over to the victors. We passed the long, imposing vista of the monuments to those who fell in Hitler's *bierhaus* putsch: a series of bronze caskets, each inscribed solely with a name, and the single word *"Hier,"* connoting that the dead were responding to the drill-call of the living; passed the wreckage of the building where the Munich *diktat* was signed by Der Fuehrer, Chamberlain, Mussolini and Daladier, so long ago, it seemed. It was a sight for which every man on the bus craned his neck to see, the expressions on his face tokened the inevitable thought.

The great Gothic structure of the City Hall was intact. We were served wienerschnitzel in the basement by sad-faced young Ukrainian slave-girls the Nazis had brought into Germany four years before. Our waitress, a round-faced lass of fifteen (an exception to the others, I later learned) struck up a conversation with the man at my side, the foreign editor of the London *News Chronicle,* a Pole who had been with General Sikorski, and who spoke her language. He introduced me as an American journalist and, hands on hips, she surveyed me frankly through blue, slightly slanted eyes. Turning to the Pole she asked him several questions rapidly, which he translated. "Will the Amerikanski confirm the German charge that Roosevelt is a Jew and that the Jews have taken over the country?" I answered the surprising question and the Pole, speaking a few moments with her, informed me that the girl had said, "It would be sad if the Jews took over such a big country." Her four years here, he said, were passed in relatively favorable circumstances as a waitress and the years of association with the Nazi idea had left their scars. I wondered at that moment what four years of the Wehrmacht occupation had done to the peasants of southern Russia: how many minds, as well as bodies, had they crippled? It was a question that troubled me in later years.

20

Resurrection in Dachau

THE ROAD TO Dachau wound through a prim countryside, gay, almost festive to the eye with the trim, gabled cottages up which rambler roses climbed. It was the Bavarian spring, the trees blossoming in early flower, the fields ariot with dandelions, the sky a cloudless blue.

The farmsides lay in that neat precision we call Teutonic, and the well-kept highways ran like ribbons of concrete across the placid country. Who stepping into this land afresh, from some remote Shangri-la, could imagine the Horror that held this natural serenity in its grip? And suddenly the evidence of that Horror manifested itself: our bus parted a stream of cyclists wearing the stripes of the concentration camp; their bony faces set as granite, they pedalled furiously in a trance of concentration. They had no eye for rambler rose of gabled cottage, sped, almost sightless, like fugitives freshly escaped from Hell.

"Russkies and Polacks," a young captain assigned to us as our guide commented. "They've liberated those bikes from the Nazis. All day long you see them pedaling God knows where." They were headed East—going home.

The bus halted at the great arched gateway to the concentration camp. We passed a big brown-stoned barracks building of the Schutztaffel, the SS, a long, three story red-brick building whose myriad windows were flung wide open as though to let fresh air in. On the walls the SS had stenciled a black silouhette of a figure eight feet high, a stealthy character in a slouch hat, hand cupped to his ear. Beneath it in great Gothic script was the legend: "Beware. The Enemy Listens."

We emerged from the bus as a squad of GI's strolled over, carrying DDT spraying guns to disinfect us against the typhus epidemic inside which took a toll of 150 lives daily in the camp that still held some sixty thousand prisoners. As the GI pumped powder on us, I stared across the courtyard at the vast stretch of wooden huts whose geometric pattern of streets reached to the horizon.

I could see innumerable men in the striped, faded prison uniforms milling around. We crossed a small wooden bridge over a medieval moat into the inner camp where thousands of men—men?—walking skeletons stared at us, their dreadful years burning in their eyes. Great sores ran across their cheeks, but most of all their fearsome boniness struck me, the blotched skin taut over the skull. My heart pounded as I stood among them, corpses granted life again and who were still uncertain of the miracle.

We were led to a one-story cement building at the extreme boundary of the camp as a horrifying stench came our way—the fearful, sicksweet odor the human corpse gives off, and turning the corner, I froze in my tracks. Before me, stacked like cordwood, lay thousands of naked corpses, piled criss-cross to a height of six feet, the naked bodies of men and women rotting in the sun three days since the GI's stormed into the camp.

The newspapermen stopped as though they had walked into a wall. Several of them pulled handkerchiefs from their pockets which they clapped to their faces as masks. The Madrid editor, my plane-mate, jammed a large square of white silk across his nose and drew a bottle of smelling salts from his pocket.

"The sonofabitch," I stormed inwardly, "oh, the mealy-mouthed sonofabitch" who had insisted that the stories were propaganda. It was loathsome even to stand near him the rest of our journey.

The colonel said, formally, surveying us curiously, that if anyone so desired he could enter and inspect the crematorium and the gas chamber. It was up to us. Or, if we preferred, we could step off a distance to escape the stench.

Four of the twenty-seven stepped forward; the Pole, the two Palestinians, and I. To approach the door of the gas chamber we passed through an aisle formed by the pillars of corpses. I looked into the faces so near that I could touch them, the mouths agape, the dead eyes staring sightless, the gaunt hands outstretched as though they were clutching for the rescuers who never came. Who can describe his emotions at such a moment? Dante, perhaps, for I have yet read nothing that faintly succeeded in describing this scene which had no parallel in all of man's time on earth. I caught a glimpse of my companions; the blood had gone from their faces, the eyes seemed as sightless as the corpses. As we entered the heavy door to the gas chamber I saw a neat little placard in Gothic letters that said, "To the Shower Bath," and I stepped inside.

Hell was a square room, windowless, of four cement walls and a cement ceiling. One door—it had no exit. Here they had stood, naked, the mothers, the fathers, the children, here the millions were driven, each to die his separate death.

How could my countrymen grasp this enormity to vow it would never happen again? And there, on the wall behind, I saw the neat, glass-covered peep-hole through which the executioner had peered.

We came out, stumbling rather than walking, and entered the crematorium—the room of the ovens. How well the accomplished engineer had calculated: the gas chamber, the gas, the death, the corpses carted through the door to the ovens a few feet off: scientific, rational, wasting neither time nor energy, the supreme accomplishment of fascism.

Oh, the Germans are a clean race, for cleanliness is next to godliness, and above the series of apertures through which they thrust the corpses to reduce them to ash another sign in Goethe's language said: "All attendants must wash their hands after the day's work." Each oven bore a polished brass plate with the name of the Munich manufacturers, doubtless a reputable firm which paid adequate dividends quarterly to stockholders who knew the Niebelungen and worshipped the Prince of Peace. They would insist, *nein,* we are guiltless. We are merely manufacturers, *mein Herr,* who honor our contracts. We are I. G. Farben, *mein Herr,* after all, we have cartel pacts with your Standard Oil, your Du Pont, and your International Nickel which Herr John Foster Dulles represents. Our pacts are inviolate, to be honored in war as in peace, and we honor them above all. *Ya,* your responsible men will understand our problems.

We came out into the open again, passed once more through the aisle of the dead, the decaying remains of the humble and the famous, the men who had paid their union dues meticulously on the first of the month and who had argued the relative merits of Kautsky, and Lenin; the men who taught children the music of Beethoven, who explored the terrains of science, the mothers who had screamed in child-birth, all lay mouldering under the immaculate Bavarian sky.

We hastened, almost ran, back to the living, the others of the delegation who had waited for us, a safe distance beyond. They stood silent, averting their eyes, it seemed to me, as though they felt that they had dishonored the dead by failing to accompany us into the crematorium; or perhaps, did they feel the dead had somehow invested the persons of those who had come near, with an awful indictment of those who stood aside? They seemed to shrink from us as though we were ghosts risen from that fearful mound.

We approached the living dead, the hordes of survivors who were even more terrible than the dead. My heart pounded as I stepped toward them but the army captain, our guide, abruptly prohibited us from shaking their hands, reminding us of the typhus. The falangist editor in his homburg absurdly fastidious in the chaos of rags and disease, plunged his hands into his pockets. But the Sikorski Pole, the Palestinian Jews and I ignored the order. I made no attempt to curb the tumultuous need within me to greet these men who were returning from Hell and I would have struck anyone who lay a deterring hand on me. Who could honor any rule, any command, of man or God this Judgment day when the dead arose?

They stood, uncertain of our intention, awaiting us. Something of anguish must have marked my face for a small, wizened, dark child with vast eyes, a boy of twelve, stepped from the crowd of survivors and plucked at my sleeve, asking *"Bist Yiddish?"* "Are you Jewish?" I replied in his tongue and he said, in a strange, cracked old-man's voice that his name was Moishe Greenspan. His father and mother, two sisters and a younger brother were "burned" here. "Now I am alone."

The boy grasped my hand, a frightened child clutching for aid, and I felt the throb through the dry bones. He did not relinquish his hold and drew me to a barracks numbered "23" which was the prison infirmary, leading me to a tall, pale, emaciated young man of thirty, the child croaking in a curious exaltation, "Doctor, a Jew has come, an American Jew." The child turned his ravaged face toward me, his great somber eyes unnaturally bright, feverish, and I suspected suddenly his reason was unhinged when he commanded me to talk to the doctor "who came from God to save the Jews." The young physician, a prisoner himself, smiled sadly, stretched out a hand to pat the boy's head, and said a few words in Polish which caused the child to laugh, unexpectedly, a strange, tortured laughter that was nearer tears than joy. The doctor's glance my way confirmed my surmise. And were a Nazi before me at that moment I believe I would have beat him to death, as the GI's did, I was told, when they broke into the camp and saw for themselves. They had thrown down their rifles and turned on the SS men with their fists.

The doctor lay aside some papers and asked me the name of my publication. My reply seemed to bring a sudden new light in his eyes, a perceptible change of manner. He seized my hand, was about to speak and checked himself. "Of course," I thought, "Of course." And even at that moment of liberation he did not dare reveal himself.

"Perhaps," he said with an intent stare, "you would wish to see my patients." Taking my arm he led me to the ward outside his office: a long, bare, wooden room holding triple-decked cots on which the typhus victims lay, two to a cot that had barely space for one full-sized man. Many were dying, and the sound of the death-rattle filled the room. A young prisoner, on a top bunk, perhaps fifteen or sixteen years of age, his face wild and skeleton-like, pointed a bony forefinger at the aisle and I turned to see a man crumble and fall to the floor, his arms outstretched and fingers clawing. We lifted him to his cot and the doctor, after examining him, turned to me with a despairing gesture, murmuring, "Just as freedom is here."

He turned his duties over to an assistant who entered and led me outside, into the air, amid the milling thousands. As we walked he told me his story: he was a Polish Jew, from Warsaw, the Gestapo captured him two years before, sent him first to Auschwitz, the death camp in Poland, and for some unaccountable reason, perhaps because doctors were scarce at Dachau, he was sent here. The words poured from his lips as though he had a compelling need to reveal his life in the hell now that victory had come.

Though he was no Communist originally he met one here and they had become friends. Knowing a few words of English, he said, he detected the word *"Worker,"* hence his involuntary start of welcome recognition, for he now knew what he had not known before—the truth about Communists. "I will explain," he said.

When he came from Ausschwitz he sensed the existence of an Underground here at Dachau despite every punishment the Nazis devised to crush it, and the penalties included crucifixion. Nonetheless, he was determined to seek out the Resistance within the camp.

His first day he discovered that some twenty babies were in his barracks, with their mothers. Treating them, and scarcely able to withstand the anguish of their mothers, a half-formed determination to save the children crystallized within him, though he realized, he said, the thought was purest fantasy. All prisoners knew that the SS planted men from the Underworld to spy upon men from the Underground. Many prisoners had no philosophy of resistance, no political affiliation or social understanding. The horror destroyed souls and many prisoners became informers, "for a slice of bread, a piece of sausage." So the SS knew, within hours, who had committed an infraction of the rules: many a good man died because he slipped a slice of bread to political prisoners, or to Jews, whose ration was least. But the majority did not inform: "most men remained men," turning away when they encountered violations of the rules.

Artisans who tended the camps, the carpenters, electricians, cooks, were selected from among the prisoners. The Nazis could not spare skilled men for work here, "only those skilled at murder." He studied the behavior of his fellow-prisoners and came to recognize that those who managed to retain a certain dignity in their bearing, a respect for others, revealed another quality, an awareness, an interest, a concern, in matters beyond themselves. This was particularly true of a certain man of middle-age, one of the camp electricians, whose air of assurance and quick understanding struck him. "He walked erect ." One day the doctor sought him out for conversation, when they were alone. "The news is not at all bad," he said to the electrician. It was the time of Stalingrad and there were ways of knowing about such things. The electrician continued to talk of other things, camp duties, but the doctor noticed some quick light in the other's eyes. Several days later the doctor repeated his words when General von Paulus surrendered. "The news is even better," he said. By this time the electrician had doubtless inquired about the doctor from those he trusted, and the doctor had confidence that the prisoners of the hospital ward respected him. "Better?" the workingman repeated cautiously, "I do not understand." "Yes, better," the Pole replied. "A certain city is liberated, a certain general is captured." Someone approached and the talk turned innocuous. "The way I spoke must have given him assurance." The next day it was the electrician who came to the doctor. "To make a long story short we probed each other's mind, and came to conclusions." The doctor surmised that the prisoner was a Communist, for though he bore the marking of a political prisoner—all wore symbols of their status here—a triangle, for politicals, a circle for common criminals—one could never be certain of the agent-provocateur, the informer. "Though I belong to no party, as I said, some intuition told me this man was a Communist, the most certain of Hitler's enemies."

One day the doctor confided his dream of rescuing the infants, the children. "I asked if he would help." The following morning the electrician outlined a plan.

As a technician he had occasion to leave the camp daily for a brief time to obtain electrical supplies at a nearby storehouse. He wore a sizeable knapsack to carry the supplies. "If I could dose the children with a sleeping drug so that they would sleep for several hours, not cry out, he could smuggle them out in the knapsack." The Pole agreed. They worked out a meticulous schedule, ascertained the best time to outwit a prying eye and they began. "The electrician had established contact outside the camp and each day I slipped an unconscious child into his knapsack; each day he smuggled his cargo through the gates to a member of the Underground awaiting him in the storehouse." The child was spirited to a nearby home, then to another, until it was safely far away.

"But didn't the Nazis keep records of their prisoners?" I asked. No, he explained, life was so cheap that the bookkeeping of death became impossible, a formality. "So many were coming, so many were going, the crematorium smoked day and night and we knew that the SS would not be aware of the missing children."

So, standing in the appalling human current swirling about us, I knew what I know: nothing on this earth, no punishment so fiendish, no ingenuity so diabolic, can conquer man. And here, in the midst of the agony, I could have sung like an angel.

We pushed forward among the men on the dusty roadway who were proceeding toward the parade ground of Dachau, for, it developed, a victory celebration was scheduled by the liberators. A bugle sounded suddenly, a clear silver note that rose above the din of many tongues: the ceremonies were beginning. We pressed our way on through the oncoming crowds that seemed to be streaming from everywhere: these thousands from all of Europe, slogging ahead in a vast tide of ragged, diseased humanity, pushing irresistibly toward the celebration. Some carried banners of their homelands: the tricolor of France, the standards of Poland, of Czechoslovakia, of Hungary, of Russia, many of the banners as ragged and tattered as they, these men so unbelievably gaunt that they could scarcely shuffle one foot before the other, their lacerated flesh barely clothing their skeletons and they marched in a strange and fearful ecstacy.

To one side of me a man passed with a scrofulous face, his eyes burning. On the other side one limped, on two canes, jerking his way forward, crab-like, clouts of filthy, blood-stained bandages on his feet. Ahead a younger man upheld and half-carried a stumbling graybeard. Two men, gasping, pushed a wheelbarrow bearing a comrade whose face had the pallor of death, his scarecrow feet protruding over the edge, his eyes feverishly scanning the scene as his lips moved soundlessly. I was startled when a tall, young, erect Negro in the prison stripes approached us and took the doctor's hands warmly, greeting him in French. "My friend," the doctor said, introducing him, "my friend who is my colleague." The black man extended a bony hand, the skin a dusky parchment over the bones. *"Mon nom est Jean Voste,"* he said in a smile infinitely sad, his white teeth contrasting brilliantly to the coal-black of his face. As we marched on he told his story: he had come from the Belgian Congo to Brussels to study medicine. When war broke out, and the Nazis overran the city, he became a Partisan with four of his classmates, three of whom were captured and executed here, at Dachau. He had survived because the SS consigned him to work as a hospital attendant, assisting the Polish doctor.

I could scarcely breathe with the magnitude of the moment. As we approached the parade ground I saw the multitude in prison stripes massed in endless rows. As far as the eye could see they stood, shoulder to shoulder, in their rags, their heads shaven, bony, corpse-like, their numbers assuming an immeasurable strength as though all mankind were assembled here on a day of Resurrection. The young Pole, his pale face incandescent now, began to sob; the African stood sternly in all his height, a black angel in rags. The Jewish boy held my hand tight in his unrelinquishing grasp. The trumpets of the honor guard, gleaming brilliantly in the high Bavarian sun, stentoriously pealed the anthems of the Allies: America, the Marseillaise, the Internationale . . . the multitudes, silent so long, began to sing, a low, hesitant rumble at first, then swelling, slowly, gradually, to a crescendo beyond belief: the majestic strains rising over the barracks, the crematorium, over the aisles of the dead, and as the child gripping my hand looked up at me, his great, wild eyes in tears, I felt life's invincibility and wept. . . .

And this is written, that no one will forget German fascism.
— and understand its class nature
Here is the true face of mans enemy —
only a working class, guided by Marxism, can prevent another